MILTON STUDIES
XXXV

MILTON STUDIES

XXXV ❧ Edited by

Albert C. Labriola

UNIVERSITY OF PITTSBURGH PRESS

MILTON STUDIES

is published annually by the University of Pittsburgh Press as a forum for Milton scholarship and criticism. Articles submitted for publication may be biographical; they may interpret some aspect of Milton's writings; or they may define literary, intellectual, or historical contexts—by studying the work of his contemporaries, the traditions which affected his thought and art, contemporary political and religious movements, his influence on other writers, or the history of critical response to his work.

Manuscripts should be upwards of 3,000 words in length and should conform to *The Chicago Manual of Style*. Manuscripts and editorial correspondence should be addressed to Albert C. Labriola, Department of English, Duquesne University, Pittsburgh, Pa., 15282–1703. Manuscripts should be accompanied by a self-addressed envelope and sufficient unattached postage.

Milton Studies does not review books.

Within the United States, *Milton Studies* may be ordered from the University of Pittsburgh Press, c/o CUP Services, Box 6525, Ithaca, N.Y., 14851, 607–277–2211.

Published by the University of Pittsburgh Press, Pittsburgh, Pa. 15261

Copyright © 1997, University of Pittsburgh Press

Manufactured in the United States of America

Printed on acid-free paper

10 9 8 7 6 5 4 3 2 1

Library of Congress Catalog Card Number 69-12335

ISBN 0-8229-4038-8

US ISSN 0076-8820

A CIP catalog record is available from the British Library.

CONTENTS

MILTON STUDIES
XXXV

THE LADY'S UNLADYLIKE STRUGGLE: REDEFINING PATRIARCHAL BOUNDARIES IN MILTON'S *COMUS*

Julie H. Kim

IN HIS TEMPTATION of the Lady in Milton's *A Mask Presented at Ludlow Castle* (1634), Comus refers to the Lady's beauty as "Nature's coin" that "must not be hoarded, / But must be current" (739–40).[1] While this particular example is one which most explicitly links economics with the Lady's beauty and ultimately and more specifically with her sexuality, it is only one in a series of such connections made in this masque. In fact, almost all the characters participate in a dialogue on the economics of female sexuality, often thinly disguised as female beauty. The brothers guarding the Lady's beauty and virginity as treasure, Comus advocating the circulation of her sexuality, and the Lady herself strenuously redefining and adjusting Comus's faulty economic discourses all deliberate on this issue. Ultimately, despite the Lady's vigorous protests—usually in debates with Comus—she cannot eradicate the notion that female sexuality is a commodity to be hoarded, borrowed, exchanged, stolen, or spent by men.

The Lady is not alone in finding herself of value, both materially and metaphorically, in her society. Modern sociohistorical studies confirm what contemporary domestic tracts from seventeenth-century England reveal: this culture's preoccupation with economics touching almost every aspect of a woman's life. While the economic association with women was most pervasive within the familial realm and conditioned domestic gender relations, women continued to be commodified and to be represented as men's actual or symbolic property outside the family as well. In fact, Milton's characterizations of the brothers and Comus illustrate the economic conflict between those within and without a woman's familial sphere. Male family members, implicitly (and sometimes explicitly) defined as rightful "owners" or guardians of their female relation's sexuality, strive to "hoard" or distribute her sexuality—and the wealth it represents—at their discretion. In contrast, outsiders with no legitimate claim to a woman venture to make her sexuality "current" and more available for themselves.

Does the Lady herself (and do other women in this period) have a voice

1

in their triangular relationships with hoarders and circulators? In a way, yes. A woman's position in seventeenth-century England was far from ideal (despite the perception abroad that England was a woman's paradise), and throughout the century their condition went from bad to worse.[2] But to understand the complexities of contemporary gender relations, we must first recognize the paradox of women's status in this period. As any text about the seventeenth century will show, patriarchal society, law, and economy tended to regard women as subordinates, as dependents, and as property. Women, especially married women or young and wealthy heiresses, were closely monitored by the men around them. Especially with the practice of primogeniture, a woman's sexuality played a crucial role in the transference of wealth (and its consequent power) between generations of men. Her sexuality had to be closely regulated and her marital chastity had to remain unquestioned for fathers to pass on most of a family's possessions and property to a child without fear of it going to a bastard. Many men were thus wary of female independence and found particularly threatening the notion of female dominance. Women were safest at home, away from the eyes of others—safest for their male relations, that is. But a large gap existed between the vision of passive and dependent women whom many men idealized and the reality of the many active and independent women. We know that women made political and religious speeches. They published books, inherited property, and managed businesses.[3] The most popular and politically stable English monarch of the Renaissance was Elizabeth I. Especially in the early part of the seventeenth century, then, many women enjoyed much more freedom and independence—both socially and economically— than a patriarchal society wished to allow. Domestic tract writers, mostly male, "doth protest too much," in fact, in conceptualizing for themselves and for their audience an ideal of womanhood that bore little resemblance to the reality; and their great anxiety over proper womanhood and their attempt to prevent women from overstepping their bounds suggest that many women did transgress their limits.

In many ways, *Comus* investigates the ambiguities of patriarchal power over women, particularly as they inform economic relationships between men. The masque responds to fears that women will be ungovernable and specifically addresses problems and questions raised by errant female sexuality. What does the Lady represent in a patriarchal economy? To what perils is she making herself vulnerable in the "outside" world of would-be seducers? While the Lady, at fifteen, is an articulate and impassioned defender of her virtue, her brothers and Thyrsis distinctly feel a need to save her from the dangers of her own independence as well as from Comus—and escort her back to her father.

In the end, the conservative patriarch in Milton puts the Lady "in her place"—amid her male guardian and relations, primary among them her father, the mostly invisible but nevertheless powerful honoree for the masque. Yet, along the way, Milton's Lady is partly successful in transcending the prescribed limits to a woman's individual identity, which is so often overlooked in favor of the larger good of the unified patriarchal family. She is able to combat, albeit briefly, Comus's attempted objectification of women. Thus, Milton reinforces patriarchal conventions at the same time that his character repeatedly transgresses her limits by asserting her individual will.

Milton's Lady, despite the fact that she ultimately succumbs to male power, is quite revolutionary when seen against the backdrop of the contemporary male concept of ideal womanhood. In the young daughter of the Earl of Bridgewater Milton combines three facets of seventeenth-century womanhood: the silent and humble woman sought by popular tracts, the chaste and supernaturally powerful Britomart celebrated in the courts, and the radical religious woman who claimed biblical authority sanctioned her actions and speech. In this amalgamation, Milton also reconciles the ideal of women proposed by many men and the reality of women which appeared threatening to patriarchy. The Lady actively strives to establish her own identity but, finally, tacitly acknowledges—with the silence imposed by her author in the conclusion of the masque—that her male relatives, even prepubescent siblings, are her proper guardians.

The Lady's struggle against Comus and eventual return to her familial fold are played out in an economic arena, economics providing both the metaphor and a metonymy for power in Milton's poetry. But, ironically, wealth—especially in that women represent wealth—is not powerful in itself. As I will demonstrate later, the signification of the Lady as gold and gems disempowers her. Conversely, she is able to assert her power when she can take herself out of the economic equation. Inevitably, however, she is, as Claude Lévi-Strauss would argue, the "exchanged" and not the "exchanger"; herself impotent, she is the conduit of power in this economic relationship between men.[4] But despite the fact that the Lady must ultimately go back home a dutiful daughter and sister, her experiences during her retreat from patriarchal guard reveal much about Milton's attitude toward women and sexuality, about her own blossoming sense of individual identity, and about the seventeenth-century English society which made coins of women.

I. Sex Scandals

In recent years, Milton critics have debated the extent of the relevance or, in some cases, the irrelevance, of two cases—the Margery Evans affair and the Castlehaven scandal—associated with the Egerton family, the family for whom the masque was written. Leah Marcus has written extensively on the Earl of Bridgewater's investigation (between 1631 and 1633, as the Lord President of the Council in the Marches of Wales) of the case of Margery Evans, a poor, fourteen-year-old serving maid who was the victim of rape. Margery Evans could not find justice and was herself unfairly thrown in jail for accusing a Philbert Burghill and his servant for their crimes. Eventually, she found aid from the Earl of Bridgewater, whose meticulous concern for details and fair handling of the case apparently resulted in greater success for her appeals for justice. Analyzing *Comus* in light of this incident, Marcus suggests that Milton must have known about the earl's involvement in the case and wanted to applaud his fair handling of it while also implicitly criticizing his colleagues present at the premiere of the masque who did not treat Margery Evans with equal justice.[5]

We cannot be certain that Milton knew of the Evans affair, although it is probable that he did know something of the investigation which ended only a short time before the presentation of *Comus* and which played a large role in the earl's most recent political and judicial reforms. The more notorious Castlehaven scandal of 1630–1631 can scarcely have failed to reach Milton's attention. In 1631, Lord Castlehaven, the brother-in-law of the Earl of Bridgewater's wife, was found to have grossly abused his patriarchal power. At his connivance, his wife was raped by his servants; and his stepdaughter, after being forced to marry his own son by another marriage, was deflowered and repeatedly raped by his servant. Apparently, Castlehaven contrived the marriage and the subsequent rapes in an effort to produce a male offspring to disinherit his own son.[6] While his actions were universally deplored and he was eventually executed for his crimes, his ordering the rapes of his wife and stepdaughter reveals to what extremes a husband and father could come to objectify and commodify the sexuality of his female relatives and use them as pawns for his own economic gain.

Barbara Breasted and others argue that the choice of the theme in his masque suggests that Milton was consciously referencing the Castlehaven scandal in an attempt, perhaps, to exonerate the virtuous family. In response, John Creaser protests that the virtue of chastity was too common and sensible a choice to celebrate and that "it was not necessary, therefore, to invoke scandal to justify the choice of theme."[7] The Margery Evans case and the Castlehaven scandal, whether or not intentionally invoked by Milton, are not, however, "irrelevant" to *Comus*. Lady Alice, who played the Lady in the premiere, was a cousin of Castlehaven's stepdaughter whose sexuality was regulated and abused by him; and Alice was, at the premiere, a year older than Margery Evans was when the latter was raped and further victimized by the law. Furthermore, the topic of chastity takes on more than casual relevance in light of the Earl of Bridgewater's political and judicial role. As Leah Marcus and Michael Wilding have pointed out, a major responsibility for the earl in the Council of Marches, as evidenced by his role in the Margery Evans case, was the protection of chastity and the punishment of sexual offenses.[8] Thus, even if Milton is not reminding the audience of the specifics of these events, he is, through the seduction plot and the threat of rape in *Comus*, doubtlessly presenting as menacingly real and particularly pertinent for the Bridgewater family the type of sexual threat and vulnerability of female sexuality found in the two cases.

To better understand the relationship between the two cases and the seduction theme in the masque, it is necessary to recognize this period's preoccupation with and exploitation of female sexuality in general. The Neoplatonic cult of love popular in Henrietta Maria's court idealized women in love and often portrayed women in Caroline masques, especially the queen, as having the power to uphold order through chaste femininity. Women in these masques exercised both verbal and physical prowess to protect their chastity and were able to command respect and admiration from courtly men for their virtue.[9] But while this Neoplatonic view appears to empower women, the true extent of women's control over men is difficult to measure. While Caroline masques may depict women as having power in their sexuality, either in use or in restraint of it, evidence from the late seventeenth and eighteenth centuries suggests that women's sexual power ultimately serves men's purposes.[10]

A woman's virginity and chastity, ideally sources of her empowerment but in reality widely associated with material wealth, represent her worth and the wealth of her male relatives—for her husband because of the dowry awarded with her and for her father or brothers because she becomes linked with family honor and to the wealth transferred with her. Chiefly in aristocratic circles, girls had to remain virgins to be valuable in the marriage market since, in the words of a contemporary, "Wives, if once known, lose their value." The coupling of female sexuality and economics was so prevalent that a girl who lost her virginity was described as "unthrifty." Angeline Goreau, exploring the seventeenth-century male attitude toward female sexuality, informs us:

A deflowered heiress could be disinherited, since her maidenhead was an essential part of her dowry and she had deprived her father of the possibility of "selling" her to a husband whose family line she would carry on. *The Whole Duty of Man*, a mid-seventeenth-century tract that documents the conventional morality, states: "The corrupting of a man's wife, enticing her to a strange bed, is by all acknowledged to be the worst sort of theft, infinitely beyond that of goods."[11]

If seducing another man's wife or daughter was considered theft, raping a woman would certainly be considered an atrocious economic crime. Even one of the early definitions of the word *rape* is "the act of taking anything by force; violent seizure (of goods), robbery" (OED). We should remember also that Castlehaven's own sexual perversions had the economic end in view of disinheriting his own son. Thus, especially in this period, sexuality of women can never be fully isolated from economic concerns.

II. Among Misers and Circulators: The Lady as "Nature's Coin"

The masque's fascination with the Lady's chastity may arise from Milton's desire to respond to the Evans affair and especially the Castlehaven scandal by showing us a noble family that successfully protects the Lady's virtue. Or, he may be reminding the audience of these recent incidents to expound his more general concerns with female sexuality and with the virtue of chastity. But while certainly not as explicitly or as exploitatively as in the two cases, female sexuality in *Comus* is similarly controlled by masculine powers. The Lady's beauty and, more specifically, her sexuality, represent wealth to be fought over and distributed among men. Wilding contends that Comus, in his argument urging the Lady to enjoy her sexuality, "reduces everything to cash terms. Beauty and morality are degraded to commodities, to cash, and the language of capitalism is the language in which he presents them."[12] But while undoubtedly Comus is a character enticed by the cash value of the Lady's sexuality, he is certainly not alone in reducing beauty to commodity and cash. When reading this masque, one is struck by male preoccupation with the Lady's chastity from the very beginning. In fact, all of the male characters in their first mention of the Lady refer to her sexuality. Comus, when he first hears the Lady's footsteps, instructs his rabble:

> Break off, break off, I feel the different pace
> Of some chaste footing near about this ground.
> Run to your shrouds within these brakes and trees;
> Our number may affright: some virgin sure
> (For so I can distinguish by mine art)
> Benighted in these woods.   (145–50)

By his art, Comus claims to know the history of the Lady's sexual experience without any previous acquaintance with her. And Thyrsis can probably credit his private magical sources (or his more intimate association with this virtuous family) for his knowledge of the Lady's chastity when he exclaims to her brothers, again in the first mention of his master's young daughter, "But O my virgin lady, where is she?" (507). But, more peculiarly, even her younger brothers, at ages eleven and nine, readily announce their interest in her sexuality. At our first introduction to the brothers, we learn that they fear the fate of "that hapless virgin, our lost sister" (350). Perhaps the older poet is attributing to his young players his own fears for female chastity. Nevertheless, it is curiously revealing that the first mention of the Lady by her nine-year-old Second Brother emphasizes her sexual innocence. What follows is a long discussion between the brothers about female sexuality, often thinly disguised as female "beauty." The Second Brother's analogy between female beauty and material wealth is unmistakable when he declares:

> Beauty, like the fair Hesperian tree
> Laden with blooming gold, had need the guard
> Of dragon-watch with unenchanted eye
> To save her blossoms and defend her fruit
> From the rash hand of bold Incontinence.
> You may as well spread out the unsunned heaps
> Of miser's treasure by an outlaw's den,
> And tell me it is safe, as bid me hope
> Danger will wink on opportunity,
> And let a single helpless maiden pass
> Uninjured in this wild surrounding waste.
> Of night or loneliness it recks me not;
> I fear the dread events that dog them both,
> Lest some ill-greeting touch attempt the person
> Of our unowned sister.   (393–407)

When the Second Brother finishes his analogy, the Elder Brother launches into a philosophic meditation on chastity. In the speeches, then, we see encapsulated and articulated by two pre-adolescents the paradox of seventeenth-century attitudes toward women. The Elder Brother, better versed in the popular philosophy of the period, lectures to his younger sibling on the classical view of love also featured in the contemporary Neoplatonic love cult, which idealized chastity and its ruling powers. He asks his brother, "Do ye believe me yet, or shall I call / Antiquity from the old schools of Greece / To testify the arms of chastity?" (438–40). Without waiting for response, he calls forth Plato in subsequent lines. In contrast, the Second Brother's analogy reminds us of the more materialistic, and perhaps cruder, conception of female beauty and chastity. That is, "beauty"—and chastity—is "gold."

While both brothers' concern is touching on one level, the acute awareness of their sister's virginity may have roots in a practical and worldly desire. Whether cloaked in philosophy or revealed in its material concern, the brothers' interest in the Lady's chastity suggests an anxiety over their own honor and wealth. While "beauty" and "gold" can be similarly stolen, in each case the woman is less a victim of the thievery than are her male relations. Englishman Gilbert Burnet proposed an economic interest in female chastity in 1679 when he wrote that "Men have a property in their wives and daughters, so that to defile the one or corrupt the other is an unjust and injurious thing."[13] Burnet proclaimed what many others implied or assumed: men have an economic stake in the sexual purity of their female relatives. Impure or blemished, a woman's price falls drastically as a scratched diamond or tainted gold might. Not only does *her* value suffer, but she would also cause the loss of her male relations' reputations or wealth.

As the Second Brother eagerly explains, beauty is golden and thus valuable but needs a guarding eye. Who better to supply this than the woman's closest male relatives? The most logical guardian is a husband. The Lady, however, is not married and therefore cannot expect protection from a spouse. And while her father and her brothers would normally watch over her, the Lady's separation from them places her in danger from attack. As the Second Brother informs us, his sister, alone, is "unowned." Her vulnerability to attack, or "ill-greeting touch," would seem to be directly related to the fact that she is not possessed by someone, either in the sense that she is lost or in that she has no male relative to claim her as his property—or both. The comparison between beauty and the "fair Hesperian tree / Laden with blooming gold" indicates that it is precisely the material value of gold blossoms that the unenchanted eye guards. Furthermore, when the Second Brother compares a "helpless maiden" to a "miser's treasure," one need not ask who the miser is. The miser/male relation is the "hoarder" against whom Comus might complain, is the one who claims economic interest in maintaining the exchange value in his possession, and who keeps a wary watch over his treasure. Despite their opposite aims, Comus and the Brothers similarly identify the Lady as valuable property to be guarded.

To help the still-young brothers watch over the Lady, Thyrsis takes on the role of guardian. As their "father's shepherd," he plays surrogate father and has the task of gathering together the flock, both animal and human. He initially informs the two brothers: "I am not here on such a trivial toy / As a strayed ewe, or to pursue the stealth / Of pilfering wolf" (502–04). Yet his task, once magnified to its proper importance, largely resembles the recovery of that "trivial toy." Significantly, while the brothers had asked Thyrsis if "any ram / Slipped from the fold, or young kid lost his dam" (497–98), his response that he is not pursuing a "strayed ewe"—gendered feminine as opposed to the masculine ram or kid which has lost *his* dam—prepares us to identify the strayed ewe with the lost Lady. The latter, like a ewe in her father's possession, has strayed and is in danger from a pilfering wolf—Comus.

Thus, perhaps even unconsciously, Thyrsis suggests an owner-property relationship between the father and the Lady.

Ultimately, the character most engrossed in his own interests is Comus, who, in his temptation of the Lady, explicitly aligns her sexuality with economic wealth. In fact, his position is defined for us even before we actually hear his own arguments to the Lady. When the Lady first encounters Comus, he asks about her "near-ushering guides" who "left your fair side all un-guarded" (283). Then, offering himself as a replacement for the lost brothers, he temporarily usurps her brothers' rightful roles as guards over the Lady and her chastity. Comus can be seen as the "outlaw" by whose den the miser thoughtlessly spread out his treasure in the Second Brother's analogy between a "helpless maiden" and "miser's treasure." After all, Comus, in the masque, rules over his rabble in "the perplexed paths of this drear wood, / The nodding horror whose shady brows / Threats the forlorn and wand'ring passenger" (37–39). The fiction does not stray far from the real. The actual setting is the Dean Forest, a place of riot and sedition; and the Marches around Ludlow, a wild and rowdy town on the Welsh border over which the Earl of Bridgewater was responsible for keeping peace, were infamous in the 1630s for drunkenness, disorder, and the practice of pagan customs.[14]

When told of his sister's peril later, the Elder Brother, unable to control his youthful zeal at the idea of confronting Comus, promises to "find him out, / And force him to restore his purchase back, / Or drag him by the curls to a foul death, / Cursed as his life" (606–09). His threat—in addition to commodifying his sister once again, this time as "purchase"—sets up an opposition between himself and Comus in economic terms. As her male relations, the brothers are conventionally regarded as rightful owners and guardians of the Lady. To Comus, however, the Lady is a "purchase." Among the many definitions of "purchase" in the Oxford English Dictionary, two that were current in the seventeenth century are worth exploring: "The acquirement of property by one's personal action, as distinct from inheritance"; and "That which is obtained, gained, or acquired; gains, winnings, acquisitions; esp. that which is taken in the chase, in pillage, robbing, or thieving." Both definitions serve to make Comus, as the one who makes the purchase, an unentitled owner—first, since he did not rightfully inherit, and secondly, since he has acquired through thievery.

Gayle Rubin draws upon the work of Claude Lévi-Strauss to analyze women in general and marriage in particular as being central to developing a network of relationships among men who profit from the "traffic in women." Lévi-Strauss theorizes that marriages are the most basic forms of gift exchange, and women the most precious gifts. More specifically—as anthropologists, historians, and feminist critics are quick to point out—the gifts of women in marriages (or in other sexual liaisons) serve to strengthen relationships between men who could develop a fruitful kinship from the exchange in women. But as Marxist critic Karen Sacks argues, an increasingly class-divided society with its aim of accumulating wealth resulted in property owners segregating themselves from their subordinate kinsmen and allying with other property owners to "preserve and defend their holdings against the claims of the nonpropertied."[15] Thus the economic traffic in women which made women valuable "gifts" to cement relations among men can also be a crucial element in creating the division between men of different classes. For property owners, one way of insuring that the subordinate classes not encroach upon their property is to monitor their women's sexuality by prohibiting marriages between their daughters or sisters and men of lower classes and protecting their own line of inheritance so that it remains pure. For instance, the Lady's brothers (and her father as well) have no intention of sharing the Lady with or making a gift of the Lady to Comus—an obvious outsider to their class—while it is reasonable to assume they must have looked forward to making a profitable match for her and for themselves among their own kind. Comus's companions are a riotous rabble; he has no meaningful kinship or class relationship with the earl's family. Comus is an interloper who cannot be allowed to penetrate their circle.

The opposition between insiders and outsiders, between misers and outlaws, is reflected in the different economic goals of the brothers and Comus. While the brothers—as misers—jealously guard and strive to "hoard" the Lady and the wealth she symbolizes, Comus—as an outsider to whom she is not immediately accessible—seeks to have her wealth circulated through making her sexually "current." In their separate ventures, Comus and her brothers resemble other men not only of the seventeenth century but of later periods as well. For instance, Ellen Pollak notes that the eighteenth-century husband defined a woman as an essentially passive object of exchange who, "whether she circulates in the open market or is, like hoarded treasure, privately secured . . . remains . . . an artifact of masculine desire, a valorizing sign not of herself but of some other (always masculine) signified."[16] Although she was writing about eighteenth-century gender relations, Pollak's language nevertheless reminds us of Milton's in his masque. In fact, her analysis clarifies for us the gender relations in *Comus* and highlights the economic discourses within the earlier work by articulating how hoarding and circulating work to commodify women. In seeing women as passive objects of exchange between men, Pollak might agree with Eve Sedgwick, who, in her study of "homosocial desire," argues that in triangular relationships involving two men and one woman, it is the competition (or, in some cases, the coordination) between men which is the central and meaningful relationship. In relations among two men and one woman, what René Girard would call the *active* members of the erotic triangle are the two men (or groups of men in the case of *Comus*).[17] While a woman in such a triangular relationship appears to be the object of desire, clearly it is the relationship among men which initiates and is most affected by her exploitation, hoarding, or circulating.

In his competition with the brothers over the prized Lady, Comus is clearly the outsider, though not necessarily an underdog. As a usurper who must circulate and cannot hope to hoard, perhaps it is only fitting that Comus uses rhetoric filled with ideas of borrowing and lending rather than those of owning and keeping. Comus depicts Nature as the generous moneylender from whom one must not "harshly deal like an ill borrower" (683); and he declares that Nature pours her "bounties forth. . . . to please and sate the curious taste" (710–14). Most of all, he asserts, so that "no corner might / Be vacant of her plenty, in her own loins / She hutched th' all-worshipped ore and precious gems / To store her children with" (717–20). Significantly, Nature, always gendered feminine, stores her most precious possessions in her loins. In the sense of the "seat of physical strength and of generative power" (OED), the word *loins*, particularly used in a seduction scene, sexualizes the image of Nature. The fact that gold and gems are stored in her loins further strengthens the link between sexuality and wealth.[18] Like the two brothers' debate earlier, Comus's own economic arguments incorporate elements of both the Neoplatonic ideal of a woman (in whose chastity lies her source of power) and this period's more overt commodification of a woman (whose sexuality is equated with material wealth).

In urging the Lady to enjoy herself and exercise her power to circulate her wealth and sexuality, Comus sounds like a possessive individualist. As C. B. MacPherson explains, various possessive individualists (among them Hobbes, the Levelers, and Locke) agreed that "the individual is essentially the proprietor of his own person and capacities for which he owes nothing to society." He adds, "Political society is a human contrivance for the protection of the individual property in his person and goods, and (therefore) for the maintenance of orderly relations of exchange between individuals regarded as proprietors of themselves." But are we to take it that all were considered "proprietors of themselves" and privy to these rights? In fact, according to MacPherson, even Levelers, when they referred to the rights of "every inhabitant," of "every person in England," were probably "understood to exclude servants as they undoubtedly were understood to exclude women."[19] Similarly, even Comus's democratic philosophy must make concessions. He admits that while the Lady may store and even circulate her own wealth, the one who should be thanked for the riches is the "All-giver," a masculine god and "master" (723–25). In fact, both participants in this debate linguistically slide between and confuse female Nature, who has generously poured forth her riches, and the male "All-giver," who needs to be thanked for his riches. Neither the Lady nor Comus clearly differentiates or distinguishes between the two. In a sense, Comus offers the Lady, and other women, more power than their own male relatives would grant them in that he insists that they themselves can effect the circulation of their riches/sexuality. But this power is illusory because its origin remains obscure, and even Comus confesses that the real master who can control this circulation and who must ultimately be thanked is a male giver. Once again, we see the power resting not with the exchanged female but with the male exchanger, whether an all-powerful God or more mundanely powerful men. In fact, when Comus suggests that he is offering avenues of freedom for the Lady's circulation of her own sexuality, he is once more insinuating himself in the role of one who can confer power and one who would ultimately exercise the circulation.

Finally, Comus's point that the Lady has the power to enjoy and share her own riches is merely a self-serving argument. In the economic circle, Comus exhorts everyone always to play the consumer. Our needs will be satisfied, somehow, as long as we consume. He urges:

> List, lady, be not coy, and be not cozened
> With that same vaunted name Virginity;
> Beauty is Nature's coin, must not be hoarded,
> But must be current, and the good thereof
> Consists in mutual and partaken bliss,
> Unsavory in th' enjoyment of itself. (737–42)

Unlike the miserly male relative who wants to hoard, the more egalitarian-seeming Comus favors mutual benefit for all involved by making current Nature's coin. In reality, however, Comus is more concerned with his own satisfaction than with "mutual and partaken bliss." He wants to be able to enjoy the Lady's riches—which he conflates with her sexuality—without interference from her male relatives who may feel they have the rightful claim to, and power over the distribution of, her wealth. In his cavalier carpe diem argument, when he pronounces that "Beauty is Nature's brag, and must be shown / In courts, at feasts, and high solemnities / Where most may wonder at the workmanship" (745–47), Comus strives more for conspicuous consumption than for giving thanks either to Nature or to the "All-giver." Appealing to pomp and ceremony and the ostentatious luxury of courts, Comus presents an argument obviously unsympathetic to Milton's own anti-Laudian, antimonarchical, anticourt beliefs. Comus throughout the masque attempts to undermine, overthrow, or usurp the power traditionally inherited by male relatives—specifically, the ability to control and hoard a daughter's or sister's or wife's wealth/sexuality—and empower himself to share in, show off, and further circulate "Nature's coin."

III. Pressing Her Limits: Radical Despite Herself?

Undoubtedly the Lady rejects, if not the coining of women per se, at least the various ways in which men exploit her coined sexuality. In opposition to both the brothers' wish to hoard and Comus's urges to circulate, the Lady takes a unique stand. She attacks Comus for his suggestion that Nature would wish "her children should be riotous / With her abundance" (763–64) and claims:

> If every just man that now pines with want
> Had but a moderate and beseeming share
> Of that which lewdly pampered luxury
> Now heaps upon some few with vast excess,
> Nature's full blessings would be well dispensed
> In unsuperfluous even proportion,
> And she no whit encumbered with her store;
> And then the Giver would be better thanked.   (768–75)

In her attacks on the unfair distribution of wealth, the Lady criticizes not only Comus in his stately palace but also the broader aristocratic and patriarchal economy that allows for the simultaneous existence of "some few with vast excess" and the "just man that now pines with want." In a discussion of sexuality cloaked in economic metaphors, it is only appropriate that the Lady responds with her own theories of political economy. She understands that Comus is trying to seduce her. But his arguments also expose the ideology of a patriarchal economy that informs and drives his seduction.

In opposition to both Comus (who wants to encroach on her wealth) and her brothers (who guard her wealth from the subordinate classes), the Lady, in a radical move, advocates economic equality and attempts to escape commodification of women by removing herself from the "traffic in women" by desexualizing herself. Late in the masque, the emphasis on sexuality shifts from temperance to chastity to virginity. Citing 1 Corinthians, John Rogers explains that, for Paul at least, "virginity liberates one from lesser, earthly structures of authority, liberating even the unmarried woman from the struggle to please her husband which is the burden of her married sisters." The virginal life, in short, is "freer from those mundane constraints at once social, physical, and psychological." But such a virtuous resistance to sexuality, preferring virginity over marital chastity, was not conducive to patriarchal dominance. Richard Halpern argues that, through promiscuous sexuality or virginal restraint, women can signal revolt from the institutions patriarchy held so dear—patrimonial inheritance and the continuation of the patriarchal family. As Halpern explains, "The virtuous resistance of the Lady may become revolt if not relinquished at the proper moment. In excess, both virginity and sexuality overturn domestic rule."[20] Thus, in her unspoken final lines (779–99, added in 1637 by Milton), the Lady's passionate defense of virginity (more than mere chastity) not only signals defeat for Comus but also threatens the larger patriarchal order.

Although the final portion of the Lady's speech was never spoken in the performance, the rest of her debate with Comus is quite radical enough. Not only is the content of her speech critical, but the fact that she even makes the speech can be construed as a rebellion against patriarchalism and as an assertion of her individual identity. Conduct books of the seventeenth century identify as two central commandments for a woman the preservation of her family's honor through protecting her reputation for chastity and the restricting of her attention to her proper concerns. While the definition of these concerns is ambiguous, most contemporary men judged debates on divinity or state affairs as unwomanly while they generally deemed discussions of household matters permissible for women. Prohibitions limiting women to their proper concerns, quite unrealistic and frequently unheeded, sometimes even "extended to the assertion that *any* talking is unfitting for a woman: 'they should be seen and not heard. . . . Their best setting out is silence,'" notes a contemporary writer.[21] Seemingly in defiance of a culture that prescribed her muteness, fifteen-year-old Lady Alice makes harsh and indignant speeches about the lecherous Comus and his beastly rabble, and also includes in her condemnation the aristocracy in their "tap'stry halls / And courts of princes, where [courtesy] first was named, / And yet is most pretended" (324–26). As if she did not stray far enough from her "proper concern" with these anticourt attacks, the Lady continues to criticize the unjust distribution of wealth created by and exhibited in these "courts of princes" in her speech advocating "unsuperfluous even proportion." Of course, hers may be a rather naive and idealistic position to take and not one Milton necessarily supported. He is not comprehensively criticizing the aristocracy here, especially not during the celebration of a noble patron. Furthermore, Milton himself profited economically (and in his education) through his father's business ventures and interests earned from them. On the other hand, it is important to note that the Lady's criticisms are aroused by Comus's cavalier lifestyle and arguments.

The Lady, in her speech, sounds like a Leveler, and it is probably not coincidental that this speech, written in 1634, reflects a growing trend in the first half of the seventeenth century—speech making by radical religious women. Women such as Lady Eleanor Davies started earning notoriety in the 1620s and 1630s as prophetesses delivering the word of God. By the 1640s and 1650s, women in increasing numbers and zeal became active in religious, political, and economic debates and prophesied wherever they could find audience. Often prophetesses portrayed themselves as weak instruments of higher powers. For example, Mary Carey depicted herself as a passive agent when she made her *Twelve Humble Proposals* to the government: "I am a very weak, and unworthy instrument, and have not done this work by any strength of my own, but have been often made sensible, that I could do no more herein (wherein any light, or truth could appear) of myself, than a pencil, or pen can do, when no hand guides it."[22] Likewise, the Lady claims to have guidance—perhaps the spiritual aids Conscience, Faith, Hope, and Chastity whom she invoked earlier in the masque (213–20) or perhaps an even higher heavenly power—when she verbally battles Comus. However, while she credits higher and external sources, she resembles less a passive instrument like a pencil or pen and more an active and confident hand that can exercise the pencil or pen on her behalf. While she believes that Comus is not worth arguing with, she insists:

> Yet should I try, the uncontrollèd worth
> Of this pure cause would kindle my rapt spirits
> To such a flame of sacred vehemence
> That dumb things would be moved to sympathize,
> And the brute Earth would lend her nerves, and shake,
> Till all thy magic structures, reared so high,
> Were shattered into heaps o'er thy false head.   (793–99)

At this speech even Comus recognizes a defeat of sorts and acknowledges, "She fables not. I feel that I do fear / Her words set off by some superior power" (800–01). Interestingly, Comus chooses to believe that the speech itself is set off by another power while the Lady clearly empowers herself and declares that her emotions could enlist the aid of superior powers.

Even as a passive speaker, but particularly as a strong and effective one, a woman poses a threat to seventeenth-century men. If she wants to speak or write in this period, the act must remain as private as possible since "the social hegemony of modesty and its attributes—virtue, honor, fame, and reputation—served to police segregation by ascribing a sexual significance to any penetration, either from within or without, of a woman's 'private circle.'" For instance, since to publish one's work is to make oneself "public" and expose oneself, women who did were thought to have "violated their feminine modesty both by egressing from the private sphere which was their proper domain and by permitting foreign eyes access to what ought to remain hidden and anonymous."[23]

Is the Lady then a subversive character who threatens patriarchy by repeatedly transgressing her limits? Not only is she lost and egressed from her "threshold of the house," but she has also strayed *away* from the place where her brothers left her. Incredibly, she has followed the sounds of Comus's riot: "This way the noise was, if mine ear be true, / My best guide now. Methought it was the sound / Of riot and ill-managed merriment" (170–02). If straying away from home, away from masculine relations, and toward the sounds of merriment were not shocking enough, the Lady, having rejected the notion of "halloing" to her brothers (226), opens her mouth and sings! And it is her singing which enraptures Comus and prompts his decision to make her his "queen." In her opening scene, then, the Lady presents a picture of a seventeenth-century nobleman's worst nightmare: a female relative away from home who opens her mouth and puts her chastity in peril.

 Yet despite any real fears that the Lady may arouse in her male relations—and in other contemporary men—she is obviously not a subversive character. Particularly when seen against the spectre of Comus's sorceress-mother Circe, the Lady's threat is quite tame indeed. Circe practices one of the chief offenses against stable social order in this period: witchcraft.[24] D. E. Underdown cites the case of Elizabeth Busher of Henton, Somerset, who "was accused of living in 'woods and obscure places without obedience to the laws of God and this land' and of being 'of lewd life and conversation, as namely the mother of divers base children, the suspected maintainer of incontinency in her own house, the continual disturber of her neighbour's quietness and threatening mischief against them.' "[25] Circe is such a witch: she inhabited a dangerous island and bore Comus from an illicit coupling, and her "charmèd cup / Whoever tasted, lost his upright shape, / And downward fell into a groveling swine" (51–53). By telling us at the beginning of the masque the real dangers of Circe to moral and social order, Milton provides a foil for his heroine and preemptively downplays any subsequent transgressive qualities the Lady might otherwise be thought to display. Circe, not the Lady, is the subversive element men ought to fear.

With the Lady, Milton offers a new ideal of chastity. As the Second Brother's material analogy is offset by the Elder Brother's philosophic zeal, and both amended by Thyrsis's more mature and spiritual vision ("here thy sword can do thee little stead; / Far other arms and other weapons must / Be those that quell the might of hellish charms" [611–13]), the Lady's initial similarity to heroines in Caroline masques or transgressive radical women is tempered by Milton's alterations or improvements. In effect, Milton retains only the positive aspects of seventeenth-century womanhood to create in the

Lady a young woman who is simultaneously silent and humble, chaste as Britomart and devoutly spiritual, but who also remains within her proper boundaries. For while Milton may be sympathetic to the Lady, he does not undermine patriarchy; he merely reinscribes the patriarchal limits. Through apparently subversive speech and behavior, Milton's Lady takes the initiative in attempting to secure for herself a greater degree of freedom and dignity than were traditionally accorded women by society. But although the Lady may transgress her preestablished boundaries, unquestionably she still has her bounds, prescribed by the masculine domain, and her radical acts are ultimately neutralized to serve patriarchal ends.

Even her speech making, her most conspicuous and problematic talent, is ultimately rendered innocent. First of all, the Lady sings to signal her brothers, though it is Comus who hears her. His reaction suggests that the Lady's singing, instead of making her appear wanton, accentuates her purity. He wonders, "Can any mortal mixture of earth's mold / Breath such divine enchanting ravishment? / Sure something holy lodges in that breast, / And with these raptures moves the vocal air / To testify his hidden residence" (244–48). Milton neutralizes the radical effect of her singing first by gendering the "something holy" in her breast as masculine ("*his* hidden residence"). She is not really responsible, or credited, for what she says because another power controls her. Further, the Lady's supposed transgression is once again provided with a foil when Comus makes a sharp distinction between the singing of traditionally more wanton women and her purer singing: he compares the hypnotic but dangerous singing of Circe and her sirens to the Lady's singing. While he admits the dangers to men of Circe's singing, which "in pleasing slumber lulled the sense, / And in sweet madness robbed it of itself," Comus claims that "such a sacred and homefelt delight, / Such sober certainty to waking bliss, / I never heard" until the Lady sings (252–64). The Lady's singing is innocent and holy, not wanton or intended to subvert male order.

Moreover, while other men of the period advise that women should be seen and not heard, Milton distinguishes between spiritually pure and impure speaking.[26] The Lady staunchly defends her chastity and argues against Comus, a masculine figure. However, she does not speak a single line in the presence of her brothers and Thyrsis. Although most seventeenth-century women probably were not so modest or oppressed that they could not converse in front of or with their own male relatives, perhaps the fact that the Lady only speaks in soliloquies and to Comus shows Milton's own prejudices or his concessions to the social mores of the period that might find a woman's vociferousness to her male relatives shocking but to a would-be seducer of her values and chastity merely righteous. After all, in repudiating Comus, the Lady is also protecting the financial and moral interests of her family. While disapproving of men elevating a woman's status to the point of idolatry (as in the Caroline masques), Milton does grant the Lady this freedom to speak to Comus, whose sophistry cannot go unchallenged.

Milton empowers the Lady to defend herself; but he does pull the Lady back into a patriarchal domain that constrains her. Since Sabrina must be invoked to save the Lady, Milton does appear to applaud again the power of feminine virtue. In one sense, he is finding one more way to praise his patron's daughter through the symbolic pairing he orchestrates between the Lady and Sabrina. The latter appears when the Lady is finally overcome by Comus, and Sabrina successfully revives her. In front of her brothers and Thyrsis, the spiritual figure speaks for the Lady and perhaps even symbolically changes places with her in that, after she has broken Comus's spell, the stage direction calls for Sabrina to descend and for the Lady to rise out of her chair.[27] More importantly, Thyrsis's failure in the face of Sabrina's obvious success in saving the Lady "indicates the feminine quarter from which the Lady must draw her strength and knowledge to achieve wholeness."[28]

But, finally, the Lady's assertion of her individuality and her awareness of her wholeness are short-lived. Her chastity no longer in danger, the Lady is silent, and her independent and passionate spirit is no longer in evidence once her brothers and Thyrsis come to save her; and while Sabrina holds the key to the Lady's disenthrallment, Thyrsis and her two brothers are her escorts back to her father's house. In fact, the "victorious dance" and Thyrsis's final speech serve to celebrate the return into the familial fold of the strayed ewe. The very public return to her family also modifies the Lady's fervent defense of virginity. Puritan thinkers like Milton advocated marital chastity and companionate marriages, and what the masque makes clear is the connection between chastity and family. Unblemished female sexuality allows for proper propagation in and of the family. Chaste daughters can be transferred in marriages and form alliances between families; chaste wives insure that property will stay in the pure line of inheritance between generations of men. Accordingly, the concentration on virginity in the masque is tempered, in the end, by the vision of the united family as the appropriate structure for the Lady. After all, even staunch Britomart, the Lady's sometime model, ultimately marries and settles down. At the other extreme, Comus's overtly sexual image of Nature as an overflowing storage vessel for riches is corrected by Sabrina's more natural and moderate bounty. The fact that chaste Sabrina's fecund powers are being celebrated by shepherds at their festivals grateful for her guidance provides more proof that chastity and fecundity are not irreconcilable in the masque.[29]

In the end, a woman's chastity is a necessary ingredient for the patriarchal family. The Lady, in turn, also needs the family. The masque's action revolves around the lost Lady: her original loss, her reunion with her brothers and Thyrsis, and then the final return to her parents. The goal of the masque is to return the Lady to the threshold of the patriarchal family and bring her back home intact—psychically and sexually. Milton is simultaneously offering his Lady more freedom than most men of the period would have wanted to allow but even less autonomy than many women actually did enjoy. We can more easily see the Lady, evaluated in her contemporary contexts, as an empowered figure who can protect her own sexuality, no matter how commodified by men. But the protection of her chastity is finally linked to the safekeeping of the family wealth and reputation. After redefining and broadening her boundaries, Milton, in the end, nevertheless suggests that the Lady's individual identity—particularly her sexual identity—is subsumed in the patriarchal family.

Northeastern Illinois University

NOTES

1. Citations from Milton's poetry are from *The Complete Poetical Works of John Milton,* ed. Douglas Bush (Boston, 1965), and subsequent references appear in the text.

2. David J. Latt, "Praising Virtuous Ladies: The Literary Image and Historical Reality of Women in Seventeenth-Century England," in *What Manner of Woman: Essays on English and American Life and Literature,* ed. Marlene Springer (New York, 1977), writes: " 'England is a paradise for women, and hell for horses' was a commonplace often uttered by travelers from the Continent after they had visited the English court" (p. 39).

3. For brief discussions on the ideal and the reality of women's lives in Renaissance and seventeenth-century England, refer to Latt, "Praising Virtuous Ladies," and Catherine M. Dunn, "The Changing Image of Women in Renaissance Society and Literature," in Springer, *What Manner of Woman.*

4. Lévi-Strauss discussed in Gayle Rubin, "The Traffic in Women: Notes on the 'Political Economy' of Sex," in *Towards an Anthropology of Women,* ed. Rayna Reiter (New York, 1975), pp. 157–210.

5. Leah S. Marcus, "The Milieu of Milton's *Comus:* Judicial Reform at Ludlow and the Problem of Sexual Assault," *Criticism* 25 (Fall 1983): 295–97.

6. Christopher Hill, *Milton and the English Revolution* (London, 1977), p. 43; Cedric Brown, *John Milton's Aristocratic Entertainments* (Cambridge, 1985), p. 20.

7. John Creaser, "Milton's *Comus:* The Irrelevance of the Castlehaven Scandal," *MQ* 4 (1987): 27. His article also provides a useful bibliography of criticism of Barbara Breasted, John Peter, Christopher Hill, and others who argue that Milton was deliberately referencing the Castlehaven scandal.

8. Leah S. Marcus, *Politics of Mirth: Jonson, Herrick, Milton, Marvell, and the Defense of Old Holiday Pastimes* (Chicago, 1986), p. 203; Michael Wilding, *Dragons Teeth: Literature in the English Revolution* (Oxford, 1987), p. 51.

9. Maryann McGuire, *Milton's Puritan Masque* (Athens, Ga., 1983), pp. 133–35.

10. Lawrence Stone's *The Family, Sex, and Marriage in England 1500–1800,* abridged ed. (New York, 1977), discusses Samuel Pepys's famous diary entries. Pepys writes of how his career

at the Navy Office allowed him to use his official position to extract special favors. In a series of mutually exploitative relationships, Pepys received sexual rewards from or chances at flirtations with women whose husbands depended on Pepys for career advancements. According to Pepys, in almost all such cases, the husband appeared to have known, if not actively encouraged, his wife's sexual intercessions on his behalf. Therefore, while it is unclear who was exploiting whom—Pepys, his upwardly mobile subordinates, or vice versa—women generally became exploited by both sides (pp. 345–48).

11. Angeline Goreau, *Reconstructing Aphra: A Social Biography of Aphra Behn* (New York, 1980), p. 37.

12. Wilding, *Dragons Teeth*, p. 69.

13. Hill, *Milton and the English Revolution*, p. 120.

14. Marcus, *Politics of Mirth*, p. 193; Wilding, *Dragons Teeth*, pp. 29–46.

15. Lévi-Strauss in Rubin, "Traffic in Women," pp. 171–73; Karen Sacks, "Engels Revisited: Women, the Organization of Production, and Private Property," in Reiter, *Towards an Anthropology of Women*, p. 217.

16. Ellen Pollak, *The Poetics of Sexual Myth* (Chicago, 1985), p. 65.

17. René Girard discussed in Eve Kosofsky Sedgwick, *Between Men: English Literature and Male Homosocial Desire* (New York, 1985), p. 21.

18. It is important that, as in these passages, the Lady's sexuality is always identified with gold and gems. As Marc Shell, *The Economy of Literature* (Baltimore, 1978), p. 137, points out, precious metals like gold serve dual purposes in the economic arena during certain periods in English history—as inherently valuable and, when made into coins, as currency of exchange.

19. C. B. MacPherson, *The Political Theory of Possessive Individualism: Hobbes to Locke* (Oxford, 1962), pp. 125–26.

20. John Rogers, "The Enclosure of Virginity: The Poetics of Sexual Abstinence in the English Revolution," in *Enclosure Acts: Sexuality, Property, and Culture in Early Modern England*, ed. Richard Burt and John Michael Archer (Ithaca, 1994), pp. 231–38; Richard Halpern, "Puritanism and Maenadism in *A Mask*," in *Rewriting the Renaissance: The Discourses of Sexual Difference in Early Modern Europe*, ed. Margaret W. Ferguson, Maureen Quilligan, and Nancy J. Vickers (Chicago, 1986), pp. 91–95.

21. Elaine Hobby, *Virtue of Necessity: English Women's Writing, 1649–88* (Ann Arbor, 1989), p. 3.

22. Ibid., pp. 27–31.

23. Goreau, *Reconstructing Aphra*, p. 150.

24. Roy Flannagan, in his section on *Comus* in *The Cambridge Companion to Milton*, ed. Dennis Danielson (Cambridge, 1989), writes that a year or so before the first performance of *Comus*, two of the Bridgewater children were diagnosed by a reputable physician as having been bewitched by a disgruntled household servant (p. 23).

25. D. E. Underdown, "The Taming of the Scold: The Enforcement of Patriarchal Authority in Early Modern England," in *Order and Disorder in Early Modern England*, ed. Anthony Fletcher and John Stevenson (Cambridge, 1985), p. 121.

26. Peter Stallybrass, "Patriarchal Territories: The Body Enclosed," in Ferguson, Quilligan, and Vickers, *Rewriting the Renaissance*, p. 126.

27. Angus Fletcher, *The Transcendental Masque: An Essay on Milton's "Comus"* (Ithaca, 1971), p. 225.

28. Kathleen Wall, "*A Mask Presented at Ludlow Castle*: The Armor of Logos," in *Milton and the Idea of Woman*, ed. Julia Walker (Urbana, 1988), p. 60.

29. Ibid., p. 60; Richard Halpern also points out, in "Puritanism and Maenadism," that Diana doubles as the patroness of virginity and of childbirth (p. 95).

MILTON'S GARDEN OF ADONIS:
THE EPILOGUE TO THE LUDLOW MASQUE

Nancy Lindheim

A PROMINENT INTERPRETER of Milton's work admitted recently that critics have never satisfactorily explained the epilogue to *A Mask Presented at Ludlow Castle.*[1] The reason for this may be that they have assumed the epilogue (specifically, the lines describing Venus, Adonis, Cupid, and Psyche) to be a comment on chastity, arising either from the thematic concerns of the masque or from Milton's own psychological state. Since these famous lines were added to the epilogue very late in the process of revision, I want to suggest instead that we see them in relation to the material they were modifying. They are not so much a new ending for the action of *A Mask* as they are a new conclusion for its epilogue.

With no "narrative" link to the masque's action, the epilogue in both its versions is an unpredictable ending for the work. An audience encouraged to contemplate "the crown that virtue gives" (9) must have expected something quite different from the kind of earthly paradise that the epilogue depicts.[2] Yet I think this idea of reward lies at the heart of the epilogue through most of its evolution; even the final revisions can be thought of as arising from questions about the eternity of virtue's reward. The Spenserian quality of these added lines, however, suggests a radical change in both meaning and poetic practice, in spite of their retaining the same subject. The change, a sudden self-conscious shift in poetic mode, is signaled by the line, "List mortals if yor eares be true" (997). It seems an invitation to interpret what follows in a different way, specifically as allegory.[3] This essay will take up the invitation and read the ending of the epilogue as an allegory—though one centrally concerned with time rather than, as critics more usually maintain, with love.[4] The idea of time, by providing the work with a clearer sense of virtue's reward, in turn illuminates the context of the whole action of the masque in a way that does not recapitulate its details or its themes. Time may be a surprising concern for an epilogue to *A Mask*, but it offers no surprise in the context of Milton's earlier and later poetry, and it will allow us to see Spenser's Garden of Adonis, his undoubted source for this allegorical material, with new eyes.

Milton's stronger concern in *A Mask*, one might think, is with space. The speeches of the Attendant Spirit consistently present an imaginative pattern based on a largely synchronic tension between this world and another world, between, for example, the world "before the starry threshold of Jove's court" and "this dim spot / Which men call earth" (5–6). Nevertheless, I want to begin with Edward Tayler's assertion that Milton's interest in time and eternity is manifest throughout his lifetime.[5] One reason that Tayler's generalization works even on the apparently anomalous *Mask* is that the Attendant Spirit's spatial pattern is in effect an alternative version of the temporal contrast between now and then, or, better, between time and the end of time. The earlier poetry—*Ode on the Morning of Christ's Nativity, On Time,* and *At a Solemn Music*—present the pattern as basically temporal.[6] It is given its simplest form in *On Time*, where clock time merely exhausts itself and gives way to Revelation's joyous eternity. In more complex formulations, the temporal impulse often seems a teleological desire to define events by their ultimate meanings. The Circumcision, for example, in the poem celebrating this event, is made to reflect the greater wound of the Passion. While the Circumcision reveals the pattern of Christ's own life and presumably the relation between Hebrew and Christian realities, Milton sees the more significant moment depicted in the Nativity ode as a turning point in the total history of the universe. The music that accompanied the Nativity recalls the past music at the Creation (*Ode*, 117–24) and, more elaborately, the future of the Last Judgment (133–64) and the ensuing kingdom of heaven.[7] By itself establishing the beginning of the "latter days" (Tayler, p. 52), the Incarnation has meaning in history as well as for the end of time. Thus the poem gives extended attention to the defeat of the pagan gods as an event that both foreshadows the apocalypse and constitutes a temporal stage in its accomplishment:

> And then at last our bliss
> Full and perfect is,
>   But now begins; for from this happy day
> The old dragon under ground,
> In straiter limits bound,
>   Not half so far casts his usurped sway.   (165–70)

Music often allows Milton to intertwine spatial and temporal figurations. The music in the Nativity ode that connects the beginning and end of time, for example, has the additional effect of providing entry to visions of heaven in *At a Solemn Music* and *Ad Patrem*. In *At a Solemn Music* a private epiphanic moment in time permits us as auditors to hear the music sung even now by the angelic host at the "sapphire-coloured throne" of God (5–16), to participate "as once we did" before the Fall and with grace will do again when we "sing in endless morn of light." The poem conveys an unusually urgent sense of time. The speaker, who is generalized to "we" talks of a renewal that will occur here "soon" and the final end that will occur "ere long": the elements together hint of millenarianism. Unlike the immediate personal reward of eternal bliss promised to the subjects of Milton's funeral elegies in the 1630s, the vision in *At a Solemn Music* presents the history of the world.[8] The Latin poem *Ad Patrem*—undatable but presumably also written in the 1630s—seems likewise to posit two stages of joy, one in time and one at the end of time, though reversed in their order of presentation. The first stage appears in the vision of Milton and his father in golden crowns playing music to which the heavens answer, a vision that will be realized at "the end of life and time and the beginning of eternity" (30).[9] The parallel second stage is the ecstatic experience of the *spiritus* while its body is still alive; this *spiritus* even now (*nunc quoque* sydereis intercinit ipse choreis [36]) is singing amid the choir of stars.[10] In these early poems, then, the need for heightened emotion and often for a natural sense of closure is reflected in movement not only from earth to heaven, but from time to eternity. The need amounts to a kind of anagogical imperative.

A *Mask Presented at Ludlow Castle* seems to ignore even those temporal means at its disposal for structural patterning. Although its basic motif, the journey, may be thought to have a temporal trajectory, Milton's masque instead employs all the resources offered by the genre for relative stasis, for "unfolding" tableau or emblem. We are made to feel the weight of the moment rather than the process of the journey. As a description of another country, the epilogue apparently repeats this spatial emphasis. Yet the history of its revisions has another tale to tell. Using the various states of the text available to us in S. E. Sprott's transcription, we can see first the gradual clarification of Milton's spatial constructions as they appear in the Attendant Spirit's "prologue" and epilogue, and then the final redefinition of the material as an allegory about human time.[11] The pattern of thought we noted in the other early poems—what I have just called an anagogical imperative— operates in *A Mask*'s epilogue as well. And like all endings, it redefines the nature of the process that it crowns.

I begin with a simplified account, based on Sprott's careful study of the manuscripts, of the complicated textual history of the material we now find in the epilogue. The opening of the masque in the Trinity manuscript (TMS), after the familiar four lines beginning "Before the starrie threshold of Iove's court," contains a passage describing the Spirit's "mansion." These fifteen or so lines are canceled at the earliest stage of the manuscript, TMS[1a]; they reappear in a much less confused version as an epilogue to the masque, in a state Sprott labels TMS[1c].[12] It is these lines, the first epilogue, that the

Bridgewater manuscript converts into a prologue, preceding even Jove's starry threshold. The Bridgewater manuscript very likely reflects the version of *A Mask* presented on 29 September 1634, but Milton seems to have preferred the material as an epilogue. Sometime before the 1637 publication of the work (probably in preparation for it [Sprott, p. 8]), he cancels the first epilogue (cancel lines occur in TMS[3a]) and copies out the final expanded version, that is, the second epilogue (also TMS[3a]).[13] We thus have three versions: a canceled or original opening, the first epilogue (used as a prologue in the Bridgewater manuscript), and the second epilogue. I include the texts of all three in figures 1–3 since the earlier ones are not readily available in most modern editions.

The original version of the Attendant Spirit's prologue (down to line 45 of the modern text), like the current opening of *A Mask,* is articulated along a spatial rather than a temporal axis.[14] In both, the Spirit contrasts the bright region of calm and serene air where he has come from with "the smoake & stirre of this dim spot," the world. The topos may have encouraged the young poet to try more than he could manage. The final lines of the deleted passage show Milton's conscious attempt to rein in his imagination: "but soft I was not sent to court yo[r] wonder / wth distant worlds, & strange removed clime[s]."[15] The "strangeness" of these climes is depicted with a stronger juxtaposition of positive and negative images than the first epilogue will eventually present. In addition to the elements Milton more or less retains—Hesperian gardens, roses and hyacinths covered with moisture, celestial songs, a fair tree with golden fruit—one finds darker ideas that he abandons: a scaly-harnessed dragon, steep falls, the waters of a jealous ocean shared between "the slow unfadom'd stygian poole" and the "wide Atlantique."[16] The first epilogue regularizes these ambivalent signals into something univocally attractive, but no longer so suggestively British. The gardens in the epilogue may still belong to Hesperus, but without being placed in the Atlantic they do not immediately evoke the blessed isles in the West that tradition allowed Shakespeare's Gaunt to associate with the demiparadise of Britain in *Richard II.*[17] Supported by the allusion to the *Phaedo*'s "true earth" that still remains in the Spirit's opening lines, Milton's geographical reference in the original passage creates a splendidly Spenserian effect, the kind of doubled description of the same place that occurs when Guyon and Arthur read the faery and "actual" versions of British history. It could not have been easy for a young poet to sacrifice such a conception.

Yet he does. The first epilogue (and therefore the Bridgewater manuscript prologue) replaces the possible allusion to a "true Britain" with a more extensive description of various literary paradises, worldly and otherworldly, that have been virtually interchangeable since early Greek literature.[18] There

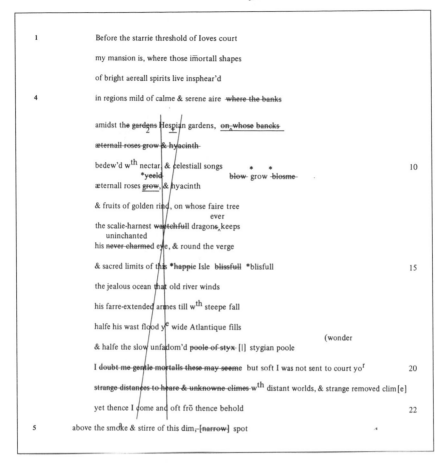

Fig. 1. Trinity manuscript, original version. From Sprott, *John Milton, "A Maske,"* pp. 44, 46.

are considerably fewer classical references in this first epilogue than there are in the second, but we can still find hints of the final form (see fig. 2 for text). Milton begins to place figures in his landscape: he replaces "Hesperian gardens" with "gardens faire / of Hesperus & his daughters three / that sing about the golden tree"; the lowercase flower "hyacinth" of the canceled opening is capitalized and perhaps thereby made ambiguously anthropomorphic;[19] the goddess Iris is newly introduced along with "many a cherub" in soft repose. The striking innovation is of course these cherubs, who lie on flower beds that Iris drenches "with manna dew." The biblical associations of cherubs and manna dew, like the references to Iris and the rainbow, all point

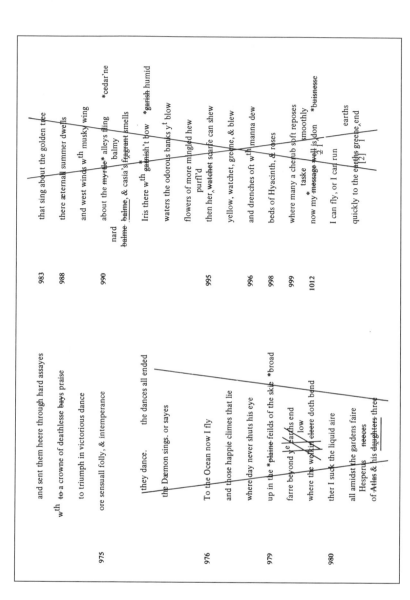

Fig. 2. Trinity manuscript, first epilogue. From Sprott, *John Milton, "A Maske,"* pp. 180, 182.

to boundary crossings between heaven and earth (messengers, messages, gifts). By blending biblical references with the many classical paradises alluded to in the earlier lines, Milton negotiates a field of potential conflict gracefully and without defensiveness. There are no invidious comparisons. The Judeo-Christian references, coming last, undoubtedly have the edge (the alternative sequence is unthinkable), but they do not assert their superiority. Instead, we are offered harmony. Biblical and classical otherworlds exist as it were in the same "place" and even perhaps at the same time—or in the same "no time," since the two temporal ideas newly introduced in the epilogue specifically deny time: these "climes that lie / where day never shuts his eye" are blessed with "æternall summer."[20]

Even after the masque's performance in September 1634, then, Milton sees his ending as presenting another world that apparently exists concurrently with ours. Because it is unpeopled, this world is not expressly a reward for virtuous living, although tradition would make it the backdrop for such an idea. The association is encouraged by the ending of the masque proper, with the song's final reference to "a crown of deathless praise" (972). Yet the very timelessness of the scene gives rise to a structural flaw: describing something that exists before the action of the masque as well as afterwards, the passage can be placed anywhere. The Bridgewater manuscript, in fact, transfers it without alteration to the prologue. Milton's final revision may thus be the result of a desire for unmistakable closure.

As I see it, the second epilogue is revised backward from the magnificent closure offered by the Cupid and Psyche material. The new ending makes at least two important changes: it introduces the idea of allegory or need for interpretation into what seemed a simple description ("list mortals if yor eares be true"), and it breaks the entire epilogue into three segments (the Hesperides section, Venus and Adonis, then Cupid and Psyche). In this scheme, the middle segment forms a seamless transition: the Assyrian queen and Adonis exist on the same plane as Iris, since he is lying on beds drenched with her dew, but the lovers are also connected (as they are in Spenser) to the following myth of Venus's son, Cupid, who dwells on another plane, "farre above in spangled sheene." The Venus and Adonis myth for Milton faces both ways here, encapsulating or extracting a truth about the "space" it shares with the Hesperides, and juxtaposing that truth to the one offered by the pendant or opposing myth of Cupid and Psyche.[21] And this truth, as I earlier suggested, has to do with time.

With this overall plan in mind, we may return to the revision that creates the second epilogue to see how it is affected (see fig. 3). Aside from the added material, the most significant change is the removal of the specifically biblical references: "many a cherub soft reposes" becomes "young Adonis oft

```
976   To the Ocean now I fly,
      and those happie climes that lie
      where day never shuts his eye
      up in the broad feilds of y^e skie:
980   there I suck the liquid aire
      all amidst the gardens faire
      of Hespus & his daughters three
            that sing about the golden tree.
      where grows the right-borne gold upon his native tree.
      along the crisped shades and bowrs
985   revells the spruce and jocond Spring
      the Graces and the rosie-bosom'd Howrs
      thither all thire bounties bring
      that there eternall Summer dwells
      & west winds w^th muskie wing
990   about the cedar'ne alleys fling
      Nard & Cassia's baulmie smells
      Iris there w^th humid bow
      waters the odorous banks that blow
      flowers of more mingled hew
995   then her purfl'd scarfe can shew
```

```
                                          Elysian
      yellow, watchet, greene, & blew
      & drenches w^th Sabæan dew
                            (list mortals if yo^r eares be true)
996   beds of hyacinth & roses
998   where young Adonis oft reposes
      waxing well of his deepe wound
1000  in slumber soft, & on the ground
      sadly sits th' Assyrian Queene
      but farre above in spangled sheene
      celestiall Cupid her fam'd son advanc't
1005  holds his deare Psyche sweet entranc't
      after her wandring labours long
      till free consent the gods among
      make her his eternall Bride
      and from her faire unspotted side
1010  tow blissfull twins are to be borne
      Youth & Ioy:  so Iove hath sworne
```

Fig. 3: Trinity manuscript, second epilogue. From Sprott, *John Milton, "A Maske,"* pp. 184, 186, 188.

reposes," and "manna" dew initially becomes "Sabæan" dew. "Sabæan" is cagey: although it may remind us of Sheba and therefore a biblical story, the basic reference is, I think, neutrally geographical, to southern Arabia. The "cedar'ne alleys . . . / nard & casia's balmy smells" already present in the first epilogue have evoked the same set of associations we find in *Paradise Lost,* where the balmy breeze of Eden is compared to the "winds [that] blow / Sabaean odors from the spicy shore / Of Araby the Blest" (IV, 156–65).[22] Not so biblical as "manna," "Sabæan" still imports difference into this largely classical paradise and shifts attention from west to east, from Hesperus not merely to Venus's Adonis, but to an Adonis mourned by "th' Assyrian Queene." One would think it the perfect transition word, but a still later revision (TMS[3c]) changes "Sabæan" to "Elysian."[23] The Renaissance status of the myth as bridging classical and Near Eastern cultures is here signaled by the way the lovers are named: he is Adonis but she is the Assyrian queen. In Milton's mind the myth seems Near Eastern. He usually calls the female figure Astarte and the male Thammuz (*Nat.* 204; *PL* I, 446, 452).[24] The cultural point, we note, is driven home spatially: Elysian dew drenches the very flower beds beside which the Assyrian goddess cyclically mourns. The paradise of Hesperus or Elysium and the paradise represented by the Garden of Adonis thus share the same "space" and, by implication, other qualities as well.

The spatial argument has a temporal correlative. If the never-ending day of the Hesperides and the sad cycle of the Assyrian queen's lament take place in the same garden, should there not be some relation between the different kind of time each depicts? Milton's further additions (984–87) to the Hesperides section heighten our awareness of the interrelation. The "bounties" brought by the Graces and Hours (987) refer to the fertility cycle just as surely as does the death of Adonis, though one emphasizes growth and the other periodic barrenness. The "crisped shades" (984) insinuate spring, I think,[25] and, together with "eternall summer" (988), set up the paradisal paradox of simultaneous seasonal change and stasis. The fact that the song of the Hesperides introduced into the first epilogue's opening lines is an allusion to a dirge, a lament for death, gains new appropriateness.[26] While originally the dragon's slaying alone was presumably relevant, now the dirge at the beginning joins with the sad Assyrian queen at the end to form a circle that encloses the garden before the scene shifts to "farre above in spangled sheene."

Since cyclicity occurs, masked, in the paradisally timeless conception of the initial Hesperidean lines of the second epilogue as well as being manifest in the closing Assyrian-Greek mythological tableau, it shapes the dominant understanding of time presented in these two sections. Whatever apparent beauty it can offer, however, cyclicity is sad because it is an entrapment: at this moment, Adonis "reposes / Waxing well of his deepe wound," but the healing process will always be followed by another wound and another period of mourning.[27] Milton's time word here is "oft": "young Adonis oft reposes / Waxing well of his deepe wound." Neither eternal nor unique, the moment (which is itself a process) continually recurs. These classical garden paradises, for all their real pleasures, are not satisfying. Either as traditionally linked to rewards in afterlife—that is, as "promised ends"—or, alternatively, as pure views of human happiness, they do not fulfill our need for permanence or meaning. The vision is not an adequate teleology, just as the first epilogue, which merely described it, did not offer adequate closure.

Venus and Adonis are brought in to epitomize the problems Milton now sees, problems to which Cupid and Psyche present a countervision. Once timelessness becomes subordinate to cyclicity in presenting the classical understanding of time, the harmony between biblical and classical elements depicted in the paradisal description of the first epilogue is no longer possible. The issue between them focuses on the way cyclicity empties *this* life of significance. Under the aegis of cyclicity, history and human time are condemned to endless and therefore meaningless repetition. "But farre above in spangled sheene" we meet a totally different conception of time. Cupid embraces Psyche "*after* her wandring labours long" and will do so "till" that moment they receive permission to marry. She will then be his eternal bride, but again at one moment Youth and Joy "*are to be* borne." "So Ioue hath sworne": the future represents Jove's plan. The strong insistence on time suggests that, in spite of the upward spatial movement, we are still talking about this world and therefore about human experience. But that experience is now freed from cycle and understood as embodying purpose and shape: Psyche's labors enable the lovers to embrace now, and in time will be crowned with marriage and eternal bliss.[28]

The contrast set up by this mythological diptych was crystallized by St. Augustine. In opposition to Greek and Roman cyclicity, Augustine's argument assumes the Jewish understanding of a "living" God whose will is manifested in (or as) history—a course of events seen (as in the Joseph story) as a linear unfolding of a divine plan.[29] The issue of Christian time occurs at several points in *The City of God*, where the opposing idea is always pagan conceptions of cyclicity and their implicit denial that history has any meaning. The challenge offered by cyclicity appears in two prominent intellectual formulations: in the personal odyssey of rebirths forecast by the Orphic idea of reincarnation, and in the absolute historical repetitions featured in the Stoic conception of the Great Year.[30] Augustine attacks the first idea, rebirth, because it denies the essential Christian tenet that everlasting bliss or damnation is the reward for actions chosen in a single lifetime (X, 30, and XII,

21). He attacks the second idea, historical recurrence, because it denies the uniqueness and meaning of Christ's life. St. Paul's statements are his proof: "For Christ died once for our sins, but 'rising from the dead he dies no more, and death shall no longer have dominion over him'; and after the resurrection 'we shall always be with the Lord'" (XII, 14).[31] The Augustinian tradition divides the issue of Christian time into two perspectives, the private and the historical, individual human life on the one hand and defining moments in the chronological unfolding of God's plan on the other.

Milton's argument in *A Mask* is similar. The Cupid and Psyche myth was understood even in antiquity as a story about the human soul; it was engraved, for example, on many early Christian sarcophagi. But the point of the myth for Milton here is the shape it offers not only to human life but to history itself. Taken as an allegory of time, it presents Judeo-Christian teleology. Even more specifically, because it offers both a defining moment that has already occurred and the promise of a better end, the allegorical narrative presents Christian apocalyptic thought.[32] In *Christian Doctrine,* Milton devotes chapter 25 to "Incomplete Glorification and the Assurance of Salvation": the Christian "will without any doubt attain eternal life, and perfect glory, since he is already justified, adopted and partially glorified by union and communion with Christ and the Father."[33] Milton's tableau suggests the emotion of this belief. The embrace of Cupid and Psyche is an allegorical action that acknowledges the soul's uniqueness and its happy security in having achieved its desired and proper place. (The assurance of salvation, the treatise says, is "a source of unspeakable joy" [p. 505].) There is a release from anxiety and "task" that will eventuate, moreover, in a still greater joy. All direction is linear and forward, creating a description not of eternity but of history itself understood teleologically, that is, with its meaning explained by and in its end. The precise moment depicted by the tableau is not clear in either the private or historical dimension, perhaps because Milton is seeking the shape of an action rather than a set of one-to-one equivalences. Historically, the defining moment was the Passion, but Milton's millenarian desires may want that moment to be reflected in some politically specific (though as yet still uncertain) time. The private allegory too can bear further probing. Cupid and Psyche are placed in the spangled sheen, but as the Attendant Spirit's didactic coda implies by urging the audience to "climb / Higher than the sphery chime" (1019–20), there is still a more exalted region to aspire to. Woodhouse's reading of the line cited in the *Variorum* seems right: "the goal is to reach the heavenly order and hear instead the angelic choir" (p. 989). That both *At a Solemn Music* and *Ad Patrem* set up parallels between quasi-ecstatic experience in this life and the final beatitude of the next can perhaps direct us in interpreting Cupid and Psyche in *A Mask*. "For the true believer," Tayler tells us, "the future Kingdom of God has been incorporated into the present, permitting the true Christian to taste of what is to come (Hebrews 6:5)" (p. 152). The joy promised by Christian time, that is, by a Christian understanding of life and of history, is available in some form in this world as well as the next; these sacred moments of joy are premonitions of the final end.[34]

Milton's handling of the myths of Venus and Adonis and Cupid and Psyche in the epilogue to *A Mask* is not so idiosyncratic as it perhaps seems. Hints of it can be found in the undoubted source of its material, Spenser's Garden of Adonis.

Spenser's basic conception is, of course, different: his garden, though called a "ioyous Paradize" (III, vi, 29), is not inspired by classical otherworlds but by medieval gardens of love presided over by Venus *genetrix*.[35] This origin seems to account for most of its themes and strategies, even its strong concern with time. A primary threat to the dream of love is temporal decay. In Spenser's garden, as in Shakespeare's mutability sonnets, time, the lover's enemy and the destroyer of "all that liues" (40, 8), is also the enemy of art, threatening "balefull night, where all things are forgot" (47, 3). Stanza 45 at first presents metamorphosis as a physical event that actually happened to such lovers as Hyacinthus and Narcissus; then its simultaneous status as a "poetic" device allows a shift to poetry's comparable battle against mortality.[36] These sad lovers who were metamorphosed into flowers are paralleled with "sad Amaranthus, made a flowre but late," and Amaranthus is explicitly linked to Aminta, whose immortality or "endlesse date" is conferred not by metamorphosis but by "sweet Poets verse." A similar swerve from metamorphosis takes place with Adonis: I shall argue in a moment that the unqualified assertion present in the words "endlesse date" gives rise to a version of Adonis's story that ignores his death and even his metamorphosis into a flower in order to concentrate instead on his triumph over time and his enjoyment of "eternall blis" (48, 1).

This shift away from metamorphosis in some ways reflects what we saw in Milton's dual nomenclature, that is, a distinction between Greek and Near Eastern versions of the Adonis myth. In describing the tapestry hanging on the walls of Malecasta's castle earlier in Book III, Spenser created a clearly linear narrative of the Ovidian myth: the story on the various panels enacts a chain of purpose, pleading, decision, prophecy, death, and metamorphosis (i, 34–38).[37] Perhaps we recall this earlier treatment when reading in the garden of sad lovers transformed into flowers (vi, 45); we certainly recall it in the stanza immediately following—"There yet, some say, in secret he does ly, / Lapped in flowres and pretious spycery" (46, 4–5)—lines that actually echo the language of Malecasta's tapestry (i, 36). But the Adonis myth presented here in canto vi is no longer the same. Gone are both linear narrative, representing the Ovidian mode of storytelling, and metamorphosis, representing one of antiquity's imaginative responses to the threat of death. They are replaced by a version of the myth whose initial assertion is cyclicity (Adonis is "by succession made perpetuall, / Transformed oft" [47, 5–6]). Moreover, the version takes the form of non-narrative tableau, as if to underline its freedom from linearity and therefore from death.

We see in this sequence of ideas one of the characteristic patterns structuring the description of the Garden of Adonis. To delineate the pattern requires something of a digression, but establishing its pervasiveness can perhaps suggest why we accept Spenser's sleight of hand with the Adonis material largely without protest. The stanzas of the garden episode as a whole (29–52) do not offer a linear progression (they present no imaginary walking tour).[38] They are most often linked merely by contrariety, a procedure that allows negation of the current idea to form the substance of the following stanza. My example will be the startling counterturn between stanzas 40 and 41; although it is the most striking of these progressions, it can stand for them all. In this counterturn, the powerful climax of Time's destructive force (39) and the subsequent lament for our helplessness to prevent its ravages (40) are merely wished away by the opening lines of stanza 41: "But were it not, that Time their troubler is, / All that in this delightfull Gardin growes / Should happie be, and haue immortall blis." The wish then becomes a "fact" as the indicative replaces the conditional. The subsequent stanzas extol the pleasures of love without jealousy or envy—and without linear time as well, since the experience is a paradisal existence of "continuall spring, and haruest there / Continuall" (42). The *mons veneris* (43–44), the central stanzas of the whole episode, offers a crescendo of life[39] exactly corresponding to the earlier destructive crescendo produced by Time as death. In the very next stanza, this joy in turn gives rise by contrariety to stories of *sad* lovers who have been transformed into flowers (45), presumably a partial (and literary) success over the death that has been silenced for so long. The next lover, sad Amaranthus only lately made a flower, shatters the success over death still further by its explicit association with the "purple gore" of Aminta's "wretched fate." The allusion, I take it, is to Sir Philip Sidney. Time and death—in their most palpable historical form—have indeed returned. The awful coincidence of Sidney's fatal thigh wound (signaled here by the "purple gore" of Adonis's and Marinell's wounds, which are, of course, to the thigh as well) drives us back to the literary tradition of Adonis's death—and thus to the end of my digression.

Within the Adonis sequence the technique of contrariety works as I noted above: a stanza that recalls the earlier Ovidian account of his wound (46) is followed with one in which an alternative version of the myth downplays the Ovidian metamorphosis by proclaiming what looks like a cyclical triumph over death. The triumph is not easy, however, and finally not satisfying. The Stygian gods remain envious, and eternity comes about not through the expected cyclical repetition of sameness but through a cyclical necessity for change:

> for he may not
> For euer die, and euer buried bee
> In balefull night, where all things are forgot;
> All be he subiect to mortalitie,
> Yet is eterne in mutabilitie,
> And by succession made perpetuall,
> Transformed oft, and chaunged diuerslie.   (47, 1–7)

The next stanza moves away from even these concessions. There is no room for an Adonis who is in any way "subiect to mortalitie," though his new positive state shows vulnerability by being defined through negation. The emerging desire for linear closure (note "henceforth," "once," "for ay") brings with it narrative reminiscences of the Ovidian tale and its recounting of a single dramatic event:

> Ne feareth he henceforth that foe of his
> Which with his cruell tusk him deadly cloyd:
> For that wilde Bore, the which him once annoyd,
> She firmely hath emprisoned for ay.   (48, 3–6)

Milton's temporal concerns in the revised epilogue to *A Mask* lead him to conflate the classical and Near Eastern myths of Venus and Adonis as "pagan" cyclicity, but Spenser's perspective remains double. His concerns seem more strongly narrative and psychologically exploratory. His two versions of the myth represent two different narrative strategies (I have suggested "story" versus "tableau"), both carrying equal weight as expressions of the human desire to overcome death. This desire too creates a bridge between Spenser and Milton: the garden of love and the otherworldly paradise each presents an incarnation of the desire for immortality.

Beyond this shared ethos, the most significant aspect of the Garden of Adonis material for Milton's revisions may well be how the Venus and Adonis story itself generates the *need* for the myth of Cupid and Psyche in terms Spenser articulates by means of time. Venus and Adonis have been so assimilated to the philosophical dimension of the garden—he is "the Father of all formes" (47, 8) in "the first seminarie / Of all things, that are borne to liue and

die" (30, 4–5)—that very little about them translates as "human." Venus and
Adonis together seem to be the principle of generation or fertility. Like the
garden's simultaneous spring and harvest, the experience rendered through
them is paradisal and magical: by fiat there is no longer any boar to trouble
them, and Adonis's love is without pain. He "sport[s] himselfe in safe felicity,"
playing with a Cupid who, "when [that is, whenever] he hath with spoiles and
cruelty / Ransackt the world," resorts to the garden and lays aside his "sad
darts" (49). Love in the "ransackt" world, then, is governed by Cupid rather
than Venus. Suddenly the garden, which earlier seemed a metaphor for some
aspect of this world, is now distanced from it. Worldly or human love experience becomes either what Psyche endured before arriving here, or what
Amoret will find outside the garden as she exercises "goodly womanhead"
(51, 9). Psyche's tale embodies the full spectrum of this love experience:

> And his true loue faire Psyche with him playes,
> Faire Psyche to him lately reconcyld,
> After long troubles and vnmeet vpbrayes,
> With which his mother Venus her reuyld,
> And eke himselfe her cruelly exyld:
> But now in stedfast loue and happy state
> She with him liues, and hath him borne a chyld. (50, 1–7)

What we notice is her mortal lot: injustice (the "vpbrayes" are "vnmeet"),
cruelty (Cupid's as well as his mother's), long troubles.[40] Appropriately for
the center of Book III, Psyche's all-too-human experience magnifies that of
the conventional lover. Being human, the experience is expressed in the
linearity of a single action that incorporates the notion of time into its meaning. The love is shaped into trial and reward. It has "lately" been transformed
into a steadfast and happy state (enduring over time rather than denying
time) and has been crowned with a child who will grow up and be nurtured
(along with Amoret) to prepare herself for the later eventuality of love and
marriage (51).[41]

Within the overarching Cupid and Psyche myth, the two main figures
seem to require a somewhat different kind of allegorical reading. Psyche—
perhaps because her name means "soul"—is the *subject* of the love experience. What she undergoes explains what it means to be a lover. Cupid's
actions, in contrast, define the range or quality of love itself. For him, playing
in the garden alternates with cruelly ransacking the world for spoils. "Ransacking" and "playing" are versions of his famous leaden and golden arrows,
suggesting that this alternation is really a bipolar timelessness: that is, allegorically, these are always the two possibilities of love. In what I have called the
overarching myth, however, Cupid and Psyche taken together share a narra-

tive that defines love as a story with a linear shape—one that, in the mode of comedy, acknowledges time as a medium, not as an enemy. This joint Cupid and Psyche myth, with its linearity and fruitfulness, is generated (through a kind of contrariety) by an unsatisfactory treatment of human time in the Venus and Adonis fertility myth, and gains fuller meaning through resonance with it.[42] In Spenser's Garden of Adonis (as well as in the betrothal of Redcrosse and Una), we can find adequate evidence for the type of allegorical conception that Milton employs in the final lines of the second epilogue.

At the end of Milton's poetic career, *Paradise Regained* returns to the ideas of linear and cyclical time that provide the allegory of the second epilogue. The narrative of the Christ event itself depicts a linear progression, but as A. B. Chambers has argued, even that linear pattern of unique events is formally accentuated with repetitions: "the poem doubles back upon itself as thematic motif, typological parallel, or significant image recurs and then recurs again. For everything in *Paradise Regained* happens not once but repeatedly. Yet the poem's line of time is rectilinear as well as circular."[43] Toward the end of the poem—indeed at its climactic moment—Milton seems to abandon this temporal inclusiveness for unmistakable antithesis, reprising the *Mask* epilogue's argument about time and history. To do so, he introduces the only elaborate classical similes in the work:[44] directly after Christ's final triumph over the Tempter—"He said, and stood. / But Satan smitten with amazement fell" (IV, 561–62)—Milton compares the action first with Hercules' victory over Antaeus and then with Oedipus's victory over the Sphinx.

That Satan himself is an actor in *Paradise Regained* seems to cause Milton's sharply constructed antithesis here. Ideas that we have seen before as merely inferior or less satisfactory now become satanic. Barbara Lewalski notes Satan's intrinsic association in the poem with historical cycles: "Satan's sense of the cyclical movement of time and his concomitant belief in recurrent and repetitive patterns in history" is evidenced, she says, in the sterile repetition of his own actions as "he returns again and again only to be repulsed as many times."[45] The two similes give more specific historical resonance to this conception. The conspicuous classical content of both the Hercules and Oedipus similes allows them to be prefigurations within ancient literature of the demise of its understanding of history. Each simile presents the victory of linear history over pure cycle. Earth's son Antaeus "strove / With Jove's Alcides, and oft foiled still rose, / . . . / [until] Throttled at length in the air, [he] expired and fell" (563–68); the Theban monster devoured whoever could not solve her riddle, but "That once found out and solved," threw herself headlong into the river (572–75). Antaeus's single death in the air ends the pattern of continued revival from his mother's lap; the second simile points not to the Sphinx's long-standing power over Thebes but to the pattern of her devourings that ends the moment Oedipus solves her riddle. As actions within classical legend expressing a redemption from the burden of cycle that Christ's Passion also represents, they figure the same action that the poem itself figures.[46] The angelic choir in celebration sings this linearity of time under Christ:

> him long of old
> Thou didst debel, and down from heav'n cast
> With all his army; now thou hast avenged
> Supplanted Adam,
>
> . . . .
>
> He [Satan] never more henceforth will dare set foot
> In Paradise to tempt; his snares are broke.   (604–07, 610–11)

The Hercules and Oedipus similes are thus conceived in an even more combative mode than was the double tableau at the end of *A Mask's* revised epilogue. But the poem as a whole is, as it must be, more ambiguous about its relation to cyclicity. Cycles had by no means been banished as an element in Christian thought and practice. The Church's own liturgy is cyclical, though each annual cycle traces the linear sequence of Christ's life; its doubleness conveys the pattern of nature and of individual human life, where linear time is made up of circling days and seasons.[47] Moreover, throughout the Christian era cycles and circles have remained relevant or attractive schemes for understanding the welter of historical experience. The forward procession of events in the Christian scheme of history itself gains meaning through certain repetitions, echoes, and reminiscences provided by the typological relation of Old to New Testament. Unlike cycles, however, they do not produce moments of exact recurrence.[48] The angels' song is clear about this typological dimension of history: Satan's being "trod down / Under [Christ's] feet" (620–21) will be repeated in his "last and deadliest wound" (622); the Paradise that Adam lost will be replaced by "A fairer Paradise . . . / . . . when time shall be / Of tempter and temptation without fear" (613, 616–17). We see not only the repetition and the measure of distinction between the occurrences, but the marshaling into an overall linear shape as well. *Paradise Regained* as title supplies the idea both of repetition and of unchanging end.

A similar doubleness can be detected formally in the poem's final action: "he unobserved / Home to his mother's house private returned" (638–39). The end of *Paradise Regained*, by depicting a "return," a homecoming, rather than a new venture, creates a shape that poetically is felt as circular. This allows Milton to draw on the aesthetic pleasure and symbolic resonance of the circle to create formal satisfaction at the same time that he denies cyclicity.

But the circular, even recurrent, action of homecoming is here preparation for the single linear act: "on thy glorious work / Now enter, and begin to save mankind" (634–35). Chambers would balance these two lines of time against each other; I rather suspect that, just as in *A Mask*'s double tableau, the cycle of return is subordinated to the linear act of Christ's being "on his way" (638).

University of Toronto

NOTES

1. William Kerrigan, "The Politically Correct *Comus:* A Reply to John Leonard," *MQ* 27 (1993): 154.

2. Quotations from Milton's poetry (except for versions of the epilogue to *A Mask*) are taken from *The Poems of John Milton*, ed. John Carey and Alastair Fowler (London, 1968). It will be cited hereafter by line number in the text and as *Poems* in the notes. Carey is responsible for all the poems except *Paradise Lost*.

3. I do not read *A Mask* itself as an allegory.

4. Even as an allegory concerned with love, lines 996–1011 provide an unexpected ending to *A Mask*. The love neither of Venus and Adonis nor of Cupid and Psyche seems significantly related to Comus's proposition to the Lady, though it may well be important for our understanding of Milton that for him a finally satisfying idea of paradise "needs" a love relation, even if only in the vehicle of his metaphor.

5. Edward Tayler, *Milton's Poetry: Its Development in Time* (Pittsburgh, 1979), p. 45, and his readings of the Nativity ode, *Upon the Circumcision, On Time*, and *At a Solemn Music* in these terms (pp. 32–42), to which my account is indebted.

6. *L'Allegro* and *Il Penseroso* are other early poems obviously structured by time, but it is diurnal. Various time patterns have been suggested for *Lycidas* as well; see, for example, Tayler, *Milton's Poetry*, chap. 2; Lowry Nelson Jr., *Baroque Lyric Poetry* (New Haven, 1961), chap. 5. Leo Spitzer, *Classical and Christian Ideas of World Harmony*, ed. Anna Granville Hatcher (Baltimore, 1963), pp. 103–05, speaks of a Greek-Jewish-Christian scheme in *At a Solemn Music*.

7. The connections between music and time are complex here: experience of such music can perhaps directly evoke the end of time seen as a kind of return to the golden age (133–48), but, in fact, history demands a linear plotting of time that encompasses the Last Judgment and the kingdom of heaven (149–72).

8. Michael Fixler, *Milton and the Kingdoms of God* (Evanston, Ill., 1964), pp. 47–48, usefully distinguishes between immediate eschatological imagery and apocalyptic eschatology, which, because it includes the idea of divine justice, must take place at the end of time. *At a Solemn Music*, like most of the elegies of the 1630s, omits the idea of apocalyptic justice. See also Katharine R. Firth, *The Apocalyptic Tradition in Reformation Britain, 1530–1645* (Oxford, 1979), esp. pp. 232–37.

9. The translation from *Ad Patrem* is from *A Variorum Commentary on the Poems of John Milton*, vol. 1, *The Latin and Greek Poems*, ed. Douglas Bush (New York, 1970), p. 244; the Latin is less clear: *Aeternaeque morae stabunt immobilis aevi* (Carey translation, *Poems*, p. 153: "and when [*cum*, previous line] the eternal ages of changeless time stand still"). The eschatological imagery of *Ad Patrem* differs in offering closure not for a whole poem, but only for its opening segment.

10. Carey, *Poems*, ad loc. thinks the *spiritus* is Milton's; I would prefer a more general identification.

11. S. E. Sprott, *John Milton, "A Maske": The Earlier Versions* (Toronto, 1973). I shall use this text, cited as Sprott, for quotations from the epilogue in all its versions. I wish to thank Professor Sprott for his gracious permission to use photographs of his text for this study.

12. TMS[1a] is the symbol for text in its first state as it was contextually emended up to line 885 (just before the song to Sabrina). TMS[1c] is text from lines 886 to 1039, contextually emended. See ibid., p. 6.

13. Sprott comments ad loc. on the neatness and evenness of the writing; there are, however, minor contextual emendations. See ibid., p. 8, for TMS[3a].

14. Compare M. M. Bakhtin, *The Dialogic Imagination: Four Essays*, ed. Michael Holquist, trans. Caryl Emerson and M. Holquist (Austin, Tex., 1982), commenting generally on golden ages: "There is a greater readiness to build a superstructure for reality (the present) along a vertical axis of upper and lower than to move forward along the horizontal axis of time" (p. 148). The only temporal reference in *A Mask's* opening concerns virtue's reward "after this mortal change" (16–21, modern text).

15. This is Milton's second attempt at these lines (see figure 1 for the original version). "Clim[e]" is what Sprott reads; "Climes" is the reading of various editions and of the first attempt.

16. Most conjectures about these changes have not had the benefit of Sprott's careful examination of the manuscripts based on shades of ink and quality of pen used. C. S. Lewis's reasons for cancellation disregard the shift in "earth" imagery that takes place within the twenty-odd lines of the Attendant Spirit's initial speech ("A Note on *Comus*," *RES* 8 [1932]: 170–76). See Stanley Fish, "Problem-Solving in *Comus*," in *Illustrious Evidence: Approaches to English Literature in the Earlier Seventeenth Century*, ed. Earl Miner (Berkeley, 1975), pp. 116–18, on this speech. William B. Hunter, "A Bibliographical Excursus Into Milton's Trinity Manuscript," *MQ* 19 (1985). 61–71, is concerned with other matters.

17. See Josephine Waters Bennett, "Britain Among the Fortunate Isles," *SP* 53 (1956): 114–40, on the ancient tradition and its uses in English literature. Bennett discusses *Richard II* but not *A Mask*. I owe the reference to my colleague David Galbraith.

18. See A. Bartlett Giamatti, *The Earthly Paradise and the Renaissance Epic* (Princeton, 1966), pp. 32–47.

19. The manuscripts and printed texts are not consistent, but through capitalization or italics they generally tend to imply the story of Hyacinth as well as merely the flower.

20. The canceled opening includes "æternall roses," but the idea becomes more particularly temporal in revision.

21. The linking rhyme pattern that F. T. Prince describes for *Lycidas* is produced here structurally in the pattern of thought. See "The Italian Element in *Lycidas*," in *Milton's Lycidas: The Tradition and the Poem*, 2nd ed., ed. C. A. Patrides (Columbia, Mo., 1983), pp. 168–69. The revision (TMS[3a]) may well have been done in 1637, the year of *Lycidas's* composition.

22. Alastair Fowler's note refers to Diodorus Siculus's description, III, xlvi, 4, of *Arabia felix*, which tells of balsam, cassia, frankincense, and cinnamon (*Poems*, ad loc., p. 612). See also *PL* V, 292–93. Virgil, *Georgics* I, 57, and II, 117, uses *Sabæan* to refer to Arabian frankincense.

23. In my reading of Sprott's apparatus, "Elysian" is the only revision Milton makes to the second epilogue upon later reflection. "Assyrian" itself may be such a transition word, since Eden is an Assyrian garden at *PL* IV, 285.

24. In *Manso*, the subject of Marino's poem *L'Adone* is described as *Assyrios divum . . . amores* (11).

25. OED 4 says the sense is uncertain when applied to trees. I take it to refer to the new

growth on darker foliage (compare "crisped yew," in Herrick's "Ceremonies for Candlemasse Eve," cited by the OED: "Then [that is, at Easter] youthfull Box which now hath grace, / Your houses to renew; / Grown old, surrender must his place, / Unto the crisped yew"). The Graces and Hours will lead on eternal spring in *PL* IV, 166–68, and the traditional association is likely already in Milton's mind (see Fowler's note, *Poems,* ad loc.). The same paradisal point is made by the coexistence of hyacinths and roses (*A Mask,* 997), which as real flowers bloom in different seasons.

26. See *A Variorum Commentary on the Poems of John Milton,* vol. 2, pt. 3, ed. A. S. P. Woodhouse and Douglas Bush (New York, 1972), ad loc. The dirge is for Ladon, the dragon slain by Heracles (in Apollonius Rhodius); the reference is apparently present in the dragon slaying of the original opening. In contrast, Woodhouse is sure that Milton merely ignores or alters this tradition because "the whole suggestion is of joy, not sorrow" (p. 979).

27. Mark Morton's unpublished dissertation, "Despair and Metamorphosis in *The Faerie Queene*" (University of Toronto, 1992), offers an interesting discussion of this problem in Spenser's poem.

28. The closest Spenserian parallel would not be his Cupid and Psyche, but the betrothal between Una and Redcrosse in *FQ* I, xii. See Angus Fletcher, *The Prophetic Moment: An Essay on Spenser* (Chicago, 1971), p. 63.

29. See the discussion by C. A. Patrides, *The Grand Design of God: The Literary Form of the Christian Idea of History* (London, 1972), chapters 1 and 2. The "living God" is mentioned on page 2; there is an extensive bibliography on pages 24–25, note 23.

30. See Ernst Hoffman, "Platonism in Augustine's Philosophy of History," in *Philosophy and History: Essays Presented to Ernst Cassirer,* ed. Raymond Klibansky and H. J. Paton (Oxford, 1936), pp. 174–77, and S. G. F. Brandon, *History, Time, and Deity: A Historical and Comparative Study of Conceptions of Time in Religious Thought and Practice* (Manchester, Eng., 1965).

31. St. Augustine, *City of God,* Loeb volumes 3 (for Book X) and 4 (for Book XII) (London, 1957–72). The first biblical citation is Rom. vi, 9, the second is 1 Thess. iv, 17. Note Origen's reaction to the idea of Stoic cycles: "If this is admitted, I do not see how free will can be preserved, and how any praise and blame can be reasonable" (*Contra Celsum,* quoted in Frank E. Manuel, *Shapes of Philosophical History* [Stanford, 1965], p. 12).

32. See Oscar Cullman, *Christ and Time: The Primitive Christian Conception of Time and History,* 2nd ed., trans. F. V. Filson (London, 1962), pp. 86–87, esp. p. 87: "The hope of the final victory is so much more vivid because of the unshakably firm conviction that the battle that decides the victory has already taken place" (italics removed).

33. *De doctrina Christiana,* I, xxv, in *Complete Prose Works of John Milton,* 8 vols., ed. Don M. Wolfe et al. (New Haven, 1953–82), vol. VI, p. 503, in caps.

34. This corresponds interestingly to the experience of grace quoted from Jansenist diaries by Georges Poulet, *Studies in Human Time,* trans. Elliott Coleman (New York, 1959), pp. 17–18. The relation between the earthly paradise and what is "farre above" is perhaps suggested in the generational connection between Venus and Cupid, a connection that in context acknowledges the Old Testament roots of Christian ideas of history. "Assyrian" thus faces both ways: to pagan myths and to the Old Testament Assyrian garden. By calling Venus the Assyrian queen while insisting that she is the mother of Cupid, Milton distinguishes Christianity from (linear) Judaism as well as from (cyclical) paganism; Judaism and paganism are associated as dispensations prior to Christianity. Like pagan otherworlds, Old Testament Eden is a physical place, whereas New Testament Eden is a state of mind. The same pattern of connections among older cultures can be found in Dante and Spenser.

35. My text is *The Works of Edmund Spenser: A Variorum Edition,* ed. Edwin Greenlaw,

Charles G. Osgood, and Frederick M. Padelford, vol. 3, ed. F. M. Padelford (Baltimore, 1934). Subsequent references are to stanza and line of canto vi, unless otherwise noted. Canto numbers are in lowercase roman numerals; I have regularized italics.

36. The connection between metamorphosis and poetry may well be unavoidable because of Ovid. See Kenneth Gross's discussion of the metapoetics of Spenser's garden in *Spenserian Poetics: Idolatry, Iconoclasm, and Magic* (Ithaca, N.Y., 1985), pp. 181–209.

37. I have switched terminology from Greek to Ovidian because the Greek versions do not place quite the same emphasis on his transformation into a flower. In Bion's "Lament for Adonis," for example, both Venus's tears and Adonis's blood are turned into flowers, rather than Adonis himself.

38. That there is no fictional perceiver makes it unlike, for example, the presentation of the Bower of Bliss or the Castle of Busyrane.

39. For those who mistakenly think a picture is worth a thousand words, I would compare Gustave Courbet's famous painting, *The Origin of the World*—though Courbet's picture likely expresses a nastier conception. Spenser's *mons veneris* is psychologically paradisal by being thought of as an always available place rather than as the attribute of a possibly "coy" person.

40. "Unmeet" (inappropriate) has a social dimension, but the idea of unfairness is what I see here (compare the OED's citation of Cowper's translation of *Iliad* I, 145: "It were much unmeet that I alone . . . should want due recompense"). The ambiguity nicely catches the lover's simultaneous haplessness and claim of deserving.

41. The child, being Pleasure, is no longer the human character in Spenser's allegory; the burden of the experience falls to Amoret.

42. That Venus and Adonis are an archetypal myth of love and fertility paradoxically generates the need for a Cupid and Psyche who have offspring. This is apparently not just a Protestant poet's dilemma; see Marcel Detienne, *The Gardens of Adonis: Spices in Greek Mythology*, trans. Janet Lloyd (Hassocks, Eng., 1977), for an unexpectedly relevant structuralist reading of the myth.

43. A. B. Chambers, "The Double Time Scheme in *Paradise Regained*," in *Milton Studies* VII, ed. Albert C. Labriola and Michael Lieb (Pittsburgh, 1975), p. 198.

44. Douglas Bush's observation, *The Complete Poetical Works of John Milton* (Boston, 1965), ad loc.

45. Barbara K. Lewalski, "Time and History in *Paradise Regained*," in *The Prison and the Pinnacle*, ed. Balchandra Rajan (Toronto, 1973), pp. 66, 68. Lewalski chooses a simile depicting recurrence in nature rather than in history to illustrate her point—the swarm of bees at IV, 15–24—and does not speak of these classical similes (p. 68). Her reading is intended to support an argument about Milton's understanding of prefiguration.

46. Tayler, *Milton's Poetry*, notes that Milton's usual practice in his poetry is to treat the figure rather than the fulfillment (p. 34).

47. The point is taken from Chambers, "The Double Time Scheme," p. 195. His argument works with the terms *kairos* and *chronos*, which characterize more technical religious discussions of this issue.

48. See Tayler's introductory chapter and his discussion of typology (ibid., pp. 22–32); Lewalski, "Time and History," pp. 66–81.

"THUS SANG THE UNCOUTH SWAIN": PASTORAL, PROPHECY, AND HISTORICISM IN *LYCIDAS*

Michael Dietz

In this Monody the Author bewails a learned Friend, unfortunatly drown'd in his Passage from *Chester* on the *Irish* Seas, 1637. And by occasion foretels the ruine of our corrupted Clergy then in their height.

Lycidas, 1645 headnote

1

JUSTA EDOVARDO KING NAUFRAGO appeared toward the end of 1637, a volume of elegies in Latin and English composed by the Cambridge circle of the drowned Edward King's friends and acquaintances. The sole poem for which the volume is now remembered, *Lycidas,* is its final and culminating work; like its companion elegies, it is attributed only by initials to its author, J. M., who would of course already be known by name to the volume's likely audience. J. M.'s poem, as befits the position in which *Justa Edovardo King* places it, is an extraordinarily self-conscious utterance, self-conscious not merely about the literary history of pastoral, toward which it adopts a subtle revisionist posture, but also about the political circumstances in which it appears, and by extension about the uses and aims of pastoral elegy in a situation of political crisis. The most forceful and engaged writing in the piece comes in a speech by St. Peter, the last of the elegy's procession of mourners, who is made to rage against Archbishop Laud in the figure of "the grim Woolf with privy paw," "devouring" the flock of English believers with the help of his party of corrupt pastors, "blind mouthes! that scarce themselves know how to hold / A Sheep-hook" (119–20).

Only a few months prior to the publication of *Justa Edovardo King,* Laud had arranged the promulgation of a new, much heavier and more thorough system of literary censorship than the already heavy one that had obtained. To write a scarcely veiled speech attacking Laud and the episcopacy was, therefore, a politically fraught act, and in St. Peter's speech, *Lycidas* dramatizes the effort required to speak directly in repressive circumstances: the abruptness of the speech, the unusual harshness of its rhetoric, "give the effect of truth bursting through censorship," as David Norbrook suggests, but also of a truth that must expend so much rhetorical energy in bursting through censorship that it all but depletes itself and its generic setting.[1] Pastoral, a courtly genre, a genre of highly coded political and social comment, cannot decode itself and remain pastoral. St. Peter's prophetic energy and overtness are all but alien to the form as *Lycidas* understands it. "Return Alpheus, the dread voice is past, / That shrunk thy streams; Return *Sicilian Muse*" (132–33), the speaker intones following St. Peter's speech, as if the gentle pastoral muse were hardly able to bear so much reality as the apostle had burdened it with. But in January 1646, when Milton published *Lycidas* under his own name in a volume that introduced his poetry to the wider literary public, circumstances had drastically changed, and with them the pressures to which Milton's elegy might have to respond. The Laudian censorship had been swept away, along with Laud and Charles. Although another struggle over censorship replaced it—Milton wrote *Areopagitica,* his defense of unrestricted publication, in 1644, against Parliament's licensing act of the previous year—the mere fact that there was a struggle, conducted with polemical vigor on all sides, demonstrates how much had changed in a very few years.

The explanatory headnote that Milton affixed to *Lycidas* in the 1645 *Poems* answers not merely the new political circumstances but the new demands of publication: set adrift from its collegial moorings of 1637 and presented to the general literary market, *Lycidas* must now be contextualized for its intended audience. That requirement to explain the elegy's occasion gives Milton an opportunity to refurbish it as well. Episcopal controversy had not, after all, disappeared with the Laudians, and Milton and the revolutionary left suspected the Presbyterians of wishing to reinstate in their synods a hierarchy as onerous as the episcopal one that had been displaced: in *Areopagitica,* Milton had asserted that the Westminster Assembly intended to "put it out of controversie that Bishops and Presbyters are the same to us both name and thing."[2] So the *Lycidas* headnote does not merely call attention to the author's past political foresight, it also advertises Milton's authority as a seer to his new audience in this new historical moment. With the headnote, *Lycidas* becomes a prophetic poem doubly prophetic: St. Peter's warning to the Laudians has been fulfilled in Laud's execution and the destruction of his clergy; now it will serve as a threat to the Presbyterians and their episcopal schemes.[3] A passage that had faced down a developed Laudian censorship thus commits itself, as the authentic voice of a prophet who has been proven successful, to denounce a nascent Presbyterian repression.

In its 1637 appearance, without explanatory headnote, firmly embedded within the memorial occasion defined by its companion elegies, *Lycidas* can afford to consider with a kind of undergraduate self-consciousness the ironies that attend upon premature but compelled utterance:

> Yet once more, O ye Laurels, and once more
> Ye Myrtles brown, with Ivy never sere,
> I come to pluck your Berries harsh and crude,
> And with forc'd fingers rude
> Shatter your leaves before the mellowing year.
> Bitter constraint, and sad occasion dear,
> Compel me to disturb your season due:
> For *Lycidas* is dead, dead ere his prime,
> Young *Lycidas*, and hath not left his peer.   (1–9)

Like a great deal of the elegy, the word *occasion* here occupies an uncomfortable space between the gesture of publishing and the act of mourning: it suggests both "reasonable or appropriate circumstance," the unconstrained compulsion under which J. M. will take his metaphorical place in a memorial volume with his fellows, and "ritual or liturgical necessity," the distressingly unfulfillable duty of mourning a man whose body can never be recovered for its funeral rites. By a kind of generic correlative, St. Peter's prophetic irruption into *Lycidas* translates the discomfort of the poem's occasion onto the metapoetic level, where a rigorous and compelled speech confronts the gracious evasions of pastoral. The 1645 headnote, though, tries to set discomfort aside. The "by occasion" with which Milton points to the crux of the poem deliberately understates the thematics of rigorous utterance there, representing St. Peter's vehemence as the product of a kind of genial opportunism: as it happens (had it not happened here it would have happened elsewhere), *Lycidas* gave its author occasion to utter a successful prophecy against Laud's "corrupted clergy."

The mood of ease is mandated for *Lycidas* by Milton's desire to assimilate the poem, and the volume in which it appears, to the period's dominant tropology of literary production. Richard Helgerson, noting that almost all of the 1645 volume consists of occasional or commissioned verse, has established its professional context; "to be a poet in the 1630s and 1640s," says Helgerson, "was, to a far greater degree than had previously been the case, to be at the service of occasion":

Most Elizabethan and Jacobean poets had written some occasional verse and some to be set to music, but never before [Charles's reign] had so large a part of the poetic output of even the most prolific and proficient writers been produced in response to such external promptings. . . . *Poems Upon Several Occasions,* Waller's title, would have equally suited most collections of the period.[4]

The mere presence of the *Lycidas* headnote as the final, authoritative site of the poem's occasion—located in the editorial space above, as well as circumstantially after, the poem itself, in a sense decathected from it—seems to enact a stance of freedom and (relative) generic unaffiliation that determines the possibility of prophecy for this early Milton.

Lycidas is—or has become, in the 1645 context—a poem committed to the emergence of the poet into a public career. The gesture by which it figures that emergence, the shepherd-singer's rising to walk into a tomorrow of "fresh woods, and pastures new," culminates the poem's movement from constrained and repetitive utterance—"yet once more"—to elegiac release: "Weep no more, woful Shepherds weep no more, / For *Lycidas* your sorrow is not dead, / Sunk though he be beneath the watry floar" (165–67). Milton's 1645 volume is shaped by the Virgilian model of the poetic career, in which pastoral is a foundational genre that succeeds to the larger, greater utterance of maturity; literally and figuratively, *Lycidas* is the work of a "rising poet," in Louis Martz's phrase. But Richard Helgerson has suggested the presence within the volume of a "strong countermovement" to the desired tendency. The gestures of inauguration Milton makes in his first published collection never quite free themselves from contingency:

Each emergence represents a deeper involvement with that from which the poet would emerge. The two monodies, *Lycidas* and *Epitaphium Damonis,* may bid farewell to pastoral poetry, but they are also Milton's most explicitly pastoral poems, the only poems in the 1645 volume that closely imitate the form of the Virgilian eclogue. Milton would seem to have chosen the genre precisely because it was one that could be left behind. The traditional association of pastoral poetry and youth, an association that [Milton] emphasizes in each of the poems, allows him to make a statement of poetic maturity. But Milton finds that such statements have to be made over and over. . . . Milton's acts of closure never quite close. No emergence sets him definitively on his way. Each time he strips off one inadequate poetic guise, he finds another underneath.[5]

There is some tendentiousness in this: what looks to Helgerson like a pathos of unemergence in the 1645 *Poems* could as easily be described as a characteristic Miltonic attention to perspective, in which the final landscape of *Lycidas,* for example, is "fresh" not by way of unattainment but as a sign of how thoroughly the poem has exhausted its prior (and lesser) landscapes. And yet the effortfulness with which *Lycidas,* like the whole 1645 collection, makes a space for such freshness belies the casual rhetoric of occasion with which Milton makes his entry into the literary marketplace. The headnote of the republished *Lycidas* may wish to erase whatever difficulties attend the poem's approaches to strenuous utterance; what it does in fact is to relocate those difficulties within the structure of the poetic career, as Milton has received it.

Genre and career in *Lycidas* are inseparable from a third term: the poem, in the context of its 1645 appearance, presents Milton not simply to the literary marketplace, it presents him to history, at once literary and social history. *Lycidas* is almost a poem specifically designed for republication; at least the gesture Milton makes in republishing the poem mimes what the elegy has always understood about its genre and the genre's implicit historical program. "Mature" song, for a Christian pastoral that looks back to Virgil's Eclogue 4 and its *paolo maiora canamus* ("for a little while let us sing greater things") inevitably figures its maturity in the historical dimension as well as in any merely personal, biographical sense.[6] The fictional occasion of *Lycidas* is the moment of a historically resonant succession of genres: the narrow spaces of classical pastoral (whose lowness is nevertheless a precursor of Christian *humilitas*) give way at last, through a series of cruxes culminating in St. Peter's speech, to the larger and freer regions of prophecy.[7] There is no final disagreement between the two genres; rather, the hesitancies and pauses that mark the poem's progress are to be thought of at most as birth pangs, since prophecy realizes and manifests the discourse of historical agency that (as Milton and the Renaissance understand it) is latent in pastoral. Republication ratifies the poem's central fiction even as it resituates the poem's occasion. In this sense, the 1645 headnote, assimilating the fictional dynamics of the poem to the period's standard tropology of the marketplace, is an essential part of the poem and the real climax of its historical argument, the site where its prophetic design becomes thoroughly readable and thoroughly public.

This essay will examine Milton's historical program in *Lycidas,* grounded in the poem's apparent desire to make its way by a relatively easy, unstrenuous passage from the argument of pastoral to the argument of prophecy. A slight but telling moment of ideological discomfort, created in the context of republication, indicates the direction of my argument: "That two-handed engine at the door, / Stands ready to smite once, and smite no more" (130–31), St. Peter warns the party (or parties) of repression, placing his own occasion within the thematic arc of a poem that moves from *once more* to *no more.* But the 1645 headnote in effect asks us to attach an asterisk to this particular appearance of the theme; the prophecy is being made to do double duty. Laud having been cast on the ash heap of history, why should *another* need arise to utter the same prophecy? For a historical imagination directed through typology toward apocalypse, the question is a fair one, and it resonates widely. By 1645, Milton's Reformation—a Reformation that has recovered the primordial Christianity, that has created a national revolution in which the former election of the Israelites is recapitulated in the election of the English people—

has both completed itself and failed to complete itself; and, as prophecy, *Lycidas* seems at once to solicit and beg those wider questions: Why has Reformation not happened once and for all? Why, having been ordained by God for England, has Reformation been left in the hands of a history at least potentially capable of thwarting its completion?[8]

This essay is interested primarily in how those questions can be parsed in the terms of Milton's poetic and prophetic commitments. What is the shape of the contradiction, to the extent there is one, between the prophetic forwardness *Lycidas* imagines for itself and the poem's literary-historical work? How far can Milton successfully negotiate between a commitment to the typological organization of history that authorizes prophecy, on the one hand, and the subjection of prophetic vehemence to the institutional and historical structures implied in pastoral on the other? The discussion that follows is organized to explore, through the medium of the 1637 and 1645 appearances of *Lycidas*, the conflict between prophecy and pastoral. Essentially this is an essay in the history of intellectuals, though my concomitant interest in what I would call the phenomenology of history—what it means for the writer of *Lycidas* to propose himself as a fully capable agent acting in a determinate historical field—means that I will only be able to make the sketchiest approaches here toward fixing Milton's place in that larger history. Having grounded the drama of prophetic self-recognition that is the central movement of the 1637 *Lycidas* in Milton's early humanism and its academic esprit de corps, I will go on to consider the ways in which the poem sees, and refuses to see, how the historically self-conscious discourse of pastoral calls any notion of a self-authorizing prophetic commitment into question. Though it would be specious to suggest that the conflict between prophecy and pastoral could ever have been absent from *Lycidas*, I will recur once more to the 1645 headnote in order to indicate how much more intractable that conflict appears in the context of the later volume. *Lycidas* is the first fully developed statement of Milton's determination to be a poet in the line of prophets; it is also, and necessarily, the first full statement of Milton's latent knowledge that the time of prophecy is already past.

2

> Thus sang the uncouth Swain to th'Okes and rills,
> While the still morn went out with Sandals gray,
> He touch'd the tender stops of various Quills,
> With eager thought warbling his *Dorick* lay:
> And now the Sun had stretch'd out all the hills,
> And now was dropt into the Western bay;

> At last he rose, and twitch'd his Mantle blew:
> To morrow to fresh Woods, and Pastures new.   (186–93)

An effort to understand the shape and full range of Milton's historicism in *Lycidas* will almost of necessity focus on the figure of the "uncouth swain" who ostensibly sings the poem and on the visionary character of his field of view at the poem's end. In that figure and in that landscape, the elegy sums up its historical momentum, offering an emblem of its own projection into its own historical landscape. The swain's sudden (but not shocking) appearance in the poem, by way of a distancing (but not alienating) turn toward the third person, has always seemed inscrutable to *Lycidas* criticism and has always required it to pause over the decorums of self-representation in the poem. Who is the swain—not as a lyric voice or a Miltonic pastoral persona, but as a historical actor—and how is his field of vision organized historically? What moment does he represent?

Among the commentators on *Lycidas*, D. S. Berkeley is one of the most appealing: however misleading ultimately, his literalist approach to the question of the swain is closer to the historical mark than most. "The swain," Berkeley insists, "is a native Briton of Druid antecedents and Graeco-Roman culture . . . without consciousness of Christianity save in the 'inspired' passage [the passage derived from Revelations beginning 'Weep no more, woful shepherds']." He is a pagan living just before the Christian advent, with the historical consciousness of a pagan—his time sense "cyclical," his typology "one of remembered archetypes," of events seen "in the light of mythic exemplars."[9] Berkeley's reconstruction of the swain's historical consciousness is faulty to the extent that it rests on the idea of a peculiarly pagan, "mythological" apprehension of historical time. The work of the comparative mythologists, from which that idea derives, postdates Milton; the idea had no currency until at least a century after *Lycidas* was written at the earliest. Nor is there any reason to think that Milton possessed a category of "historical" representation in general, in the modern meaning: representation grounded in a thematics of historical difference, a sense of distance from past consciousness that mandates a special system of mimetic canons.

Berkeley's focus on the swain as a specifically historical figure in *Lycidas*, and as potentially a problem for the poem's historical argument (in the relation between his historicity and that of what Berkeley calls the "inspired" passage near the end of the poem), is nevertheless shrewdly chosen. Critics have tended to ask what occasions *Lycidas*—what factors of biography or genre or politics or even doctrine motivate the poem. *Lycidas* itself asks *what its occasion is*. The poem is world-historical, like much of Milton's early work especially, in the sense of its being reflexively concerned with its moment; the play of consciousness in the poem (its digressions, the interruptions of its elegiac "narrative") is determined by Milton watching himself write and asking what sort of an era it is in which he could write this sort of poem. Milton's answers, typological and apocalyptic as they are, cannot be said to exist for *Lycidas* prior to the activity of self-representation.

Lycidas moves through a series of rhetorical expansions—which are also gestures toward the realization of prophecy in history—followed by stock-taking pauses or defensive regressions. The poem gives itself access first to the voice of Phoebus, a Virgilian "strain . . . of a higher mood" (87) from which the pastoralism of the elegy must recoil and reassert itself in a new invocation ("O Fountain *Arethuse,* and thou honour'd floud, / Smooth-sliding *Mincius,* crown'd with vocall reeds" [85–86]); then to the voice of St. Peter, "the Pilot of the *Galilean* lake" (109), whose prophetic outburst requires an even more defensive reassertion of the limitations of the pastoral medium; and last the consolatory and "inspired" passage, a vision of Lycidas in heaven hearing "the unexpressive nuptial Song, / In the blest Kingdoms meek of joy and love" (176–77). The poem's return from that final strenuousness of vision and voice is an envoi that shifts into the third person—"Thus sang the un-couth Swain to th'Okes and rills" (186)—an envoi that reflects, in other words, decisively and in the mood of leave-taking on the terms of pastoral self-representation in general, and specifically of pastoral self-representation in the face of a historical momentum that carries beyond the bounds of pastoral. It is in the never-completed dialectic between pastoral and a pro-phetic energy which pastoral cannot accommodate without strain that, as Berkeley's comments suggest implicitly, the historicity of *Lycidas* resides.

The open-endedness of dialectic in *Lycidas* is not something that crit-icism of the poem has tended to acknowledge. The elegy's ultimate consola-tions are phrased in the language of types and, as most critics understand typology, that means that the poem works inexorably to reveal—and to insert itself into—an achieved, absolute order of historical significance. Many critics see an accumulating conceptual and christological rigor in the poem—all typological relationships articulated, all earlier, merely latent significances brought forward through the consciousness of the swain into the self-consciousness of the poem. Northrop Frye offers as clear a statement as any of this critical attitude:

Each aspect of *Lycidas* poses the question of premature death as it relates to the life of man, of poetry, and of the Church. But all of these aspects are contained within the figure of Christ, the young dying god who is eternally alive, the Word that contains all poetry, the head and body of the Church, the good Shepherd whose pastoral world sees no winter, the Sun of righteousness that never sets, whose power can raise

Lycidas, like Peter, out of the waves, as it redeems souls from the lower world, which Orpheus failed to do. Christ does not enter the poem as a character, but he pervades every line of it so completely that the poem, so to speak, enters him.[10]

But such readings underestimate Milton's ambivalences, especially as the pastoralism of *Lycidas* represents them. The elegy never really abandons its "pagan" pastoral, a fact that has made most of the poem's critics rather uncomfortable. As the poem's envoi represents it, the progressive gesture involves a recathecting of pastoral motive within the social and historical commitments of a prophetically oriented humanism.

The landscape at the end of the poem is a typological landscape in which types are never fully articulated as such. The lines in which "the Sun had stretch'd out all the hills, / And now was dropt into the Western bay" (190–91) culminate the typological momentum of the poem in a punning equation of the sun with Christ the Son, and a near insertion—but only a near one—of the swain within that equation. "At last he rose, and twich'd his Mantle blew" (192): for an instant, the "he" that rises in the poem's penultimate line is simultaneously the swain, the sun, and a power encompassing both.[11] The sunset that Milton's singer watches at the end of the poem is at once natural and eschatological. Its earlier emblem, the day-star, has figured Lycidas's resurrection:

> So sinks the day-star in the Ocean bed,
> And yet anon repairs his drooping head,
> And tricks his beams, and with new spangled Ore,
> Flames in the forehead of the morning sky:
> So *Lycidas* sunk low, but mounted high,
> Through the dear might of him that walk'd the waves
> Where other groves, and other streams along,
> With *Nectar* pure his oozy Lock's he laves.   (168–75)

The anonymous oaks and rills, woods and pastures of the swain's final landscape are like the "other groves and other streams" of Lycidas's rest—they have the anonymous "otherness" of anagogical completion. But this landscape will support figural identification only insofar as it rests on a naive tropology of natural resemblance. In that sense it remains always a pastoral landscape. Despite the pressure of the "inspired" passage toward a full expression of typological understanding, in such "paganizing" details as the periphrasis for Christ ("him that walk'd the waves") or the encomium to Lycidas ("henceforth thou art the genius of the shore"), it continues to maintain the social decorums of Renaissance pastoral. Swains are rude folk whose language exhibits a natural and thus restricted consciousness, as E. K. notes in Spenser's *Shepheardes Calender,* glossing the April eclogue's use of "Elisa" for Queen Elizabeth: "in all this songe is not to be respected, what the worthinesse of her Majestie deserveth, nor what to the highnes of a Prince is agreeable, but what is moste comely for the meanesse of a shepheards witte, or to conceive, or to utter. And therefore he calleth her Elysa, as through rudenesse tripping in her name."[12]

As Berkeley's comments will suggest, taken less literally than he does himself, in *Lycidas* the social decorum of Renaissance pastoral elaborates a concomitant historical decorum—though certainly not the historical decorum of novelistic or psychologistic historiography. The "natural," pastoral restrictedness of the swain's consciousness, particularly as it appears in the poem's antidigressive turns and stock-taking pauses, represents a certain pleasantly limited capacity for historical feeling and historical self-awareness, a capacity against which prophecy seems like a strain and an interruption. The third-person envoi with which *Lycidas* ends does not place the swain directly in the country of Revelation (and the typological system that country images) into which Lycidas himself has been assumed, but allows him and the poem to pause on the threshold of that country. The elegy's final, "Dorick" landscape is bathed in a light that intimates the possibility of a completely articulated historical vision without imposing on the swain, or on the reader, the responsibility of achieving that vision. Nevertheless, the envoi is *Lycidas*'s most extensive projection of its rustic pose into history. The pastoralism that has resisted the progress of prophecy becomes progressive itself, a continuous perspective, a vanishing point, and, in that more limited sense, prophetic; *Lycidas* ends with the swain placed under the sign of the interminable, specifically the interminably self-conscious.

Since Johnson (though subsequently with more circumspection and nuance), criticism of *Lycidas* has assumed a kind of contempt for pastoral and has wanted to rescue the poem (or watch the poem rescue itself) from its pastoral mechanisms. Thus the decisive rupture, the moment where the poem is supposed finally to switch its allegiances from pastoral, occurs dialectically at its extreme of pastoral statement:

> Bid *Amaranthus* all his beauty shed,
> And Daffadillies fill their cups with tears,
> To strew the Laureat Herse where *Lycid* lies.
> For so to interpose a little ease,
> Let our frail thoughts dally with false surmise.
> Ay me! Whilst thee the shores, and sounding Seas
> Wash far away, where ere thy bones are hurld.   (149–55)

"False surmise," according to the mainstream of *Lycidas* criticism, is exposed here as *radically* false: the rhetorical prerogatives of pastoral (and of poetry *tout court*) must finally collapse when faced with the twinned "realities" of death and Christian mystery. J. Martin Evans considers the classical background of Milton's "elaborately and self-consciously poetic" writing in the flower passage—valedictory speeches in Theocritus's first Idyl and Virgil's Eclogue 10—and notices in the Miltonic version a kind of deathly evacuation that has almost metaphysical implications:

> The vision is still essentially pastoral but now it is unpopulated by any living human presence. Whereas Gallus [in Eclogue 10] imagines himself lying in a pastoral bower beside his mistress, Lycidas lies on a laureate hearse alone. . . . the attempt to interpose some pastoral "ease" (152) collapses in the face of reality; decking a drowned man with flowers, Milton realizes, is like feeding the sheep with wind. So the preceding fiction *and all it stands for* is dismissed as a "false surmise."[13]

Evans's reading of the classical sources is sensitive, but his idealism understates the crucial contingency: it bears remembering, obvious as the point is, that surmise fails at this moment in the poem not in itself but because there is no real "laureat herse" to strew with flowers. With King's body lost, so too the occasion for any competent cultic acts of mourning, for which the flower passage is a self-consciously inadequate synecdoche. That synecdoche points beyond *Lycidas* itself to the whole of the 1637 volume: *Justa Edovardo King* is the only "hearse" Edward King will ever have.[14] The flower passage, in other words, represents the moment in which the 1637 *Lycidas* confronts, in practical terms, its own occasion and its own historical present, and we should expect that confrontation to have an image of some praxis as its issue rather than a merely theoretical elaboration of doctrine.

The death of King is a college death, and the consolatory task of *Lycidas* is to recover the college feeling lost in that death. Milton is hardly different, in proposing himself that task, from anyone even now who has lost a school friend too early in life. Where his difference lies is in the ideology of college feeling implied in a memorial volume like that in which *Lycidas* first appeared. In the moment of "false surmise," Milton is examining with some urgency not merely the competence of *Justa Edovardo King* as an object of attachment and memory, but the historical and professional competence of the humanistic career itself. The idea that books can enshrine human presences is a founding myth of Milton's profession; we need only remember *Areopagitica:*

> For Books are not absolutely dead things, but doe contain a potencie of life in them to be as active as that soule was whose progeny they are; nay they do preserve as in a violl the purest efficacie and extraction of that living intellect that bred them. . . . As good almost kill a Man as kill a good Book; who kills a Man kills a reasonable creature, Gods Image; but hee who destroyes a good Booke, kills reason it selfe, kills the Image of

God, as it were in the eye. Many a man lives a burden to the Earth; but a good Booke is the pretious life-blood of a master spirit, imbalm'd and treasur'd up on purpose *to a life beyond life*. (YP II, pp. 492–93; italics mine)

"If 'Lycidas' affirms the value of the academic as opposed to the courtly life," David Norbrook writes, "this is only to be expected in an elegy for a college fellow" (p. 274), indeed in an elegy placed emphatically at the end of a volume of elegies. However, we may not expect the degree to which the academic correlates with the historical. *Lycidas* is orchestrated so that the significance of King's death ramifies until it attains the widest conceivable historical reach: touching the question of fame (at the level of personal ambition), of priestly vocation (at the level of Cambridge and of English politics), finally of the possibility of secure revelation (at the level of the "life beyond life," an emblem of typological signification itself). The fact that there is no recoverable body to mourn occurs in *Lycidas* at the point of that final articulation as a challenge, implicitly, to the entire humanist doctrine of recovery—of human presences, of forgotten or occluded history. That fact is also the means by which the poem opens itself at last, overtly, to typological argument and a historicity based on the substitution of type for type.

The figure of the uncouth swain in the last stanza of *Lycidas* occupies a typological vantage conditioned by the poem's elaborately orchestrated turn to Revelation.[15] The turn moves not from pastoral "convention" to anti-pastoral "reality" but from a partial text to a fully realized, fully inclusive text, even to an ekphrastic landscape of the book. One sees in the image of the swain among the oaks and rills a representation of the humanist scholar-poet, turning to walk into the landscape of his profession, a landscape whose anagogical saliency—whose prophetic worth—is guaranteed by the poem's "discovery" of biblical revelation from within the humanist experience of classical pastoral. The envoi offers the emblem of a continuing expectancy: the pictorialized distance that supervenes in the last, framing lines of the poem—a kind of memorial or epitaphic distance—asks one to imagine that the swain has always occupied this landscape and will always remain to occupy it, always just on the point of moving fully into it and away from view.[16] That the swain, as a figure, appears before the reader at the end of the poem where no figure had been before, serves to mark the place of the dead shepherd while retaining the region of a crucial *as if:* the swain both is and is not a recovered Lycidas. From this perspective, the elegiac motive in the monody requires a turn to the third person—"Thus sang the uncouth swain"—because nothing other than the elaboration of humanist self-consciousness repairs the loss; the poem's high ideological achievement is to recover the human presence in texts as humanism itself, as the typological saliency of the humanist commitment.

Put perhaps too compactly, pastoral is insufficiently self-conscious because it does not realize its own typological dimension, but in Milton's hands it will be brought intact, still as pastoral, to the very borders of that realization. For Milton, at least in this early phase of his career, there is nothing ideologically to discriminate between the recovery of classical learning and the recovery of the church to the true image of Christ; they occupy the same historical space, follow almost the same historical logic. A passage from the 1641 tract *Of Reformation Touching Church-Discipline in England* measures the world historical background of the swain's position within a landscape of sunset already becoming sunrise:

When I recall to mind at last, after so many darke Ages, wherein the huge overshadowing traine of *Error* had almost swept all the Starres out of the Firmament of the *Church;* how the bright and blissfull *Reformation* (by Divine Power) strook through the black and settled Night of *Ignorance* and *Antichristian Tyrrany*, me thinks a soveraigne and reviving joy must needs rush into the bosome of him that reads or heares; and the sweet Odour of the returning *Gospell* imbath his Soule with the fragrancy of Heaven. Then was the Sacred BIBLE sought out of the dusty corners where prophane Falshood and Neglect had throwne it, the *Schooles* opened, *Divine* and *Humane Learning* rak't out of the *embers* of *forgotten tongues,* the *Princes* and *Cities* trooping apace to the new erected Banner of *Salvation;* the *Martyrs*, with the unresistable *might* of *Weaknesse*, shaking the *Powers* of *Darknesse*, and scorning the *fiery rage* of the old *red Dragon*. (YP I, pp. 524–25)

The leap Milton makes in *Lycidas* is to put himself at the point where revelation is about to emerge as "historical" (as a typological imagination would understand history): that is, when it is about to reveal itself concretely as a fulfillment, or to reveal the terms in which fulfillment must happen. It is not important that the swain actually be somebody living just before Christian revelation; his historical position is like a before, but a before in this ethical sense—the moment is any moment before revelation manifests itself.

The end of *Lycidas* is almost programmatically disinvested from the idea of "prophetic strain." If there is a merger of perspectives in the *Lycidas* envoi it is restricted to one in which the swain's pleasures—vision without visionary strenuousness, movement forward without movement beyond (beyond the bounds of pastoral)—are to become compatible with, "natural" signs of, a prophetic self-representation for which vehemence is unnecessary, even outmoded. What remains to be asked is whether that merger can, in fact, be maintained; whether there can be a prophetic position that avoids looking intently at the consummation that ends prophecy; whether the interminability of pleasant historical self-consciousness at the end of *Lycidas* masks a more difficult, even repressive economy of history. The answers to those questions will be found in a closer consideration of the thematics of the career, and its historical shape, in the *Lycidas* version of pastoral.

3

The "mantle blew" that the swain takes up in the penultimate line of *Lycidas* is a densely allusive figure that, unpacked, opens an avenue to the poem's sense of its literary-historical mission, and to the increasing difficulty Milton has in managing, in one set of gestures, a commitment to the prophetic stance and a competent version of careerist self-authorship. But to elaborate a reading of that figure requires some prior sketch of the problematics of social power that lie behind the *Lycidas* envoi so that we can understand what Milton feels he must do, and must avoid doing, in order to articulate a self-sufficient prophetic stance.

Several commentators have noticed that the mantle image, which immediately alludes to the first eclogue of Spenser's *Shepheardes Calender*, also encodes a reference to the transmission of prophetic authority. Joseph Wittreich sees in it the poem's ideology of reception: "The primary allusion here is to the relationship of prophets: just as Elijah passes on his mantle to Elisha [2 Kings ii, 8–14], Lycidas bestows his mantle on the uncouth swain and Milton passes on his to us." Alastair Fowler reads in the same allusion a broader access to humanist as well as prophetic commitment: the mantle "is the robe of a rededicated student body, the bands of a *Musarum sacerdos*, even a prophetic mantle fallen from the ascended King to Elisha-Milton below."[17] The allusions are apt—the text of Elijah's ascent appears frequently in seventeenth-century funeral sermons—though neither of these comments suggests the rather etiolated version of prophecy that Milton offers in his distant, if not gingerly, handling of the Elisha reference.[18] And the ratios of the reference seem misstated: the crucial analogy has Elijah stand to Elisha not as Lycidas to the uncouth swain, but as Spenser to Milton in the figure of the swain. Neither Wittreich nor Fowler seems to have noticed that their reading of "transmission" rests on a pious fiction that *Lycidas* itself does not authorize. There is no act of transmission in the envoi (or anywhere else in the poem) by which the mantle of Lycidas can actually come to the swain; like all the tropes in which *Lycidas* concludes, this one is fundamentally natural, since the swain's mantle is simply his and carries, for him, no weight of otherworldly reference along with it.

But if the two readings I have cited make a mistake about the texture of allusion in *Lycidas*, it is a mistake with a venerable antecedent, one that can help us understand something of the dynamics of literary and prophetic transmission which *Lycidas* may be resisting. Andrew Marvell, in his "First Anniversary of the Government Under His Highness the Lord Protector," pays a verbal and imagistic homage to *Lycidas* that situates the mantle allusion in just the context Wittreich and Fowler do. Contemplating the riding accident in Hyde Park in which Cromwell narrowly averted serious injury or even death, Marvell composes a mock elegiac tribute to the Lord Protector that at its climax sees him translated:

> But thee triumphant hence the firy Carr,
> And firy Steeds had born out of the Warr,
> From the low World, and thankless Men above,
> *Unto the Kingdom blest of Peace and Love:*
> We only mourn'd our selves, in thine Ascent,
> Whom thou hadst left beneath with Mantle rent.[19]

Marvell's compliment to Cromwell is also a cautionary tale: had you died, it says with a kind of delicate hyperbole, had you gone to the final kingdom without establishing a kingdom in the here and now, you would have left England "perplexed" after you, the "mantle" of its prophetic national election rent.[20] The advice Marvell implicitly offers here rests both on a commonplace about the historical chosenness of the English and on a typological equation between meanings of *kingdom:* the heavenly and anagogical "kingdom blest of peace and love," and the possible earthly kingdom of a new Cromwellian dynasty, suggest, as a middle term that links them in the progress of history, the millennial kingdom that at least some of the revolutionaries hoped to establish with the overthrow of the Stuart monarchy. Marvell's politics here has access to, but no real investment in (certainly no prophetic investment in), a typological rhetoric that may help advance the cause of legitimist rationalism: a millennialist argument is suggested in these lines; Cromwell in effect can take it or leave it as he chooses, but, as between one political realist and another, both Marvell and the Lord Protector understand the uses and limits of such argument.

Like Wittreich and Fowler after him, Marvell seems unaware that the fiction of transmission is actually absent from the envoi of *Lycidas.* Unconsciously, perhaps, the "First Anniversary" has straightened out a kink in the earlier poem. The prophetic allusion in Milton is fleeting and in a sense dissipates almost before it can be grasped, and there is a paradox in this—the fleetingness of the allusion, the near evacuation of direct prophetic reference in the *Lycidas* mantle figure, seem to be produced exactly as signs of the extraordinary privilege that *would* attach to the prophetic reference if it were quite there.

In contrast to *Lycidas*, one notices how Marvell has stabilized the vanishing reference in Milton's mantle figure, resituating it into a determinate, and familiar, associative context. Marvell's poem reads the mantle allusion self-confidently (if not complacently) within a figural and institutional nexus—of national election, apocalyptic possibility and state power—that one recognizes as an ineluctable feature of dissenting political thought in the Elizabethan-Stuart period. The associations are so familiar, in fact, that we may plausibly think that Milton has actively resisted them at the end of *Lycidas* and may wonder why the mantle figure there has been divorced from a set of meanings that—reading backward from Marvell's handling of the figure in the "First Anniversary"—seem almost native to it.

The notion that in the envoi of *Lycidas* Milton has deliberately un- (or under-) written an easily available associative context for the figure of Elijah's mantle will gain some credibility if we examine a similar, more sharply outlined instance of such an unwriting that also appears in Milton's early verse. At issue is a passage in *Ode on the Morning of Christ's Nativity* that parodies a moment in the April eclogue of *The Shepheardes Calender* where—again in the context of panegyric—the poem attempts to merge the rhetoric of divine authority in history on the one hand and state power on the other. As in the last lines of *Lycidas*, Milton takes up an image of the sun in uncanny movement (or lack of movement), fully aware of all the anxious typological resonance that image has; the moment is one of the several false dawns in the Nativity ode:

> The Sun himself with-held his wonted speed,
> And hid his head for shame,
> As his inferiour flame,
>   The new-enlightn'd world no more should need,
> He saw a greater Sun appear
> Then his bright Throne, or burning Axletree could bear.   (79–84)

Milton is remembering Spenser's compliment to Elizabeth:

> I sawe *Phoebus* thrust out his golden hedde,
>   upon her to gaze:
> But when he sawe, how broade her beames did spredde,
>   it did him amaze.
> He blusht to see another Sunne belowe,
> Ne durst againe his fyrye face out showe:
>   Let him, if he dare,
>   His brightnesse compare
> With hers, to have the overthrowe.   (73–81)

Like Marvell's lines to the Lord Protector, but without their explicit apocalyptic reach, these lines from "Aprill" center on a missing typological third term:

the contest of Phoebus, the pagan sun, and Elizabeth, the English sun, winks at the Christian sun/Son figure even as it suggests that Elizabeth's preeminence over Phoebus is founded in that figure, as the historical preeminence of Christian empire over pagan. "Overthrowe" is a possible English translation of "hyperbole" (Puttenham calls hyperbole "the overreacher"), and it seems that Spenser, oddly, has pointed to the inflation of his rhetoric in the very word that completes the gesture of imperial compliment.[21] But the pleasure of the compliment is located exactly in that irony, which is by no means subversive or self-undermining. The language of the stanza and its imagistic setting refer to the plein air theater of an Elizabethan progress; Spenser is offering Elizabeth an illusion of mastery, an atmospheric pun, greater than any a merely staged pageant could give her. He is thus recommending poetry to her use and offering her his services as an exemplary poet in the typical double gesture of panegyric; but he wryly withdraws his compliment and his service even as they are proffered, an admission that the atmospheric effect is, after all, not real, and neither in Spenser's power to make real nor in Elizabeth's power to command. The actual compliment here is to Elizabeth's intelligence and her ability to discriminate between herself and the rhetorical position she occupies. In the very grandiosity of Spenser's hyperbole, side by side with it, there is a delicacy of what might be called moral effect, a fine measuring of the distance between the real and its imperial representations. We both know, Spenser in effect says to Elizabeth, that what is sayable and what is possible are two different things; but as realists we also know that what is sayable and impossible often has its uses.

A rhetorical performance like this is not in Milton's repertoire. Commenting on the effective anti-Spenserianism of *Paradise Lost*, Maureen Quilligan suggests that

there is one large difference between Milton and Spenser in the way they offer the reader a choice: Milton does not hold out Spenser's plurality of possibilities, his leisured sense of time to select among and possibly synthesize potential interpretations, to acknowledge the mediate nature of the truth-bearing fiction. Milton offers instead a binary either/or choice about a single truth.[22]

When he rewrites the April eclogue for his Nativity ode, Milton takes a stand censoriously (not to say puritanically) against the earlier panegyric, reminding Spenser that there is only one true Phoebus, as there is only one true monarch. Paradoxically, Milton's parody works by refusing to draw the line between representation and reality upon which Spenser's hyperbolic ironies depend. After all, who can tell that the sun did not withhold his wonted speed, on this day of days? Milton deploys the rhetoric of compliment, here and throughout the ode, against compliment and against the pleasures and privileges of trope that the genre of compliment advertises. John Guillory remarks on Milton's bias against tropes, though outside the context of the ode, in a way that brings the question of figuration into the historical dimension as a question of the appearance and structure of authority in history:

We find it difficult to conceive of authority except in terms of signs and symbols, linguistic displacements or tropes, as though authority *were* this mediation. Two important problems are touched on here. . . . Authority without mediation is a Protestant dream, a desire fraught with nightmarish possibility. . . . It may be that we preserve our humanity in the willingness to distinguish between power and authority, even to deny the priority of power on moral grounds. This is as much as to say that we remain human by granting priority (fictively) to the figurative rather than the literal. Milton can be seen to move toward a reversal of this gesture, or a restoration of the literal origin.[23]

The "shame" that the sun of the Nativity ode feels is not the blush of "amaze" with which Spenser's sun confesses inferiority in the contest of natural powers, it is the intrinsic and permanent condition of unredeemed figuration. Like the Nativity ode, though without that poem's effortfulness, the *Lycidas* envoi seems intent on avoiding a "realist" and thus merely figurative historical rhetoric—even when that avoidance requires the sacrifice of an authoritative and ready-made fiction of prophetic election. Milton in this is a genuine bourgeois, who disdains to offer his services to any merely temporary institution or to accept any sponsorship that cannot reveal itself to be finally and genuinely on the side of history. The implicit continuity of figuration through the medium of state power that makes Phoebus, Elizabeth, and Christ—and would make Elijah, Cromwell, and Christ—all versions of one another arrayed on a single indifferent historical plane, is anathema to Milton, for whom all figures are unhistorical that do not herald the imminent arrival of the one true Figure. The rhetorical imagination of the Nativity ode, in its ultimate bias against tropes, is organized by a typological sense of history: whatever is not transparent to anagogy is just a delaying tactic. Though the pleasure of visionary self-consciousness at the end of *Lycidas* is largely founded on the pleasure of delay, Milton will not allow that pleasure to be shadowed by any allegiance to an unredeemed historicity, by anything that would cheat on the implications of the poem's last word: "new."

Milton's commitment to what we might call typological rationality, absolute in such ideologically charged moments as the rewriting of Spenser in the Nativity ode, is nevertheless not so absolute as Milton might wish it to be. In fact, a disabling contradiction lies at the center of that commitment. For Milton, the idea of typological completion can never actually dissolve or fully subsume even the redeemable past, while the unredeemable past can never really be "lost" in the sense of being utterly under condemnation. The rhetoric of the past—a rhetoric that values the past simply in its being past—and the real practice of the recovery of the past are at the cornerstone of Milton's sense of his career and of its commitments, including its culminating and justifying prophetic commitment. Of course, this is still an abstract formulation, and the discussion of the last few pages, with respect to *Lycidas*, is only speculative. But it is possible to watch in some detail the play of avoidance, and the pressure of literalization, as they determine the concluding position in which *Lycidas* finds itself, that of the swain in his landscape. Milton's stance toward his poem *as* a poem—specifically as an arrangement of tropes, thus as a structure at least potentially allied to mere and unredeemed figuration and its temporality—is conditioned by his knowledge of pastoral and of the resources of pastoral self-representation. To put it another way: Pastoral, in the sense of a Renaissance pastoral that sees itself descending from Virgil's *Eclogues*, is a genre directed toward the early founding of a poetic career, toward establishing a poet's claim on literary history. The last clause of that sentence cannot be overstressed. For Milton's 1645 volume of poems, careerist as it is, pastoral is the privileged figure for the priority of the marketplace, for its literary-historical authority: the gesture of self-presentation (and self-representation) encoded in pastoral is made in a social dimension capable independently of and athwart any typological authority of organizing and addressing itself to history. The entry of *Lycidas* into this new, competing historical arena of the marketplace represents as well the entry of Milton into a history that is not as "Miltonic" as it needs to be to secure a place for prophecy. And *Lycidas*, in its struggle to maintain sole allegiance to prophetic self-consciousness, ends by all but evacuating the historical competence of literary prophecy.

4

In the "mantle blew" that clothes the swain appears *Lycidas's* culminating gesture of literary-historical self-consciousness. Milton alludes here to Spenser, to the end of the January eclogue in *The Shepheardes Calender,* when Colin Clout has broken his pipe and finished his complaint over the beloved (but unloving) Rosalind in despair:

> By that, the welked Phoebus gan availe
> His weary waine, and nowe the frosty Night
> Her mantle black through heaven gan overhaile.
> Which seene, the pensife boy, halfe in despight,
> Arose, and homeward drove his sonned sheepe,
> Whose hanging heads did seeme his carefull case to weepe. (73–78)

Spenserian metaphor has a cosmic reach in this passage that Milton explicitly disavows, not censoriously but, as in the Nativity ode, according to a rhetoric of literalization. *Lycidas* assumes its intertextual descent as a literal burden—the swain carries his mantle on his shoulders—but, with a kind of reductive wit, makes the burden light. An almost coy *sprezzatura,* so easy it seems scarcely Miltonic, sees the blue of early evening where Spenser saw black night; the swain "twitches" his cloak around him as if to smile at the menacing sweep with which night "overhailes" Spenser's sky.

The conclusion of "Januarye" represents a complex, agonized Virgilianism informing the project of the *Shepheardes Calender:* the shadow under which Colin retreats homeward summarily combines all the shadows that populate Virgil's *Eclogues,* the "maiores umbrae," into an ultra-Virgilian darkness of erotic and poetic failure. The closest referent in Virgil is the end of Eclogue 10, where—as in *Lycidas*—pastoral song turns aside from lament and offers a picture of the shepherd-singer himself:

> surgamus: solet esse gravis cantantibus umbra,
> iuniperi gravis umbra; nocent et frugibus umbrae.
> ite domum saturae, venit Hesperus, ite capellae.   (75–77)

[We must go: the shade can be a burden to singers, the shade of the juniper: and the shadows even harm the crops. Go home with full bellies, Hesperus rises; go little goats.][24]

Commentators have long understood that this supervening shadow represents Virgil's farewell to the pastoral mode; William Berg calls this shade the "equivalent to that retirement from the real world, to the *otium* in which Virgil composed the *Bucolics.*"[25] But retirement has become a burden; it even weighs down, by anticipation, a georgic which has yet to appear in Virgil's career, suggested in the slightly distracted half-line "nocent et frugibus umbrae."[26] Virgil must move away from the leisure, now debilitating, that has always constituted the pastoral occasion. In "Januarye," Spenser has drawn the shadow of Virgil's farewell over his own work. Here the Virgilian *umbra,* literalized even before Milton in Spenser's rather earnest manner, has become graver and more pervasive. The harm, in particular the feeling of bearing a burden, alluded to in Eclogue 10 only to be sidestepped, affects everything in Spenser's pasture—the boy "pensif," the sheep "sonned" and dry of milk, their heads hanging, Phoebus "weary." Ironically, Virgil leaves pastoral because it is not forward or engaged enough; his mission is not to avoid a burden but to take up the greater burdens of the career before him. In Spenser, the burdensomeness of pastoral things has already become all but world-historical, the consequence of a pastoral prolonged beyond its time by a poet who has only just begun his pastoral. Spenser knows, and posits himself *as* knowing, what is present in Virgil only (to Spenser's eye) as an intuition or a presentiment: to paraphrase Eliot, the difference between Spenser and Virgil is that Spenser knows more than Virgil, and Virgil is what he knows.[27]

Milton appropriates Eclogue 10, and its turn toward pastoral self-representation, through the medium of Spenser's historicism. He means the end of *Lycidas* to overturn the intertextual descent from the *Eclogues* to *The Shepheardes Calender*. The typological saliency of the swain's position is not to be distinguished from his specifically Virgilian earliness—from a more-than-Virgilian earliness which is the obverse of Spenser's more-than-Virgilian lateness. Milton's shadows contain no burden or harm at all; there are no crops to be damaged; the singer rises of his own motion, not "pensif," not chased by darkness, into a "tomorrow" which has all but risen with him. Nor are there any sheep, sated or "sonned," to be driven home—an odd lacuna that seems an index of Milton's historical self-consciousness. Writing about Eclogue 10, about its "pastoral questioning of pastoral" (p. 236), Paul Alpers assesses the quality of farewell in its last lines:

Virgil appears [more] fully as a shepherd here [than anywhere else in the *Eclogues*] precisely because his poem has taken him to the limits of pastoral self-consciousness. It is a kind of writing that seems normal to readers of Renaissance and modern pastoral, in which a consistent, external pastoral world is often attenuated or nonexistent, and in which it is a normal function of pastoral—in the form of images, gestures, modes of feeling, and ethical attitudes—to reveal an individual sensibility and its reflections on itself. But for Virgil, the heir of Theocritus, to represent himself as he does here means an end to representing shepherds, and therefore an end to writing pastoral and to the *Eclogue* book. (Pp. 239–40)

The swain's inattention to his flock—what amounts to the same thing, his lack of a flock—represents at a considerable extreme this attenuation of the external—not, however, in the Renaissance mode of self-reflection. *Lycidas*, too, contemplates the end of pastoral self-representation, but in a transition from one naiveté (rustic) to another (prophetic), as if the history of pastoral self-consciousness had never happened. The lack of sheep is an emblem of that unwritten history, of that early naiveté; it banishes the pathetic sympathy of Spenser's "pensif" boy and the hung heads of his flock as it banishes the more delicate but equally self-reflective contrast between Virgil's full-bellied goats and the shadow-haunted consciousness of *his* swain.

Renaissance pastoral—particularly in Spenser's case—founds itself in the knowledge of the Virgilian career, that is, in the knowledge of the supersession of pastoral. For Spenser, pastoral is already a genre of limitation and failure, but its failure is its resiliency: *The Shepheardes Calender* sets itself the task of elaborating and articulating the historical space of that failure as Spenser's own arena of opportunity. The conclusion of *Lycidas,* though, imagines a pastoral that does not know failure yet, a pastoral that exists before Virgil and the characteristic Virgilian moment of shadow. Milton's singer is "uncouth": "Incognitus," like the singer of *The Shepheardes Calender* rustically unknown to fame, but in addition unknown to the pastoral text which has yet to descend. What is still to come—the failure of representation that constitutes the history of pastoral—will not come, and from this perspective no longer needs to come: the apocalyptic sentiment, the feeling that history is finally remaking itself in one's own moment, must obviate or set at one side any history not organized by apocalypse.

The artificiality of perspective in this moment is not the sign of an intertextual struggle. If the swain is early, he is less a figure of priority (in what would be a Miltonic claim to have surpassed Spenser by having preceded him) than a figure of latency. *Lycidas,* so flamboyantly influenced a poem, can hardly be said to forget the history of pastoral, but it concludes by finding a position in which it can remember that history precisely and merely in order to disremember it. Milton in effect allows his reader to be in two dissonant historical locations at once. The dissonance is pleasurable, but of a different order than the pleasure in genial, innocently unstrenuous commitment otherwise represented by the swain and his landscape. In the discrepancy between these two types of pleasure we have in fact reached the point of contradiction in *Lycidas*'s programmatic effort to elaborate a "modern" version of prophetic commitment. The question for Miltonic prophecy is: Where and how is history made? In Reformation is one answer, an answer given in the humanist self-awareness that posits the swain in his landscape as a type of Lycidas; outside Reformation is the other, given in the willful, repressive opacity of the swain's pastoral self-consciousness. The historicity of pastoral, as Milton experiences it in *Lycidas,* exerts a pressure not toward self-recognition but toward self-misrecognition, not self-placement but self-displacement. In this respect, and through the filter of Renaissance historicism, the end of *Lycidas* is somewhat like the end of Virgil's Eclogue 10: the brief, distracted anticipation of georgic there oddly seems more reminiscence than anticipation—like a backward eddy from the forward movement of the goatherd—already marking a possible unwriting in which georgic is no longer georgic but has been assimilated to pastoral in the pastoral eclipse. Substitute *prophecy* for *georgic* and the formula is virtually the same for Milton.

Milton criticism has more than once attested to the appearance of a double consciousness in those moments where Milton faces history, or faces apocalyptic duration. In a discussion of *Comus,* John Guillory remarks that

Milton's early poetry is much informed by motifs of the prefigurative, the annuncia-
tive. We can take as a motto for the sublimity of this stance, the line Wordsworth liked
so well, from *Paradise Lost:* "He onward came, far off his coming shone." In such a
line we hear the excitation of standing on the threshold before the advent of the
"superior power." The attraction of this deferral is very great. . . .

Prefiguration is related to a matter of anxiety as well as pleasure in Milton's early
career, his concern with the danger of *prematurity,* or a precociousness that might
possibly spend itself before the great work is accomplished. The lingering of "paganism" in his work, even in those poems . . . that seem impatient to herald an apocalypse,
is a necessary and self-imposed restraint, a continuous purgation and deferral. (P. 91)

The self-imposition that shapes what Guillory calls the prefigurative, and I
call the prehistorical perspective, is its crucial component. Guillory's comments remain within the terms of a deliberately Miltonizing tropology, but
we must push *Lycidas* a little past the boundaries of its own consciousness if
we hope to take its historical measure. The "lingering" of paganism in poems
like *Lycidas* or the Nativity ode—the supposed conflict between pagan and
Christian perspectives—is not really at their center of contradiction and is
thoroughly available to them for the organization of a kind of historical pleasure. A deeper conflict is being fought out, to which this pleasurable one
bears repressive relation. Milton (in the figure of his swain) does not defer
the arrival of the "superior power" of Christ—the anagogically superior
power, whose arrival will set aside Milton's moment and his prophetic work—
in favor of the "before" of paganism. What is really on the verge of arriving is
a fully articulated critical historicism—the humanism without prophecy already intimated in Spenser's more disabused pastoral—that will subject the
prophetic position itself to critique, that will deny it its desired historical
independence, its privilege to interpret the terms of historical agency. Milton, as a prophet, must defer an advent in which *Milton himself,* in the
apparent independence of the new critical subjectivity, will have to set aside
everything beyond his own present and the determinacy of his own historical
moment. The threat of that advent calls forth so great an energy of repression
that even the transmission of prophecy itself, in the trope of the swain's
mantle, is subject to misrecognition—*Lycidas*'s own half-Virgilian "backward
eddy." Milton's famous prophetic egoism has its source and boundary in this
deferral. The vanishing point of the swain's gaze, like all crucial Miltonic
ironies, is meant to maintain the diminishing prerogatives of apocalypse and
figural historicism, "superior powers" now on the verge of losing their power
to organize and guarantee the prophetic mode.

The last lines of *Lycidas* offer a wishfully unanxious choice of two competing tracks, parallel nevertheless in that both move forward into the historical landscape:

"Tomorrow to fresh woods and pastures new" can imply continuity with the life that seemed to be disrupted (emphasis on "woods" and "pastures") or a turning point, a decisive resolution prompted by the recognitions of the poem (emphasis on "fresh" and "new"). In either case, it is clear what is at issue.[28]

The issues are clear and they can be resolved without strain, almost casually, with a gesture like that of the swain twitching his mantle over his shoulders. In 1645 Milton seems to have made his choice, the choice for prophecy and apocalyptic fulfillment, "the ruin of our corrupted Clergy then in their height." And the gesture the headnote makes, standing apart from the poem, referring to its grand expression of commitment as having been produced "by occasion," is in its own way as casual and as circumstantial as that of the swain. Yet here too we are presented with the same systematic ironies found in the perspective of the swain at the poem's end. Milton's headnote represents St. Peter's speech as the true prophetic occasion of *Lycidas*, the source of its historical momentum—and thus points inexorably to the one turn above all others in the poem that represents the structural occlusion of prophecy:

> Blind mouthes! that scarce themselves know how to hold
> A Sheep-hook, or have learn'd ought els the least
> That to the faithfull Herdmans art belongs!
> What recks it them? What need they? They are sped;
> And when they list, their lean and flashy songs
> Grate on their scrannel Pipes of wretched straw,
> The hungry Sheep look up, and are not fed.   (119–25)

"Return *Alpheus*, the dread voice is past, / That shrunk thy streams" (132–33): Thus the swain's reaction to St. Peter's speech, a reaction that shows his consciousness at its most reductively prehistorical. Pastoral is weaker than prophecy, a less developed form of literary speaking, and must be coaxed back onto the scene in prophecy's aftermath. But we may suspect that Milton protests too much here, that prophecy in *Lycidas* can speak with its full vehemence only where pastoral authority—the institutional authority that pastoral represents—has been artificially limited. Pastoral, for the Renaissance preeminently a genre of memory, must be made forgetful in *Lycidas;* that is the only means by which Milton can secure his sense of prophetic commitment within the structure of the humanist literary career. A consciousness like the swain's, situated before the advent of Christian revelation, has no access to the pun on *pastor* (shepherd/priest) that ideologically grounds the literary history of Christian pastoral and organizes St. Peter's intervention in *Lycidas*. Aware of the struggle against episcopacy, the 1645 headnote tells a grim and in some sense final joke, that Milton's pastoral cannot allow itself to perform the central recognition that justifies pastoral—

justifies it in the terms of prophecy and figural historicism, as the Christian completion of a pagan mode. The pastoral pun is constrained to appear in St. Peter's speech strictly, and antihistorically, as *anti*pastoral. In 1637 the return of the swain's voice marks only a pause, but in 1645 it draws an absolute limit, a double perspective beyond which Milton cannot—or will not—pass, an irony that constitutes his prophecy.

Lycidas is haunted by the shade of an antithetical historicity, an intermediate and interminable temporality whose presence, to the extent that it must be addressed, debilitates typological certainty. The effort to change, restrict, even end ecclesiastical authority, whatever its apocalyptic rationale, has by Milton's era made itself felt as a contradiction in the organization of historical consciousness.

The reformers of the sixteenth century and after could hardly avoid attacking the papal Church as anti-Christian. The ambiguity of the biblical phrase permitted its use as meaning no more than "opposed to Christ." However, this meaning always carried with it the more complex signification "he who puts himself in the place of Christ." . . . The papacy became the Antichrist as well as a thing anti-Christian. Joachim's followers, from the thirteenth century onwards, had laid the basis for the complex as well as the simple identification. But the Joachite prophets had attacked a papacy which had recently been corrupted and which would promptly be defeated. They did not consider it necessary to give antichrist a history; its true history, for Joachites, occurred as the valid church of the second dispensation was taken over by antichrist on the eve of its displacement by the Church of the third age. . . . These shapely proportions were precluded by the Reformation necessity to attack the papacy as such, all fifteen (or so) centuries of it.[29]

Put perhaps too simply in terms of the history of intellectuals and their careers, Milton's allegiances have cast him outside the cultural formation in which the ecclesiastical institution, of whatever shape, could serve as the center of interpretive authority and the place from which those intellectuals who thought to project themselves into history could work. The result of such a movement, as *Lycidas* displays it, is a kind of institutional vacuity at the center of the prophetic commitment. Consequently we find an insuperable nostalgia in the very pose of historical forwardness that critics have long thought the most characteristically Miltonic thing about Milton. The movement into a landscape, and into the future which that landscape serves to trope, is famously Milton's preferred gesture of closure, whether lyric, pastoral, dramatic, epic. In *Lycidas,* that movement is merely lateral, through the unmarked and vacant space of an indeterminate landscape—a bright enough landscape, but one that resists visibly figuring its own anagogical completion. Unlike Virgil's goatherd, unlike Colin Clout, Milton's swain is given nothing (except his own history) to turn aside *from,* and nothing certain to turn aside to. The "unexpressive nuptial song" of Revelations that Lycidas hears "in the blest regions meek of joy and love" is meant, ultimately, to complete the swain's "Dorick lay" of today and tomorrow and the next day—to *be* his song, by way of typological fulfillment—but the third-person turn of "Thus sang" tells us only that the swain has sung, not where or how he carried the song forward or what finally the song has to do with him. The *Lycidas* envoi places the anagogical song at an epitaphic distance from its own singer; it has no aftermath for him, nor is he its aftermath.

   In *Les grecs ont-ils cru à leurs mythes?* [Did the Greeks believe in their myths?], an extraordinary essay in speculative historiography, Paul Veyne attempts to describe the historicity of Greek mythology and legend in the era of Pausanias. At one point Veyne has reference to the historicity of Christian hagiography in a way that bears on the pathos of the swain in the last lines of *Lycidas:*

> The legendary worlds [of the saints] were believed in as true in this sense—no one doubted their existence, but no one believed in them the way we believe in the realities surrounding us. For the faithful, the miracle-filled lives of the martyrs were located in a past without age, a past about which they knew only that it was anterior, exterior, heterogeneous to real time: it was "the time of the pagans." Likewise the myths of the Greeks: they took place "before," during the generations of the heroes when the gods still walked with humans. The time and the space of mythology were, on a hidden level, heterogeneous to ours; a Greek placed the gods "in the heavens" but would have been amazed actually to see them there; he would have been just as amazed to be taken at his word on the subject of time and told that Hephaestos had recently remarried or that Athena had aged a great deal lately. He might then have "realized" that mythic time, in his own eyes, had only a vague analogy with quotidian temporality, but also that a kind of lethargy had always prevented him from seeing that heterogeneity. The analogy between these temporal worlds had in fact camouflaged a hidden plurality. It does not go without saying that humanity simply has a past, either known or unknown; one no more sees the limit of the centuries one remembers than one sees the line that bounds the field of vision; there are no shadowy centuries stretching out beyond the horizon: one ceases to see, and that is all.[30]

Veyne's is a genealogical fantasy about what might be called the euhemerist moment, written from within a historical imagination founded in part on euhemerist criticism. I offer it here as a kind of parable for *Lycidas* and early Miltonic prophecy: Veyne fantasizes about a critical juncture at which a double perspective becomes single, two historical landscapes subsumed within one horizon of temporality. It is a fantasy we can perhaps read back, by way of the repressive defense I have just outlined, into Milton's own consciousness of prophecy. However much he wishes to give Greek belief its phenomenological due, Veyne is drawn irresistibly to imagine a repair of "heterogeneity," a reduction that collapses mythological time into the quotidian. Already in Milton's time such a reduction or merger of perspective has become at least virtually possible—possible enough that the desire to remain prior to that juncture, within the moment of "lethargy," as Veyne has it, feels obscurely like a choice. The vacuity of landscape in which *Lycidas* ends seems exactly like a trope of lethargy, a metapoetic appearance, by way of the economy of repression, of the "burden" or shadow given concrete form in Virgil and Spenser. It would be too much to say that the Christian tropology of history presents itself to Milton now as merely legendary, but in some half-conscious sense it must seem under an indictment and in need of defense. The Renaissance invention of the classical and of a historical duration appropriate to it is figured for *Lycidas,* and occluded in it, as the careerist, self-consciously historical specificity of pastoral. That duration *must* be occluded if anagogy and apocalypse are to remain categories properly historical—capable of receiving the kind of cathexis that, for Milton and the radical English left of his time, was invested in prophecy and in the activity of revolution—rather than, in effect, stranded, transcendentally outside of history and historical action.

Louisiana State University

NOTES

I owe thanks, for their helpful responses to this essay in its various stages of completion, to Harold Bloom, Deborah Karush, and Sharon Aronofsky Weltman.

All citations of Milton's poetry in this essay refer to *Poems of Mr. John Milton: The 1645 Edition,* ed. Cleanth Brooks and John Edward Hardy (New York, 1951).

1. David Norbrook, *Poetry and Politics in the English Renaissance* (London, 1984), p. 277.

2. The contention that "New Presbyter is but Old Priest writ large," as Milton put it in the 1646 sonnet *On the New Forcers of Conscience,* was an integral and familiar part of the debate over the legislating of compulsory Presbyterianism from 1644 to 1646, and was made in one form or another by critics both to the left and to the right of the Presbyterian Assembly. Ernest Sirluck, in his introduction to *The Complete Prose Works of John Milton,* 8 vols., ed. Don M. Wolfe et al. (New Haven, 1959), vol. 2, pp. 120–30, offers a very clear summary of the controversy surrounding the role of the state in church government in the immediate post–Civil War period. The Yale prose edition will be hereafter cited in the text as YP.

3. My identifying the "grim Woolf" and his pastors with the Laudians may seem dubious, given that *A Variorum Commentary on the Poems of John Milton,* vol. 2, pt. 2, *The Minor English Poems,* ed. A. S. P. Woodhouse and Douglas Bush (New York, 1972), identifies a "general consensus [among Milton scholars] . . . that the *Woolf* stands for Roman Catholicism" (p. 638). That consensus did not exist prior to the late nineteenth century; the eighteenth-century editors Newton and Warton take it as a given that, in Newton's words, "Milton meant to accuse Archbishop Laud of privily introducing popery and therefore in his zeal threatened him with the loss

of his head." Scott Elledge, *Milton's "Lycidas": Edited to Serve as an Introduction to Criticism* (New York, 1966), pp. 289–97, compiles the commentary of the eighteenth-century editors, along with Jerram's revisionist, apologetically Anglican nineteenth-century notes. Milton's own later use of *Lycidas*'s devouring wolf image, in the 1652 sonnet to Cromwell, would seem to endorse Newton; the sonnet asks the Lord Protector to "Help us to save Free Conscience from the paw / Of Hireling Wolves, whose Gospel is their Maw."

For purposes of my argument it is immaterial whether the identification with Laud is firmly established or not; indeed, given the censorship that existed when *Lycidas* was first published, the language of St. Peter's speech of necessity had to be at least formally opaque to readers outside the circle of political sympathy, a point Christopher Hill also makes in *Milton and the English Revolution* (New York, 1977), p. 50. It is more important that Milton's 1645 headnote makes the identification with Laud (for all practical purposes), not as evidence of a prior 1637 intention but as evidence of what the change in the poem's circumstances meant and could be made to mean. The headnote claims a transparency of allusion in St. Peter's speech that it cannot have had, or wished to have, in the poem's earliest appearance; thus Milton himself, in his 1645 temper, becomes the first revisionist critic of *Lycidas*.

4. Richard Helgerson, *Self-Crowned Laureates: Spenser, Jonson, Milton, and the Literary System* (Berkeley, 1983), pp. 259, 196–97. We can estimate how thoroughly *Lycidas* is structured by Milton's sense of the decorum of literary professionalism if we contrast the poem's commitment to graceful self-presentation with the rhetoric of the early polemical prose. David Loewenstein, *Milton and the Drama of History: Historical Vision, Iconoclasm, and the Literary Imagination* (Cambridge, 1990), remarks of the prophetic stance of the tracts: "The wrath of God in history finds its counterpoint in the wrath of the militant polemicist: because God himself may speak in a 'vehement character,' this polemicist's only regret [in the *Apology for Smectymnuus*] is that he has 'had not vehemence anough' (I, 902, 878) in combating his opponents" (p. 21). Milton's desire to shape a poetic career for himself, and his sense of the terms that shape the poetic career, means that, unlike the controversial prose, *Lycidas* can only be ambivalent, and provisional, about its approaches to vehemence.

5. Louis Martz, "The Rising Poet, 1645," in *The Lyric and Dramatic Milton: Selected Papers from the English Institute*, ed. Joseph H. Summers (New York, 1965); Helgerson, *Self-Crowned Laureates*, (p. 269)

6. Milton's reliance on the *rota Virgilii*—the sequence of bucolic, didactic (georgic), and epic poetry defined by Virgil's corpus—as a model for his own career extends well beyond the boundaries of *Lycidas* or the 1645 volume; nor are the historical implications of the Virgilian model confined to the elegy. Fuller discussions of the model are available, in terms of Milton's own early career, in Albert C. Labriola, "Portraits of an Artist: Milton's Changing Self-Image," *Milton Studies* XIX, ed. James A. Freeman and Anthony Low (Pittsburgh, 1984), pp. 179–94, esp. pp. 184–86; in terms of the larger cultural-historical context, in Richard Neuse, "Milton and Spenser: The Virgilian Triad Revisited," *ELH* 45 (1978): 606–39, esp. 609ff. I will have more to say about the historical meanings of pastoral, and the descent of the genre from Virgil to Milton through Spenser, in the final section of this essay.

7. Edward W. Tayler, *Milton's Poetry: Its Development in Time* [Pittsburgh, 1979], one of the few important critics to insist on the *essentially* pastoral character of *Lycidas*, speaks of the poem "recapitulating the history of pastoral": "The forward movement of the monody may be viewed in one of its aspects as an exercise in the critical history of literature, for Milton has in the first two sections dealt with classical and Old Testament 'pastorals' in such a way that they find their proper fulfillment in the 'pastoral' of the New Testament" (pp. 50–51). Tayler's corrective emphasis on pastoral as the generic ground of meaning in *Lycidas* in a sense overshoots the mark, however: his account has no room for prophecy as an independent if not competing phase

of the poem's historical agenda, and in that way fails to see—a point this essay will develop at length—the urgency of Milton's desire to *make*, more than merely recapitulate, his own history.

8. The early tracts confront versions of these questions at any number of points: in *Animadversions*, for example, Milton speaks of "our forescore yeares vexation of [God] in this our wildernesse since Reformation began" (YP I, p. 703), and in *Of Reformation* bemoans "the *Precedencie* which GOD gave this *Iland*, to be the first *Restorer* of *buried Truth*, [which] should have been followed with more happy successe, and sooner attain'd Perfection; in which, as yet we are amongst the last" (YP I, p. 526). Loewenstein, *Milton and the Drama of History*, pp. 8–34 (esp pp. 8–12), gives a useful, brief summary of the millennial historical thinking that developed in the English Reformation and that shaped Milton's own historical imagination. As Loewenstein sees it, the antiprelatical tracts "show Milton actively struggling with a labyrinthine historical process. They vacillate between celebrating the imminent millennium in England and lamenting the perversity of church and national history" (p. 13).

9. David Shelley Berkeley, *Inwrought with Figures Dim: A Reading of Milton's "Lycidas"* (The Hague, 1974), p. 31.

10. Northrop Frye, *Anatomy of Criticism* (Princeton, 1957), pp. 121–22. More recently, Joseph A. Wittreich Jr., "'A Poet Amongst Prophets': Milton and the Tradition of Prophecy," in *Milton and the Line of Vision*, ed. Wittreich (Madison, 1975), has insisted that the poem progresses "from Orpheus to St. Peter, to St. Michael, to Christ—from type to type, to manifestation, to the reality. This procession of types . . . brings Christ to the center of this prophecy" (p. 127).

11. Peter Sacks, *The English Elegy: Studies in the Genre from Spenser to Yeats* (Baltimore, 1985), notes the blurring of antecedent in the envoi's last couplet, seeing there "an assimilation of the elegist to the guiding figure and power of the poem, the sun. . . . The way in which the elegist preempts the rising of the sun reflects back on Christ's power to effect a spiritual sunlike rise for man. But Milton has calmly assumed that power himself. . . . We find it hard to avoid the recognition that it is, after all, the poet who has Christ raise Lycidas" (p. 116). Elegant as it is, Sacks's formula merely preserves, by way of inversion, the christological focus of readings like Frye's and Wittreich's.

12. *The Yale Edition of the Shorter Poems of Edmund Spenser*, ed. William A. Oram et al. (New Haven, 1989), p. 78. All subsequent citations from *The Shepheardes Calender* will refer to this volume.

13. J. Martin Evans, *The Road from Horton: Looking Backward in "Lycidas,"* English Literary Studies Series, no. 28 (University of Victoria, 1983), pp. 56–57; italics mine.

14. The OED does not record a usage in which "hearse" means "volume of memorial poetry," but does record a very near relation from which Milton obtains his pun: "a temple-shaped structure of wood used in royal and noble funerals. . . . It was decorated with banners, heraldic devices, and lighted candles; and it was customary for friends to pin short poems or epitaphs upon it" (2c). The article cites predominantly seventeenth-century sources for the usage.

Brooks and Hardy are the only commentators I have seen who stress how the real emptiness of the hearse grounds the meaning of "false" in "false surmise," though they do not extend the referent of "hearse" to include the funereal occasion of the 1637 volume itself. Yet they, too, assume that the rejection of false surmise decisively rejects the "wishful return to conventional pastoral" of the flower passage (p. 183).

15. For echoes of the Book of Revelations in *Lycidas*, lines 168–81, see the *Variorum Commentary*, pp. 728–30.

16. My use of terms like *ekphrasis* here bears comparison with Richard Hooker's in his essay "*Lycidas* and the Ecphrasis of Poetry," *Milton Studies* XXVII, ed. James D. Simmonds (Pittsburgh, 1992). That essay is primarily interested in the device of the end-frame and fills an important gap in the discussion of the device by noting its background in the "framed poetry

recitals" of Theocritean and Virgilian pastoral, in which the lyric is "always absolutely dissoci-
ated, sometimes problematically, from the world of the frame. These lyrics demand to be
evaluated on their own formal terms as works of design and skill. . . . If there is such a thing as a
basic narrative in *Lycidas,* this narrative lies in Milton's framing, or ecphrasis, of the speaker's
monody" (pp. 60–61). Unfortunately, Hooker's dogmatic, retro–New Critical insistence that an
ekphrastic framing "defines the lyric as a self-contained, self-referential work of deliberate craft,
and one that is to be evaluated on its own narrow, formal terms without reference to or bearing
on the world of the frame" (p. 60) seriously mars his treatment of both *Lycidas* and its classical
background. Pastoral song has its archetypal occasion in the contest between two shepherds for a
skillfully made artifact such as a bowl or a pipe. The Theocritean frame, by casting the lyric
record of that contest as itself an artifact, simultaneously repeats and represses, on the metatex-
tual plane, the poem's prehistory of labor and agon. Such is also true with *Lycidas:* reacting
against the critical tendency to assess Milton's monody in biographical terms, Hooker claims
instead that "the elegy becomes immediately obsolete following its production or reproduction":
"Through [the lyric's] autonomy and fixity, it loses any dialogic or interactive relation to the
constantly changing world of actuality, the world of 'Tomorrow' and 'Pastures new,' and so loses
any (temporary) claim it may have had on the swain's—and the reader's—attention" (p. 73). But
this view fails to recognize that Milton's frame, like those of Theocritus and of Virgil, is designed
to memorialize and subsume the history of its own production in the poem, precisely (and
ideally) in order to mark the completion of one phase—of a career, of a history, of a representational mode—and the commencement of its successor.

   17. Joseph A. Wittreich Jr., *Visionary Poetics: Milton's Tradition and His Legacy* (San Marino, Calif., 1979), p. 142; Alastair Fowler, " 'To Shepherd's ear': The Form of Milton's *Lycidas,"*
in *Silent Poetry: Essays in Numerological Analysis,* ed. Alastair Fowler (London, 1970), p. 174.

   18. On seventeenth-century funeral sermons, see John M. Wallace, *Destiny His Choice:
The Loyalism of Andrew Marvell* (Cambridge, 1968), p. 127.

   19. *Andrew Marvell: Complete Poetry,* ed. George deF. Lord (New York, 1968), 215–20;
italics mine.

   20. For a detailed account of the political argument in and behind "The First Anniversary,"
see Wallace, *Destiny His Choice,* chap. 3 *passim,* esp. pp. 127–36: "Marvell followed conventional exegesis in ascribing Elisha's anguish to his sorrow, not for Elijah, but for Israel. . . . Elisha
tore his clothes, and Elijah's were consumed, but the cloak which symbolized the succession and
the double portion of his father's spirit vouchsafed to Elisha was whole and inalienably his. If
England were not to be left shivering with dissension, the succession ought to be assured at
once" (p. 129).

   21. George Puttenham, *The Arte of English Poesie,* facsimile rpt. of 1906 rpt. (Kent State,
1970), p. 202.

   22. Maureen Quilligan, *Milton's Spenser: The Politics of Reading* (Ithaca, N.Y., 1983), p. 42.

   23. John Guillory, *Poetic Authority: Spenser, Milton, and Literary History* (New York,
1983), pp. 102–03.

   24. Virgil, *Eclogues,* ed. Robert Coleman (Cambridge, 1977). The English translation is
my own.

   25. William Berg, *Early Virgil* (London, 1974), p. 189, where he also gives a brief account of
the Augustan context of Virgil's image. See as well Paul Alpers, *The Singer of the Eclogues: A
Study of Virgilian Pastoral* (Berkeley, 1979), pp. 238–40.

   26. Michael J. Putnam, *Virgil's Pastoral Art: Studies in the Eclogues* (Princeton, 1970), p.
389, also notes this anticipation of georgic.

   27. Paul Alpers, *The Singer of the Eclogues,* notes the "doubleness" of the last lines of
Eclogue 10:

The poet proposes no more for himself than to pursue his task to its appropriate end by taking his flock home. This diffidence produces beautiful suspensions—normal relations and cycles held against the sense of a decisive ending—and a corresponding opacity about where the poem has left us. . . . It is very difficult to pursue [the] implications . . . in Virgil's line: its suspensions must be stated in terms of the pastoral fictions of the *Eclogues*. (Thus from the perspective of Renaissance pastoral, Virgil himself seems a "naive" poet). (P. 240)

"Naive" in Schiller's sense, but perhaps also "naive" in the more common use of the word: Virgil, to Spenser, may have seemed—in this moment at least—not quite "allegorical" enough, not quite to have caught all the allegorical implications of his own pastoral.

Richard Neuse, "Milton and Spenser," makes a similar point when he discusses the odd "flatness" of the debates that occur throughout *The Shepheardes Calender:*

The pastoral characters have as a law of their being an unselfconsciousness that signifies precisely their inability to imagine a variety of possible perspectives. But the authorial persona Colin Clout, as his laments make clear, is no longer a part of the seasonal round. . . . Colin's estrangement from his fellow-shepherds . . . is an implicit, not yet fully conscious, rejection of the pastoral world. (P. 612)

28. Alpers, *The Singer of the Eclogues*, p. 240.

29. W. H. Oliver, *Prophets and Millenialists: The Uses of Biblical Prophecy in England from the 1790s to the 1840s* (New Zealand, 1978), pp. 31–32.

30. Paul Veyne, *Les grecs ont-ils cru à leurs mythes? Essai sur l'imagination constituante* (Paris, 1983), pp. 28–29. The English translation is mine.

FIRE, ICE, AND EPIC ENTROPY:
THE PHYSICS AND METAPHYSICS
OF MILTON'S REFORMED CHAOS

Catherine Gimelli Martin

At certain revolutions all the damn'd
Are brought: and feel by turns the bitter change
Of fierce extreams, extreams by change more fierce,
From Beds of raging Fire to starve in Ice
Thir soft Ethereal warmth, and there to pine
Immovable, infixt, and frozen round,
Periods of time, thence hurried back to fire.

Paradise Lost II, 597–603)[1]

Some say the world will end in fire,
Some say in ice.
From what I've tasted of desire
I hold with those who favor fire.
But if it had to perish twice,
I think I know enough of hate
To say that for destruction ice
Is also great
And would suffice.

Robert Frost, "Fire and Ice"

1

WHETHER ROBERT FROST had Milton's lines in mind in a poem which, with evenhanded irony, considers the alternative eschatologies of "fire" and "ice," the polarity was neither new nor remains without general significance. Milton seems to have adapted Dante's image of Satan embedded in ice at the bottom of hell, but in doing so sets up a radically revised equivalence between these extremes which captures the paradoxical complementarity of their antithetical cosmogonic states. Much as in Revelation the omega becomes equivalent to the alpha to which it recursively points, here the fire of the infernal pit into which Satan is cast seems both the eschatological equivalent of the chaotic deep or void of Genesis i, 1, and its latter day antithesis, the "ice" of the entropic stasis or "heat death" of a universe burnt to cold solar dust, ashes from which no "new heavens and earth" can arise. Such at least was the state that late nineteenth- and early twentieth-century thermodynamics projected as the fate of all closed systems, including ours—and to which Frost teasingly seems to allude as an analog of human hate and desire.[2]

Entropy is the tendency of heat in a closed system to dissipate until it reaches stability at the lowest possible temperature. But we now know that chaotic entropy is only a single aspect of a double-aspected universal process within which disorder appears not so much alternatively as along with the "negentropy" of the self-reflexive process by which everywhere, and in all large-scale, open-ended systems like our universe, order self-organizes out of chaos.[3] Translated into literary terms, such dualities tend to seem paradoxical, even though such paradoxes also govern the self-referential processes wherein meaning itself is constructed, as it were, "negentropically." Chaos here then means either one or both of two things, depending on whether we focus on the textual representation of things, or on the condition itself. Yet in either case, chaotic entropy or "noise" (to borrow the language of information theory) is at once a real and not a metaphoric dissipation of apparent coherence and intelligibility in seemingly or actually closed systems, and also a temporary state of disorder which in open-ended systems tend toward new forms of order.[4] Moreover, this duality applies equally to the material world as we know it and to the world as Milton saw it—whether from the personal perspective of his "chaotically" self-organizing literary career, or from the larger perspective of the breakdown of historical meaning and the reemergence of new orders of meaningfulness from the ongoing "void" of God's concealed plans, his "meaning" for a universe.[5] If there is a providence in the fall of a sparrow or the blindness of a John Milton, then order arises apperceptively, emerging out of the apparent disorder of such things as failed marriages, or the failures of the Puritan revolution.

In more technical language, the far-from-equilibrium-state characteristic of all systems living off of constant input and output requires negentropy both initially to order its generation and to sustain the play of entropy within its self-enclosed systems. For our universe, like that of Milton's God, is both open and closed. It is as open-ended as the boundless deep from which he creates the world out of himself, the illimitable godhead. But it is also closed in that everything that proceeds from this all-thing, no-thing must return to him who limits the extensions of his own substance through Raphael's recursive "one first matter all."[6] It is a paradox, but paradoxes, like oxymorons, abound in *Paradise Lost*, as they abound in Christianity. Yet they also inhere in a kind of latter-day post-Gödelian logic within which the "undecidable" propositions of self-referential language mirror the universal condition of self-recursivity that structures the dynamic processes at play in the self-organization of order out of chaos. Since entropy is a necessary aspect of the breakdown of intelligibility and coherence, Milton's intuition of hidden principles of reconstitutive providential meaning could tap into what now seem like universally valid principles of dynamically self-ordering physical processes. Nor, given Milton's evident use of Lucretius, is his intuition entirely surprising, since the principles in question have been traced by chaos theory pioneers such as Ilya Prigogine and Isabelle Stengers to Lucretius's atomic speculations upon the nature of things.[7]

There is no point, however, in forcing a Lucretian analogy to current chaos theory in order to make Milton a prophet of twentieth-, and possibly twenty-first-century science. The focus here is rather on Milton's self-reflexive hermeneutics, his emplotment of principles corresponding to modern-day entropy and negentropy which may be taken as a symptomatic reflection of a Kuhnian type of cultural ecology in which criticism is necessarily intermeshed within the concerns of science, whose theories, for all their superficial autonomies, are part of the breakdown and buildup of holistic, open-ended systems.[8] Arguably in its time Milton's poem reflected a similar and massive paradigm shift linked to the Cartesian moment, which in its dissolution now reveals vast interanimating networks of older and newer paradigms in the process of crumbling and reorganizing new niches out of their own chaos. With this in mind, his epic, as it has been and continues to be read, embodies a cultural niche that serves as an exemplary extension of what in chaos studies has been called the "autopoetic" principle.[9] From this perspective the current situation represents the breakdown of an older hermeneutical order out of which a new one organizes by a recursive feedback process, though in the case of *Paradise Lost* it is as if we also return the poem to itself through new readings. For neither the old nor the new historicism will capture this dissipative/reintegrative aspect of our participatory recreation of Milton's work within the larger cultural cycles of constitution, growth, decay, and extinction leading to new formations, particularly when so much contemporary work along these lines remains trapped in a mistaken ego psychology and its Freudian anxieties of influence, or its parallel anxieties of subversion and containment. Instead I would suggest that the line following "fire and ice" from Milton and Dante back to Lucretius and forward to Frost offers a model of a completely different kind, one far more consistent with the realities of dynamic systems theory. It is from this standpoint that Frost's epigram on "Fire and Ice" may be read as an appropriately ironic remark upon the paradox implicit in Milton's most ironic epic innovation: a benign poetic universe founded upon the "wasteful" void of Chaos.

There is no room here to discuss its hermeneutic counterpart in any detail: the inevitable and productive grounds of undecidability, incompleteness, self-contradiction, and paradox in self-referential language which is directly or indirectly propositional. Nevertheless, in the inspirational convention by which *Paradise Lost* is mediated, the poet's "I" is a self-referential projection by Milton of himself upon a mirroring virtual bard. Thus, as Kurt Gödel's famous undecidability and incompleteness theorem would predict, in any critically generalizable class of formally self-referential propositions, undecidability or incompleteness—and correlatively self-contradiction—cannot be avoided.[10] Poetically, this undecidability may register as uncertainty, equivocation or "noise" entropically tending toward chaos, though it just as surely creates the conditions for a pluriform meaningfulness. When we invoke chaos here, it should then be understood in this "fecund" communicational sense, which obviates both of the extremes in which Milton's allegorical or "capital *C*" Chaos is generally taken: either as covertly complicit with purely dissipative or "hostile" disorder—and thus as a recurrence of the classical dualism Milton sought to avoid; or as overtly allied only with life-giving creativity or divine order—and thus a return to the preordained, univocal monism by which Milton's argument attempts to justify God's ways to man.[11]

Instead, Milton's Chaos would seem to embody preordained, ongoing, and quasimechanistic functions, the clarity of which easily or entropically dissipates, but which supply the dynamic drive and underlying power of his art. Loosely speaking, since entropy denotes the tendency of complex systems to dissipate into simpler ones, its "noisy" functions also invert Milton's more typical idealization of simplification as a purifying form of order and complexification as a symptom of premillennial disorder. When eschatologically the saints are finally "unmixt" in the Son's protoapocalyptic apotheosis during the final stage of the War in Heaven, the pure return to the steady state of bliss within the bosom of God, harping "Unfained *Halleluiah's*" (*PL* VI, 744). Yet in a memorable passage in *The Reason of Church-Government*, Milton contrastingly describes this state as an astonishing mixture of sameness and difference: "it is not to be conceiv'd that those eternall effluences of sanctity and love in the glorified Saints should . . . be confin'd and cloy'd with repetition of that which is prescrib'd, but that our happinesse may orbe it selfe into a thousand vagancies of glory and delight, and with a kind of eccentricall equation be as it were an invariable Planet of joy and felicity."[12] No mere harping of endless hallelujahs here, but order, so to speak, as perpetually wandering "vagancies" (YP I, 752) reborn out of their own tendency toward mixture or chaos.

Yet these "eccentrical equations" have their rules. While God can use evil to create "more good" (*PL* VII, 615–16), Satan cannot actually make "a

Heav'n of Hell" (I, 255) except to the extent that he succeeds in making it reflect the perversely dissipative form of entropy he introduces into heaven. Nor does heavenly desire ever truly "mirror" the satanic variety, since the very glory of divine majesty rests upon its plan to bestow this capacity to bring good out of evil (order out of chaos) not only upon its more "ethereal" creatures but upon all material creation—a process that also suggests how Milton "conceived" his own readers. Collaterally then, although destruction is inherent even within the *ex deo* structure of creative matter, some fires are fertile, while others burn out into frozen lakes filled only with "black tartareous cold infernal dregs / Adverse to life" (VII, 238–39). As a state at once anterior and posterior to "one first matter," chaos is thus the deity's most paradoxically "mixed" (or low) and "free" (or high) form of material existence, lacking form but filled with *relatively* random energy. But for that very reason, here if anywhere God's most ambi-valently charged forces are able to meet and "substantially" compete: creation perpetually vies with destruction, and the two ambiguously related forms of entropy (stable nonorder and dissipative disorder) interchange with the reintegrative phase of negentropy. All three phases are definable as the oppositely inclined though *not* unproductive ingredients of the random motion of elementary particles: entropy as the randomness of matter in its state-steady, which in the absence of an energy source tends toward increasing disorder (its dissipative phase); and negentropy as the disorderly but regenerative phase of systems far from equilibrium.

Although the laws of thermodynamics describing these phase states were not formalized until two centuries after Milton's epic was written, these terms are only anachronistic where science and literature are misconceived as ascending separately and/or linearly to the successively higher plateaus projected by the Hegelian dialectic of history. But when conceived as the by-products of irregular and local processes of historical disintegration and reintegration, these forms of cultural representation can be shown to evolve neither separately nor linearly, that is, to evolve according to the general model of culture that Milton shares with most contemporary historians. For as the poet clearly perceived, without a fully formless plasticity governing both the primordial and the emergent level of material history, "logically" God or good would have to be at least indirectly responsible for Satan or evil. As a result, creation's monistic if chaotic protomatter not only counters but also *conserves* dualism in a scientifically prophetic sense. For Milton's mythical materialism is actually a version of the "mixed" monism of twentieth-century cosmology and physics—which is *not* strictly speaking a pure monism, but rather a postulated unity expressible as the joint function of its two fundamental binaries, entropy and negentropy.

In the largely animistic terms of this synthetic binarism, then, essentially the same forces described by modern chaos theory are expressed in the allegorical figures of Chaos and Night, who also model the paradigmatic alternation of light and darkness extending throughout the universe, from the "grateful vicissitude" within the Mount of God to its reflection in "Male and Femal Light, / Which two great Sexes animate the World" (VIII, 150–51).[13] Here what must be borne in mind is that by deriving everything from God's "one first matter all," Milton sets up a universe in which everything with respect to his *ex deo* substance must in some sense be self-referential, and therefore subject to the Gödelian rules whereby the language of self-reference is necessarily paradoxical. As the primary mediator between the multiple levels of these paradoxes, Chaos must perforce model the coincidence of opposites. In its most typical form, this realm must thus *always* interpose some undecidability either between God and prematter or between his alchemical *materia prima* (represented by Night) and the higher differentiae of an incipiently ordered creation (Raphael's "one first matter"). Alternatively, as both positive and negative "sameness," the dual aspects of entropy reflected in an active Chaos and a passive Night also equivocally "order" the negentropic differentiae capable of reorganizing into life just across their threshold, leaving themselves and their realm "undecideably" and dynamically both positive and negative.

Though these processes in different phases may seem alternately hellish, heavenly, or merely neutral forms of change, the initial balance between Chaos and Night more immediately personifies the noisily mutable rather than the more truly threatening forms of change that occur once their realm is tyrannically invaded by hellish fire and ice. Without in any way weakening the qualifications raised above, these distinctions remain important to any reader concerned with preventing these distinctions from immediately degenerating into pure incoherence, which is in any case hardly the same thing as Gödelian undecidability. Quite the contrary, Gödel's theorems merely point to the logical impossibility of at once maintaining a system's internal coherence and externally demonstrating its truth value. In poetic terms, this means that from the standpoint of hell (from which, as the epigraph suggests, the reader approaches their realm), the allegorical persona of Chaos seems to preside only over the self-consuming or destructive aspects of fire and ice alternately feared and embraced by the demons as their "natural" ally. But from the standpoint of heaven, his realm appears in a more positive if still equivocal dialectical light, as *both* "the Womb of nature and perhaps her grave" (II, 911); or as both entropic and negentropic.

Thus here as everywhere in Milton's cosmos a calculated indeterminacy is sounded whenever the *summum bonum* of the divine will and its material manifestations seems to emerge as a revelation of the temporal embodiment of the mysterious Providence that the poem at once requires and conceals. For from the external standpoint of eternity—or its spatial equivalent, the eternal de- and re-evolution of matter—chaotic variability will always ultimately follow the divinely negentropic or regenerative direction of divine Providence rather than the malignly entropic drift sought by hellish revenge. But from the immanent standpoint from which the meaningfulness of a text emerges, the world as God's providential book is best served by those calculated and even practiced Miltonic ambiguities wherein uncertainty may seem at first a distracting noise, but later turns out to be a rich enlargement of a higher logic of poetic coherence. This paradigm of reading in turn presupposes a construction of textuality and history as noisy and sometimes dissonant matrices of emergent revelation which are not therefore meaning-less or, ultimately, unharmonious.

This apparently postmodern valorization of Milton's "chaotic" poetic form is actually historically consistent with his lifelong valorization of patience as the highest virtue of the saints, which necessarily requires a patient regard to the apparently contradictory signs of God's providential design. Contributing to this characteristically Reformed orientation is the older Renaissance sense of uncertainty as itself a productive matrix for understanding divine order, as in Tasso's allegorical claim that the "art of composing a poem resembles the plan of the universe, which is composed of contraries, as music is."[14] This conception seems to have directly influenced the organization of Milton's epic around dynamic contraries of the kind with which he had been experimenting as far back as the composition of *L'Allegro* and *Il Penseroso*. The countervailing energies of their alternately "swift or light" and "heavy or damp" muses will in his later epic be translated into the dissonant "consent" of elements enacting his post-Restoration revision of *concordia discours*, a vision which at once inverts the privileging of harmony in the standard representation of this theme and subverts any univocal description of chaotic ambi-valence as inherently hostile *or* benign. To overturn this inversion is thus also to overlook its subversive relation to the Royal Society's proto-Newtonian paradigm of order, thereby losing sight of the subversive implications of his continuing adherence to the idea of Lucretian indeterminacy *as* order, or at least as the passive, plastic counterpart of the deity's active cosmogonic creativity.

This vital reciprocity is maintained by the fact that, *except* for the deity who maintains their mutability, *all* physical states, malign or benign, dissipative or reintegrative, are both materially and metaphysically reversible in orientation. In this context, Satan's irreversible attachment to heaven's fixed "Orders and Degrees" (V, 792) is therefore as prejudicial to creative order as

Beelzebub's pseudochaotic preference for physical *and* moral Confusion (II, 365–72). Moreover, since varying forms of order and disorder permeate the entire universe, fallen and unfallen, they can be differentiated only by the tendency of demonic entropy to degenerate into the "extreams" of hellish fire and ice. Thus this degradation of matter and energy is caused less by God's absence from hell (where his traces appear even in "Vallombrosa," the valley of the shadow of death shepherded by his concealed presence) than by the active material and metaphysical dissipation generated by the demons' determined blockage of fluid entropic energy, the essence of *ex deo* matter itself. As when Satan diverts heavenly rays to the "hollow" purposes (VI, 552–53) of his cannon fire, his perverse "fixation" of heavenly light brings "into Nature . . . / Miserie, uncreated till [his] crime" of troubling the benign entropy of God's "Holy Rest" (VI, 267–68, 272). In perverting energies which in this benign atmosphere would naturally bring order out of chaos, Satan can then most accurately be accused of the "sin" of replacing the divine disorder of the heavenly dances with his own more determinate disarray—which is *not* most "Eccentric, intervolv'd, yet regular / Then most, when most irregular they seem" (V, 623–24).

The structural irony inherent in this situation is that such disorder is "negentropically" necessary both to the reconstructive nature of creaturely freedom, and to whatever recuperative powers Satan himself retains in his progressive descent and decay.[15] Without it, there would only be a static creation with no potential for the "rebellion" so harmlessly waged by Chaos (II, 894–97) and so disastrously by Satan. In exercising his God-given freedom to intervene in the evolutionary processes that symbolically culminate in the Son's anointing, Satan's sin can be further defined as his opposition to the entropic "lowering" of divine energy that enables the transfer of creativity from creator to begotten creature; a process which, as Raphael at once demonstrates and promises, allows all life gradually to rise (V, 491–500). Within this network of paradoxically benign ascent *and* descent, Chaos should be understood as the complex vehicle of those free metaphysical transactions which, in fully expressing their subjective wills, must first become physical. His volatile realm thus provides the sphere of indeterminacy that permits degenerate energies to be alternately "entombed" in their own "tartareous" waste or "enwombed" in the matter of "new worlds," individual or cosmic. These contrary phases of entropy explicitly emerge as the Almighty ordains the "dark materials" of Chaos "to create more worlds" in the same sentence that we see the "warie fiend" preparing to convert it into a precinct of hell (II, 915–17).

The situation is repetitively varied as Satan, cormorantlike, surveys the earthly paradise from the Tree of Life, whereon he sits "devising Death" (IV,

197) much as he had sat upon the edge of the abyss devising how to introduce deadly "ice" (X, 291) into its "pregnant" expanse (II, 913). Inherently more disordered than Eden, the void is also more inherently susceptible to multiple and conflicting forms of order, including not only Satan's hyperorganized "universe of death" (II, 622), but the spontaneous "warmth" of earthly creation (VII, 221–37) and negentropic recreation (VI, 871–77; X, 635–38). This strangely mixed but consistently libertarian expanse thus supplies the single, continuous, and extended substance mediating between God and "one first matter all." For this very reason, it neither can nor ever shall be subdued by a godhead who privileges discord *as* concord.[16] In short, as a poet for whom differentiation and ambiguation of the scale of "one first matter" was in a manner literary *materia prima,* Milton seems to have made an imaginative Lucretian leap whereby the potential (in every sense) of the Grand Anarch Chaos as a neutral and plausible mediator of the scale of one first matter's extremes could be used to supply an incipient or emergent condition of good.

2

Both Milton and many of the seventeenth-century natural philosophers with whom he was conversant were attracted to Lucretius and his "great Original," Hesiod, because in contrast to the earlier preference for a sinisterly metamorphic, Ovidian Chaos, the early empiricists were free to imagine the void of primal flux as the place of a creative *en-tropos* or in-turning, a generative "swerve" in a nature whose Venus principle counters the more negative or violent Mars principle.[17] However, like entropy and negentropy, *both* Mars and Venus principles appear as alternatively creative and destructive when viewed from different perspectives—the "higher" Venus of love and procreation being the alter-ego of the lower one who (as Virgil classically warns) destroys the empires that Mars collaterally rebuilds. These alternate scenarios in part suggest why even though Milton's validation of chaotic disorder as a vitalist force akin to the providential mysteries of his God is plainly stated in such texts as the *Christian Doctrine,* it would be ignored by generations of critics steeped in the opposing view of order as originating *only* in an "external, objective, self-consistent, and authoritative system" such as that posited by Newtonian mechanics. As an aesthetic informed by this "authoritative system," neoclassicism would further reinforce the critical aversion to the equivocal resonances in the role of such figures as Chaos and Night, Sin and Death, as agents of choice in the cosmogonic process.[18] Yet the fact that these choices change the course of the epic action for good as well as ill in itself eloquently testifies to the depth of Milton's departure from the dominant

cosmogonic tradition, where matter/*mater* is unequivocally the "evil" opponent of the creative voice who *does* permanently silence it, not the vehicle of
a freedom whose fecundity (as in Lucretius, and to a lesser extent, Hesiod)
ultimately allies it with divine mutability.[19]

The essential alterability of all choice enacted in and through matter
thus penetrates to the deepest strata of the epic's ideology, which in dramatic
contrast to the fallen Nature of Spenser's *Mutabilitie Cantos,* literally rests
upon Chaos itself. As such, it cannot *in itself* be malign, though it may
become so when corrupted by external agents, whose higher form of organization not only can but *must* include the ability to express itself in suitably
"plastic" material manifestations, that is, in its ability to reorganize matter out
of chaos. This logic applies even to Sin and Death, who though genetically
descended and psychically linked to Satan, possess an initiative every bit as
real *and* as limited by the constraints implicit in applying creaturely liberty to
all. Physically, this means that Sin must be free to choose to open the gates of
hell, while metaphysically she cannot "shut / [what] Excel'd her power" (II,
883–84). That is, she may choose to advance Satan's cause, but she cannot
close a temptation that divine freedom decrees open to all. In this sense, hell
is as ever "open" as the satanic mind, that peculiarly and typically Miltonic
"everywhere" (IV, 75), to be sealed only by the individual will, or by its
regeneration through the "grave" of Chaos and the "womb" of Night. At the
apocalyptic level this sealing occurs once Sin and Death have had their self-
destructive day, so that all that remains are hardened dregs no longer capable
of choice, their "draff and filth" which, having "At random yeilded up to their
misrule," will finally "obstruct the mouth of Hell / For ever" as heaven and
earth are renewed (X, 628–39).

A similarly Lucretian endorsement of randomness as the road to self-
renewal applies to the pointed contrast between satanic confusion and the
truly chaotic kind. At once bounded by the higher creativity of the encompassing Word (VII, 216–31) and permanently "open" to change, Chaos
"naturally" *excludes* the destructive sedimentations that produce the "fierce
extreams" of fire and ice.[20] Thus while blasts of nitrous fire may randomly
rebuff and even inadvertently assist Satan's confused progress through this
random realm of self-discovery and recovery (II, 935–38), its very randomness prevents its being permanently misshaped by the organized "Confusion" with which Beelzebub would "with Hell fire / . . . waste [God's] whole
Creation" (II, 364–65, 371–72). For in Chaos there can only be temporary,
not any such satanically "inbred" enmity (II, 785) as that which sets Sin
against her son, and both against their common father. The abyss ruled by
"*Rumor* next and *Chance,* / And *Tumult* and *Confusion* all imbroil / And
Discord with a thousand various mouths" (II, 965–67) is in fact far too

irregular and noisy to obey either hell's king or their own Anarch, who is in any case too weak, wavering, and confused to be limited by his own decisions, much less by logic itself.

Yet on some things Chaos does express a firm and consistent commitment, as when he reacts "indignantly" to his betrayal by Satan's hyperorganized forces, which along with Sin and Death "scorn" and "scourge" his libertarian domain (X, 311, 418). As the prior and inherently divine principle of pure *potentia*, chaotic mutability inevitably resists their divisions and desolations, which are but cause and effect of a single inclination (X, 410–20). Thus, as the Shawcross edition notes, contemporary logic would construe the "pregnant causes mixt / Confus'dly" (II, 913–14) in Chaos as representing "Ramus' forces by which things exist: nothing has been born yet from their confusion but potential birth is imminent" (p. 294*n*49). By situating these forces at the degree-zero of his ongoing material universe, Milton represents irregular and indeterminate matter as essentially benign, chiefly *because* its causes cannot be permanently diverted into the satanic "fixations" which Chaos quite rightly if weakly resists. This resistance is appropriate both to its predetermined plasticity and to its continuing receptiveness to new forms, which absolve it of guilt even in the actual presence of evil. Unlike the *hyle*, *sylva*, or uncreated substance which in the more standard Christian schemas of Silvestris, Spenser, and Shakespeare are aligned with evil, chaotic matter now partakes of the same positive mutability assigned to Raphael's "one first matter."[21] For as the dark "root" of its monistic stalk, chaos quite literally informs the "more aerie" flowers in which creation blooms (V, 470–90). Evil then takes root only in the perverse will's relentlessly *regular* and *spiritual* disposition to halt the spontaneous tendency of all created substance to return to the "one Almightie . . . from whom / All things proceed" (469–70). Although the malign will is manifest through the agency of chaotic matter, in this monistic universe the mutable spirit is the physically evolving and metaphysically corruptible source of the transformations formerly associated with matter.

This Protestant adaptation of Lucretius's materialist theodicy thus characteristically reshapes the latter's Epicurean resignation to the nature of things into a celebration of Christian liberty. Tracing mankind's only "fatal" necessity to the limitations of nature's fundamentally self-empowering laws, Milton also completes a process underway in the earlier poems and prose and clearly emerging in his "transcendental" or genre-rupturing masque.[22] Here, in anticipation of the epic reconciliation between Chaos and "one first matter," the masque presents first a conventional and then a corrected version of Chaos, which emerges during the peripeteia at its center. At this point, no longer regarding Chaos as threatening (334–35), the Elder Brother imitates the epic voice in predicting that its elemental energies will ultimately cause "evil on itself . . . back [to] recoil." Much like the epic narrator, he reaches this conclusion by confronting his fears of the error, darkness, and "barbarous dissonance" (*PL* VII, 16–32) at work in the "navel of this hideous Wood" (550, 520). This challenge then permits a renewed understanding of Chaos as an *affirmative* realm of trial:

> Yes even that which mischeif meant most harm
> Shall in the happy trial prove most glory.
> But evil on itself shall back recoyl,
> And mix no more with goodness, when at last
> Gather'd like scum, and settl'd to itself,
> It shall be in eternal restless change
> Self-fed and self-consumed; if this fail,
> The pillar'd firmament is rott'nness,
> And earth's base built on stubble.   (591–99)

Here, as in *Paradise Lost*, mutability is not opposed to good but, through trial, becomes not only its precondition, but the final condition whereby "self-fed and self-consumed" evil will resolve back into the purer random-ness of "eternal restless change." And as in *Areopagitica*, where the very fabric of the temple of Reformed truth is woven from disharmonious ele-ments, difference defeats evil much as the freedom of the press unmasks error: by allowing its abortive by-products to choke upon their own self-consuming waste (YP II, pp. 515, 549, 555), the same "natural" fate awaiting Sin and Death.

The result is that far more than Satan, God can justly say "Evil be thou my good," thereby making even Death no more the mortal enemy of Donne's famous sonnet. Instead, it becomes mankind's "final remedie" which, assisted by internal resolve,

> after Life
> Tri'd in sharp tribulation, and refin'd
> By Faith and faithful works, to second Life,
> Wak't in the renovation of the just,
> Resignes him up with Heav'n and earth renewd.   (XI, 62–66)

In this passage as throughout Milton's mature work, the older tradition of *memoriam mori* has been so inverted that uncreated matter and natural flux rather than the Platonic immutability of the immortal soul are now linked to spiritual good, a condition attainable only through freedom, mobility, self-determination, refinement, and change—the central values of this most radi-cally "Reformed" epic. Though its cosmos still ideally reflects a transcendent order, its structure remains both physically and metaphysically consonant with the good only through the immanent compliance of its agents, who in choosing life by definition choose freedom over the tyranny of the satanic will. Since the entropic decline of prime matter results from the endorsement of this malign will, Chaos itself remains innocent of what has been externally imposed upon it. Here, as in the disordered realm of dreams, evil "May come and go, so unapprov'd, and leave / No spot or blame behind" (V, 118–19). Containing the potential but not the inclination toward evil, Chaos's unformed matter thus becomes Satan's unwitting ploy, which like our Grand Parents falling "deceiv'd / . . . therefore shall find grace" (III, 130–31). However, in his case even the Anarch's inadvertent guilt is called into question by his final appearance, which shows his realm indignantly resisting the infernal triad's fire and ice (X, 416–18) when it invades him

> As when two Polar Winds blowing adverse
> Upon the *Cronian* sea, together drive
> Mountains of Ice, that stop th' imagin'd way
> Beyond *Petsora* Eastward, to the rich
> *Cathaian* coast.   (X, 289–93)

Besides imposing an icy solidity upon Chaos (which also means blocking the entrance to the earthly paradise) and "fixing" (295) its "rich[es]" (292) with "*Gorgonian* rigor . . . / And with *Asphaltic* slime" (297–98), the adversary's northerly "adversity" punningly emphasizes the effects of their harsh new "reign" of rigor mortis.[23] Here once again the enormous contrast of the satanic offspring's icy fire with the far more benign anarchy of chaotic fluidity (283) underlines the central physical, metaphysical, and political distinctions between these opposing kinds of confusion. Swooping down into Chaos's fertile "damp and dark" and "hovering upon the Waters" (283, 285) like an insane parody of the Holy Spirit's "brooding" upon the abyss (VII, 234–35), Sin and Death immediately begin to parch and freeze its mutable seas into an "aggregated Soyl" (X, 293) pointedly compared to the bridge with which Xerxes tried "the Libertie of *Greece* to yoke" (307). With tongue not much in cheek, the poet calls this imperial "scourge" a work "of wondrous Art / Pontifical" (311–13), a sign of the ultimate spiritual tyranny: a specious "liberation" (368) enforced by "reducers" (438) who would in every sense *pontifically* bridge, subject, enchain, and diminish the metaphoric Greek "home" of liberty itself.[24]

The injustice of their enslavement of this once-libertarian realm is further underscored in the following simile, which again describes Satan's legions as waging the moral equivalent of imperial war, mounting a barbaric invasion resembling that of the Tartar who "leaves all waste beyond / . . . in his retreat" (431–35). Here punning on the double meaning of their "wasting" or ruin of Chaos's once fertile "waste" (282) or *undeveloped* expanse, the passage then concludes by prophesying the reciprocal "wasting" of those who "waste and havoc yonder World" (617), the continuum that explicitly connects Chaos to the earthly paradise. Thereafter punished in the fashion of their crime, the satanic cohort is sympathetically reduced to the "sharp and spare" (511) shapes reminiscent of the bars that Sin and Death had used to restrain chaotic energy (417), until in their "true" mythic dimensions these groveling serpents chew the "bitter Ashes" (566) of their hellish fruit, the proleptic equivalent of the "tartareous dregs" they are later destined to become. Accordingly, they must "taste" the fire that Chaos's damp "Anarchie" would have put out (283), had they not "wasted" it. In this allegory of material action and reaction, God's judgment serves chiefly to clarify the naturalistic consequences of interfering with physical entropy, including the negentropic reaction that will inevitably restore its benign balance. Thus not even "the folly of Man" which "Let in these wastful Furies" (619–20) can forever alter the quenching capacities of Chaos's pregnant deep, which if not unalterable, is more resiliently reactive than the forces of Sin-ful rigidity. For once the Sin-ful family's energies have at once allegorically and actually exhausted themselves, the bitter morsels of their rigor mortis will "naturally" be digested and excreted by the very chaotic organs they had attempted to enslave; so that finally, those great reducers King Death and Queen Sin will themselves be reduced to stoppers of that cosmic "bung hole," the giant "mouth of Hell," whose "ravenous Jaws" they "for ever . . . seal" (636–37).

The framing of this final appearance of Satan, Sin, and Death as the oppressors of both Chaos *and* the creation it conceives plainly indicates that all such forces, even Satan's, monistically participate in material principles that constitute a "voluntary covenant between human will and divine commandment."[25] Rather than the Platonic impression, reflection, or cloudy shadow of an eternal macrocosm of ideas, matter here takes on the Lucretian shape of the dynamic substance sustaining and evolving the whole. Moreover, because matter is no longer the "merely" mutable shadow of an ideal form, its ambiguous negentropy mediates between the eternal and temporal dimensions of time much as between the formed and formless dimensions of space. As a result, to "conquer" Chaos is really to diminish one's own vital substance, producing a victory as pyrrhic as the theft of the Holy Spirit's transforming warmth, which indeed describes the metaphysical level of Satan and his Sin's actions. Finally, then, his metaphysics will recapitulate his physics, as he and his progeny are bound to a frozen lake of fire, the "natural" effect of their ever-burning ice (Rev. xx, 14).[26]

3

As outlined above, some antecedents of this vitalistic Christian metaphysics are apparent in Milton's earlier poems and prose, which similarly valorize the dynamics of becoming rather than the stasis of being, the space of Raphael's "worlds and worlds" (V, 268) and the time of Michael's "Ages of endless date" (XII, 549). A cosmos founded upon an "abyss / . . . whose end no eye can reach" (XII, 556–57) rather than upon a plenum implies a discontinuous universe which must affirm degeneration as an aspect of regeneration, as a significant if somewhat obscure strain of Christian thought similarly does.[27] In line with the Reformed emphasis upon returning to the original, unobscured roots of its tradition, Milton is particularly inclined to rehabilitate forgotten and/or "primitive" modes of inquiry, which throughout his work produce a characteristically skeptical yet sympathetic attitude toward the early Greek materialists and their myths as "fabling" (*PL* I, 741) vehicles of the light God gives us "to discover onward things more remote from our knowledge" (YP II, p. 550). In the dawning beams of this reforming zeal, the early pagan poet/philosophers (*almost* although never fully equal in authority to the biblical authors) can be used to provide a Greek gloss on the Hebrew text, a way of filling in the interstices of the notably terse and even contradictory accounts of Genesis. Hence what overtly or covertly inhibits more conventional readers from participating in this rehabilitation is the deeply entrenched opposition between "evil chance" and "divine necessity" in standard Christian theology, which if sustained, would indeed render Chaos a suspect if not wholly dubious ally of God.[28]

Thus here most of all this historical inquiry must emphasize the monistic implication of Milton's metaphysics. Moreover, *because* the simultaneous processes of entropy and negentropy (or dissolution and evolution) govern historical inquiry itself, not only broad concepts like "the Christian tradition" but far more specific ones like Protestantism or Puritanism are all but empty of content except in relation to the specific attitudes, ideas, and practices informing the phase in which they participate.[29] The task of accurately assessing this juncture is all the more demanding in that, like ours, Milton's period was in rapid transition (to take its furthest extremes) between establishing the paradigms of objectivity still current throughout much of the scientific world, and forecasting science's recent "shift from Newtonian to relativistic physics."[30] Yet far from endorsing either extreme, Milton like most progressive thinkers of his day was unwilling to endorse either/or forms of rationality, even while upholding the standard of reason itself.[31]

In theology as well the Reformers were divided between the conservative or Presbyterian faction's emphasis upon plain speech, concrete methods, and clearly established doctrine, and the Independent faction's insistence upon truth as the product of random inspiration, providential conjunction, and a concerted refusal to "make . . . a dogmatic absolute" capable of exact definition. Earlier condemned by his enemies as evincing a characteristic Independent "mutability," Milton consistently insisted upon the right "to reverse himself and reassess his positions with respect to changing situations," a principle that remains central to his core beliefs. This spiritual and political analog to the philosophy of "chaotic" inspiration most notably developed in *Samson Agonistes* is compared by Michael Fixler to the tenets of the dissenting ministers, who in their *Apologeticall Narration* explain that

for all such cases wherein we saw not a cleare resolution from Scripture, example or direction, we still professedly suspended, until God should give us further light, . . . we having this promise of grace for our encouragement in this, . . . that in *thus* doing the will of God we should *know* more.

A second Principle we carryed along with us in all our resolutions, was, Not to make our present judgement and practice a binding law unto our selves for the future . . . to alter and retract (though not lightly) what ever should be discovered to be taken up out of a misunderstanding.

In this emergent view of both human accountability and divine providence, mutability, reversibility, and indeterminacy provide a decentered though not thereby deconstructive view of the logos, whose "most *sacred law* of all other" is to reflect these most unbinding and disjunctive of principles.[32] Because this waiting for leadings or "rousing motions" and a corresponding embrace of their ambiguity is one of the most notable aspects of Milton's post-Restoration poetry, it makes neither aesthetic nor philosophical sense to postulate his "conversion" to the antimetaphorical plainness of the Royal Society (as Maureen Quilligan and others have done). Such a stance would not only ally him with political and theological adversaries like Hobbes, but would condemn the very principles of Christian liberty emphatically maintained in the final books of *Paradise Lost*.[33]

A revalidation of Chaos as well as a reevaluation of its ambiguous relationship to eternal "necessity" is thus essential not only to an adequate understanding of the poem, but to its place in the foundational debates of the seventeenth century. As the cosmic counterpart of his God, Chaos recasts necessity as varying in accordance with the stance of the observer, thereby accommodating an "indeterminate" human understanding of the deity who exists before, after, and *within* time. These different "phase states" have been already been traced in Chaos, which (as we have seen) acts as a spatial analog to the temporal eternity of God's "Holy Rest."[34] Like the activity of the simultaneously "boundless" yet "fateful" godhead (VII, 168–70), the void is

at once spatially circumscribed and temporally dimensionless, at once negentropically evolving and entropically the same. This analogy at once expands
and unifies a universe where both time and space, divine *and* fallen, cohere
not in their hierarchical linearity or preordained fixity, but in a benign alterability that remains providentially "pure." Raphael explains these cosmic
paradoxes to Adam as upholding both continuity within difference as simultaneously necessary *and* fortuitous aspects of the irregular creation history
embedded within God's mysterious plan.[35]

Thus just as the narrative voice embeds the reader's view of Eden within
the circumstances of Satan's visit and subsequent temptation, so Raphael
frames the prior deviation within the divine plan (which *does and does not*
"decree" it) within the very covenantal moment meant to celebrate "Heav'ns
great Year" (V, 583).[36] This simultaneously circular and linear period of time
then provides two contrary events whose lineages nevertheless meet in an
expanded providential circle: the moment in which God begets the Son and
Satan begets Sin. Although material history now acquires a newly degenerative form of entropy even as the negentropic new covenant is announced, this
day's inscription of evil within good no more taints an anointing that will more
loosely unite the angels "as one individual Soul / Forever happie" (V, 610–11)
than Chaos's kingdom is tainted by Satan's entry into its

> Illimitable Ocean without bound
> Without dimension, where length, breadth, and highth,
> And time and place are lost; where eldest Night
> And *Chaos,* Ancestors of Nature, hold
> Eternal *Anarchie.*   (II, 892–96)

If Chaos like Night here acquires an Erebusian shading through its mere
propinquity to hell, the former's "Eternal *Anarchie*" is originally as neutral as
the latter's darkness, which even in heaven is a fundamental component of
the "Grateful vicissitude" (VI, 8) everywhere inherent in a creation which is
divine in and through the very dissonances of its concords.

Although this open-ended model of time and space conflicts both with
the Newtonian and the dominant Christian-Greek paradigms of the universe,
it has an equally long and respectable lineage of its own, not only in Hesiod
and Lucretius, but also in Plato's mythopoetic dialogues (especially the *Phae-
drus* and the *Timaeus*), the Gnostic gospels, and the important strands of
Jewish mysticism synthesized by Philo. This "demiurgic" tradition counters
the syncretic Stoic/scholastic tradition in which creation is eternally and
inalterably in place as a static form present to "the mind of God" and the
enlightened observer. Here instead any "objective" representation of reality
must be understood as the result of an emulation of divine *creativity* within

the feminized deep (Tehom), that is, as an active re-creation of an original word or work trapped in subsequent layers of imperfection. As a result, the human mind is regarded as worshipping the deity chiefly by participating in its ambiguous energies, not by reflecting its eternal constructs. Although these traditions are not only often confused but actually overlap (both tending to cite Genesis and Plato as ultimate authorities), in their most powerful and distinct forms they produce fundamentally different conceptions not only of the deity and his relation to his creation, but of the nature and metaphysics of matter. As we have seen, in the mainstream or Augustinian tradition matter is associated with nothingness and/or evil, while in the demiurgic tradition that produces atomists like Milton's contemporary John Ray, chaotic matter constitutes a neutral state whose elements are "variously confused and confusedly commixed, as though they had been carelessly shaken and shuffled together; yet not so but that there was order observed by the most 'Wise Creator' in the disposition of them."[37]

The roots of this tradition are themselves somewhat shaken and shuffled together, it being uncertain whether they precede or antedate the dominant Indo-European creation myths which celebrate the silencing of primeval feminine "disorder" by antithetically masculine, law-giving deities. Here the forces of Yahweh/Marduk/Zeus (the younger, law-giving sons) definitively conquer and contain Tehom/Tiamat/Titans (the first children of Gaia, the original *mater*/matter). In the later (though perhaps originally earlier) pre-Socratic myths the precedence is reversed, so that in this strand of thought feminine Venus or Love orders the unruly forces of masculine Mars or Strife. Both myths are thus structured by binary oppositions conducive to philosophical dualism, though the latter far less so than the former. As in the two conflicting accounts of gendered creation in the Hebrew bible ("in his *own* image . . . male and female he created them," Gen. i, 27, which precedes the more patriarchal or "priestly" account of Eve's secondary derivation from Adam's rib, Gen. ii, 22), the more androgynous account of creation is also more favorable to a mutable matter/*mater*.

Yet in part because *Paradise Lost* seems to favor the second and more narratively explicit Genesis account, and in part because of the continuing hegemony of that tradition, the common critical tendency has been to assume that the poem maintains its dominant, antichaotic, antifeminine conventions despite the abundance of contrary evidence. For however "not equal" Adam and Eve may appear in the early stages of Milton's epic, their "filial freedom" (IV, 294–96) thereafter emerges in much the same dialectic terms as "Male and Femal Light." Yet the same dialecticism prevents Chaos from simply being God's "woman" in the purely positive sense outlined by John Rumrich, who fails to note the extent to which Chaos is never fully subdued *or* informed either by Satan *or* by God. For much the same reason, Chaos cannot cogently be coopted by a fashionable reading which would make it unequivocally in league with the "benign" forces of feminist disorder.[38]

For in an opposite and ultimately more positive sense, the realm of Chaos is *pure* disorder. While any member of Satan's "family" could have affirmed with its Anarch that "Havock and spoil and ruin are my gain" (II, 1009), his own anarchy prohibits him from understanding either Satan's deliberate disingenuousness or *any* organized mode of being, whether in hell, heaven, or earth. As a result, Satan is as usual lying when he claims to advance "the Standard of . . . ancient *Night*" (II, 986) on earth, when he is only advancing a vastly more infertile form of confusion to "encroach" upon her "Scepter" and circumscribe her reign (II, 1001–05). Even so, any dialectical view of Chaos necessarily implies its own troubling inconsistencies, most notably the following: if matter becomes "good" by remaining unstable, how can Chaos be materially linked to the eternal *im*mutability of the God from which, through light (III, 1–6), it physically seems to originate? How can the still traditionally omniscient and beneficent deity create a fully indeterminate form of matter? Given the dominant and almost insurmountable theological dichotomy between the liberty of the rational spirit and the irrational license of matter, *and* confronted with an unruly Anarch who does at times seem to oppose the divine monarch, the unwary reader might well suspect that, at some level, Milton's epic inadvertently resurrects a classic hierarchical dualism. Despite being praised as nature's "eldest birth" (V, 180), the material "cause" upon which God builds when he is "late[ly] . . . moved" to lay aside "his holy Rest" (VII, 90–93), Chaos would then remain an inchoate if not overt opponent of divine order, the force that must traditionally be silenced lest its "troubl'd waves" (VII, 216) overturn creation with their "loud misrule" (VII, 271–72).[39] Not merely a passive symptom but also an active ingredient of Sin, Chaos would thus with good reason "tamely endure" (II, 1028) satanic "confusion."

Yet even this modified dualism, like that latent in Cartesianism itself, provides a plausible but hardly compelling explanation of Milton's largely anti-Cartesian epistemology. A far more plausible source of what R. A. Shoaf calls Milton's poetics of "duality, not dualism" is the emergent paradigm which, rather than classically "abhorring" a vacuum, affirmatively exploits it and all its analogs (the null set, nothing, the margin, void, or gap). Departing from the fixed *horror vacui* that demonized open systems as at once irrational and atheistic, the more mystical heirs of Pythagoras and Philo grounded their systems in invisible "nothings," systems which would not only reemerge in both Kepler and Pascal, but also deeply influence a significant number of the period's mathematicians and scientists as well as Milton.[40] At a time when the zero/void was coming into its own as "the completion of an existing semiotic paradigm" previously current among the "linguistic, cultural middlemen" of Europe (its artists and merchants), thinkers like Milton could begin to cancel the traditional opposition between what Brian Rotman calls "the Devil's Nothing" and "God's All," thereafter claiming this vacuous "other" as his missing other half, at least in a limited sense.[41] For God cannot truly inhabit the "no place" of Chaos any more than he inhabits any other place: though he may "fill [its] infinitude" which like the rest of space is therefore never "vacuous," he remains "uncircumscribed" in his retirement from *any* space or time (VII, 168–70), including that of his purely metaphoric heavenly throne, dark with the "excessive bright" of his inscrutability (III, 380).

By returning to this older and apparently more "original" mystical/atomistic tradition, the Protestant poet could thus ingeniously *and* progressively turn a neutral if necessarily dark Chaos into the subatomic counterpart of the empty galactic expanses Galileo's telescope had newly charted *ad majorem Dei gloriam.* As in all syncretic literary systems, the precise materials woven into Milton's reformed Chaos must remain somewhat conjectural, not least of all because no single classical source contains a parallel revision of the atomist tradition, which more typically converts Hesiod's primitive association of "dark" matter with evil into a neutral state where it is *neither* good nor evil. Milton creatively adapts this Epicurean model by making it *either* or *both,* which makes the exact nature of his debt to his sources still more speculative. Nevertheless, the textual evidence strongly suggests that he used his classical learning in much the same way that modern scholars use the Bible: by separating it into distinct stylistic strands or additions, early and late. For if Milton had no access to modern methods of source criticism, his own examination of the conflicting biblical precedents for divorce clearly anticipates these methods. In any case, his adaptation of Hesiod's Chaos more or less exactly isolates the same three separate strands or phases that modern scholars detect in the *Theogony*'s successive depictions of this state, which in common with the Orphic poets he slightly reorders by making Night rather than Chaos the "original, inchoate state of things."[42]

While this resequencing of Hesiod provides the most likely understanding of Night (who is *so* inchoate that she never speaks), its real importance lies in showing how Milton methodically constructs an external historicization of these creation myths upon their intratextual evolution. In Hesiod's first reference to Chaos as the foundation of the universe, the void appears as the ancestral "mother" of order, grandmother of "broad-bosomed Gaia [earth], a firm seat of all things for ever, and misty Tartaros in a recess of broad-wayed earth" (*Theogony,* 116–19). If initially only the predestined underside of earth, Chaos next appears as a *gap* between Tartaros, earth, and sky, where it becomes a mutable *state* capable of participating in the general upheaval caused by the war of the Titans, when "A marvellous burning took hold of Chaos; and it was . . . as if earth and broad heaven above drew together; for just such a great din would have risen up" (*Theogony*, 700–03).[43] Yet once the Titans are defeated and the cosmos acquires its final shape, Tartaros is described as having been removed to the utmost limits of earth, where its

unharvested sea and starry sky, of all of them, are the springs in a row and the grievous, dank limits which even the gods detest; a great gulf, nor would one reach the floor for the whole length of a fulfilling year, if one were once within the gates. But hither and thither storm on grievous storm would carry one on; dreadful is this portent even for immortal gods; and the dreadful halls of gloomy Night stand covered with blue-black clouds.

There are gleaming gates, and brazen threshold unshaken, fixed with continuous roots, self-grown; and in front, far from all the gods, dwell the Titans, across murky Chaos. (*Theogony*, 736–39, 811)

In this final transformation, which bears an obvious and close resemblance to Milton's epic description, the fallen Titans "detest" Chaos's "unharvested" seas and skies mainly from their standpoint as losers in the cosmic confrontation.

Hence as in the much later epic, in the Hesiodic original Chaos takes on a different appearance after the entry of the fallen immortals, the Titans who have become "uncreated," dispossessed of what they mispossessed through their titanic tyranny and fraud. From this as from other perspectives Chaos is dreadful, though for the Christian poet its dread could be linked to the dispensation of divine justice, the law that in hurling Satan and the other fallen angels into hell also reechoes throughout the "roots" and "springs" of the rest of creation. This linkage to the deity allows a *transformative* Chaos to become the ancestor not only of the Greek Gaia, the "broad-breasted" nurturer revitalized in Book VII of *Paradise Lost* (276–82), but also to produce her apocalyptic antitype, the cleansed earth of Book X. This mythopoetic transformation becomes even more suggestive when the creation and recreation myths of the Bible are fused with atomist understandings of the void. As "fabling" yet also prophetic scientific speculation, the glosses of Heraclitus, Empedocles, and Democritus upon Hesiod could then be understood as prototypes of the far more sophisticated atomism that Lucretius bequeathed to the seventeenth century. Yet because in either ancient tradition nothing can come from nothing, this line of thought resurrects the logical paradox that had long beset the dominant Christian/Greek tradition: if non-being (which is evil) is incompatible with God, how can God build upon the void?[44]

Could not his priority to creation be understood as implying a previous absence or gap in the divine plan, and thus a preexisting condition of "evil"?

The canonical solution to this dilemma is Augustine's, who follows Plotinus in placing God in a static realm of eternal being wholly divorced both from the world of becoming and from the "nothing" in which it originates.[45] In rejecting this solution along with the inheritance of the Eliatic school generally, Milton embarks on the path leading not only to the "heresies" of the *Christian Doctrine* but also to the cosmic innovations of *Paradise Lost*. Characteristically suspicious of scholastic as well as of all other elenchic arguments (as he remarks in *Areopagitica*), he instead embraces the "sensuous" Lucretian logic of *ex nihilo nihil fut* and with it both the idea of *ex deo* creation and of flux as the logical corollary of creative growth, since time exists even *in* eternity: "For Time, though in Eternitie, appli'd / To motion, measures all things durable" (V, 580–81). Still, as a Christian poet Milton could scarcely follow Lucretius in endorsing *mere* flux, which for him implies a theistic origin. In general, because the Epicureans resolve the elenchus of the Eliatic school by positing the randomness *and* the eternity of matter, for them matter can come neither from nothing nor from God. Instead, the gods (characteristically Venus or Eros) impose order upon an eternally preexisting substance, thereby insuring that, as Lucretius says, within the generative void, "nature resolves everything into its component atoms and never reduces anything to nothing."[46]

Here the first law of thermodynamics applies: matter is neither created nor destroyed, but interchanged and renewed through the Democritan principles of collision and attraction. Yet this state prohibits further evolution and/or mediation; for Lucretius, there is no "third substance that can either affect our senses at any time or be grasped by the reasoning of our minds." Eliminating the mediation of Heraclitan fire (which seems originally to have been a rationalized version of Zeus's thunderbolt), Lucretius thus proposes a Miltonically untenable vision: that of a cosmos held together by an invisible but nondivine physical force, a "vortex" or "swerve" that may be far more easily linked to gravity or to Venutian attraction than to the Christian God.[47]

To accommodate the ongoing mediation of his creator God, Milton seems to have fused Lucretius with Heraclitus, in the process splitting his deity into two functions: the feminine or "passively" Venutian role at once associated with the Son or receptive "Word," with Chaos's "fluid Mass" (VII, 237), and with Night's womblike "vast vacuitie" (II, 932); and the masculine and Martial functions associated at once with the Son's infusions by "Paternal Deity" (VI, 703–05, 750) (swords, chariots, golden compasses) and with the warlike or regenerative aspect of Chaos as a mythic *"Bellona"* (II, 922). In this dual but not dualistic mode, the Almighty not only spans the gap between spirit (or Son) and matter (or Chaos), but in doing so becomes the fully active universal mediator which, like Heraclitan fire, provides "the common connecting element in all extremes" without which nothing would exist.[48] Yet in his *most* mysteriously passive aspect, the Almighty recedes not merely into light, but behind it, into that oxymoronic "dark . . . bright" (III, 380) quintessence suggesting the subatomic and invisible absence *behind* his emanations. Yet this quintessence represents only the standpoint of eternity; from the temporal standpoint of creation, his emanations descend from light's "Coeternal beam" (III, 2) not only to the Son and through the Spirit or "Urania" to her invisible sister Wisdom, but also *into* the curiously bright/dark, fe/male kingdom of Chaos, the dark root in which he is both implicitly present and absent, the place or fertile "nothing" where the circle at once begins and ends. Thus when the "wasteful" void of Genesis is "redeemed" through the *ex deo* generation of matter, Chaos can become the physical counterpart of God's largely inactive though not anticreative energies, those resources always immanent in a deity eternally "free to act or not" (VII, 171–72).[49]

More analogous to Heraclitan flux than fire, Chaos therefore functions as the passive residue and/or reservoir of the divinely androgynous mutability that governs "the total balance in the cosmos [that] can only be maintained if change in one direction eventually leads to change in the other, that is, if there is unending 'strife' between opposites." Here as in the Nietzschean strife between Apollo and Dionysus, or as in the recent scientific strife between macrocosmically steady-state and microcosmically evolutionary principles of order, these generative oppositions exist as dichotomies susceptible not to reduction but only to sublation, their poles at once both canceled and upheld. Or, as Ilya Prigogine and Isabelle Stengers alternately state the case, the most recent findings of chaos theory now suggest that the classic opposition between chance (randomness) and necessity (order) seems no longer tenable, since these "dissonantly" yet generatively work in tandem to create life.[50]

Finally, then, whether or not Milton can be securely or only tentatively tied to this particular version of a subdominant tradition once again in ascendance, in purely textual terms *Paradise Lost* clearly *does* develop all three functions of classic cosmic flux (balance, change, and reordering strife) as the trifold form of epic entropy embedded in Chaos. Hesiodically imagining its original balance in flux as benign, Milton reserves the state of "grievous" strife for the influx of his demonic Titans, the fallen angels who precipitate an alien and opposite but "equal" reaction. Yet as the cause of these defects, they also negentropically resolve the resulting imbalance once they are consumed by the negative inertia they initiate. Although his Nature is still "Not

Subject to Old Age," Milton now makes it renewable rather than "merely" immutable in order to accommodate the inevitable duality introduced by the fall of angels and men.

As suggested above, this continuity of order with disorder comes startling close to anticipating the three phases of modern thermodynamics. That is, both the threefold reversible processes at work in his Chaos *and* the irreversible time that they transact roughly conform to the current understanding of the three phases through which matter evolves: equilibrium (the condition implied by the first law); inertial or entropic decline (the "linear" condition implied by the second law); and reintegrative flux (the self-organizing principle postulated by modern molecular biology and chaos theory).[51] Transposed into metaphysical terms, these phases suggest that only when a determined alienation from God replaces an indeterminate one, that is, only when evil enters chaos, does the second physical sense of the word *entropy* replace the first: instead of existing simply as a "measure of the amount of energy unavailable for useful work in a system undergoing change," evil makes entropy "a measure of the degree of disorder in a substance or a system [where] entropy always increases and available energy diminishes" (*Webster's New World Dictionary*). Yet finally, if like energy itself Chaos is evolutionarily *available* to degeneration or evil, it also conserves an immanently benign order by remaining available to regeneration.

The profound subtlety of this fusion of metaphysics with physics may be briefly illustrated by an otherwise well-informed scientific commentator's quandary over how precisely to describe the place of Chaos in Milton's epic. Ignoring its ambiguous evolutionary potential, and like Rumrich considering it only in its precreation or "God-filled" state, Harinder Marjara unwittingly overemphasizes a positivity that is implicit in but not necessary to that state. Yet precisely this lack of necessity explains how it passively mirrors Milton's God, the deity who pronounces that "Necessitie and Chance / Approach not mee" (VII, 172–73). Although both are maximally free of necessity, the fact that God provides the positive ground of freedom rather than its negative or neutral counterpart makes their creative potential differently if distinctly divine. Divine liberty is infinitely integrative, while its chaotic counterpart is infinitely disintegrative except in the presence of a positive will to good *or* evil; a distinction that makes Chaos the ground of absolute or "negative" freedom, and God the ground of a positive freedom tempered by grace and mercy. Yet only *through* this antithesis can the immutable godhead be reconciled with the "chaos" of free will, whose indeterminacies are both physically and metaphysically (as an absence of external determination) essentially the same. Yet as *Sonnet XII* suggests, liberty is *only* supremely good *and* free insofar as it counters its own negative potential, the tendency of liberty to degenerate into license.[52]

Hence while Marjara is undoubtedly right in supposing that Milton's revision of the traditional Chaos is facilitated by the revalidation of vacuous space that "came into prominence with the revival of Platonism, Stoicism, and especially atomism" (nature no longer "abhors" a vacuum), he overlooks the extent to which this revision of the "abhorrent" void makes the divine immanence within Chaos no longer a contradiction.[53] *Because* it contains both vacua and unformed matter, Chaos can now represent the unimaginably pure potentiality of a God who is no longer a traditional *actus purus,* but the supreme metaphysical counterpart of a divine efflux which can be at once empty and full.[54] Applied to Chaos, the dictum suggests that its apparently paradoxical womb/tomb principles are no more logically contradictory than the laws concerning the conservation of matter/energy that underlie the laws of entropy. In terms more familiar both to seventeenth-century science and to Milton's imagination, these principles are described by Marjara as follows:

The process of change from one element to another and from one substance to another is not, in Milton, a mechanical process of rarefaction or condensation, though the images of "dense" and "rare" occur frequently in *Paradise Lost*. A qualitative change is taken for granted, but at the same time, Milton assumes that the essential matter which they are made of remains the same. There is no real duality between corporeal and incorporeal substances, and the vertical rise is merely a change from a lower to a higher degree, and not a transformation into a different kind.[55]

Hence matter is conserved, even as it becomes alternately more dense or more rare, more entropically stable and "heavy," or more negentropically active and "light."

4

There thus remains only the task of demonstrating how these physical processes can elucidate a number of the textual cruxes that have haunted the critical reception of Milton's Chaos. Mainly these revolve around its original confrontation with and supposed seduction by Satan, although, as we have seen, these passages are in part problematized by neoclassical standards of allegory which parallel those of classical physics in idealizing a static world of being as opposed to a dynamic realm of becoming. But additionally, the complexity inevitably introduced by this dynamic cosmic framework makes the initial task of distinguishing the perverse entropic energies of Satan, Sin, and Death from those of the "embryon Atoms" randomly clashing in the abyss (II, 900) particularly difficult, especially for the modern reader less attuned to the wealth of contextual detail embedded in Milton's epic similes. Here apparently small but actually substantial differences between the confusions of its "vast vacuitie" (932) and those that plan and propel Satan's fatal journey to earth gradually emerge as antithetical aspects of Milton's epic design. A case in point is the little-noted simile in which, as he slogs through a chaotic liminality which is "neither Sea, / Nor good dry Land" (939–40), Satan is described

> As when a Gryfon through the Wilderness
> With winged course ore Hill or moarie Dale,
> Pursues the *Arimaspian,* who by stelth
> Had from his wakeful custody purloind
> The guarded Gold: So eagerly the fiend
> Ore bog or steep, through strait, rough, dense, or rare,
> With head, hands, wings or feet pursues his way,
> And swims or sinks, or wades, or creeps, or flyes.   (II, 943–50)

At one level, this description foreshadows Satan's degenerative descent into the "creeping" and "flying" animals that the spread of Sin and Death will turn into beasts of prey (the half-lion, half-eagle griffin shape here being surrounded with amphibious or serpentine verbs and adjectives). Also implicated is the griffin's traditional moral alienation from the "warmth of the Holy Spirit," though not without a characteristically monistic emphasis. The material continuum of this evolution is underscored by the trifold energy or light symbol associated with epic gold, which may either be hoarded (as by both the griffinlike Satan and his colleague, Mammon) or benignly dispersed, as it is both on the floor of heaven and in Eden's "vegetable gold" (IV, 220). The latter image, like the heavenly one, suggests that gold excels chiefly in being variable, transformative, and free; so that unlike heavenly gold, which is at once the common ground and gleaming foil for the living roses and amaranth which "crown" both angelic and human immortality, its true "fruit" (III, 350–54, 362–65; IV, 218–19), hellish gold is hardened by Satan's crew into the deadly temple and capstone of Pandaemonium, the native seat of the griffin.[56]

Thus when evil enters Chaos, its originally mobile matter is entropically enclosed, limited, and objectified—that is, "purloined" from both the native indeterminacy whose heavenly flux "Rowls o're *Elisian* Flowers her Amber stream" (III, 358–59), and from the "pregnant" tumult of "hot, cold, moist, and dry" (898) in Chaos. As a result, Satan does not actually seduce but "tartareously" *reduces* its potent mixture by subduing volatile elements which in a "pure" state of entropy would remain "in thir pregnant causes mixt / Confusedly" (913–14)—but fertilely. In accordance with another characteristic epic pattern, this simile recontextualizes and illuminates an earlier image of contracting entropy. When challenged by a son whose kingdom serves only "to enrage thee more" (II, 698), Satan confronts his own diminished alter ego, a shape "tenfold / More dreadful and deform,"

> Unterrifi'd, and like a Comet burn'd,
> That fires the length of *Ophiucus* huge
> In th' Artick Sky, and from his horrid hair
> Shakes Pestilence and Warr. (II, 705–06, 708–11)

Structurally, this confrontation with Death confirms Satan's status as a "combiner of fire and ice" which, like his astronomical counterpart, the "serpent-bearer" comet, favors the "'cold' instruments of death, pestilence, and war."[57] In the lower realms, the result of this collision of satanic or diminishing entropy with the utter negation of Death thus appears as

> when two black Clouds
> With Heav'ns Artillery fraught, come rattling on
> Over the *Caspian,* then stand front to front
> Hovr'ing a space, till Winds the signal blow
> To joyn thir dark Encounter in mid air:
> So frownd the mighty Combatants, that Hell
> Grew darker at thir frown, so matcht they stood;
> For never but once more was either like
> To meet so great a foe. (II, 714–22)

As the passage suggests, the logical opponent and final fate of the father is found in his still "icier" son, whose midair encounter threatens Satan with a premature head wound (compare *Paradise Regained* IV, 568).

The grim appropriateness of Death's misappropriation of the Son's role here is signaled not only by the substitution of the latter's righteous sword for the former's mortal dart, but also by the halting or "freezing" effect that this encounter has upon hell, whose fires thereupon grow darker, not brighter, as they might in a more naive epic cosmos. Allegory thus receives a further ironic twist, since Sin's "merciful" preservation of Satan from Death's "mortal dint" (813) or thunderclap (*OED* 1b) at once dialectically delays and permits an even deadlier collusion of cold energies diverted from their proper source, the divine balance of benign warmth and energy. Dramatically enacting this irony, Satan initially tries to distance himself from these children, to whom he declares that "I know thee not, nor ever saw till now / Sight more detestable then him or thee" (II, 744–45). Yet this perverse echo of the final judgment upon those who fail either to give or receive God's mercy—"depart from me, I never knew ye"—only increases his alienation both from his own creation and from God's. Precisely because he has carnally known Sin he now knows her not (this incestuous experience and its fruits having deformed her beyond recognition); so like a gothic self-portrait his "perfect image" more closely resembles him the more he attempts to disown her, who is indeed the "perfect image" of his internal freezing and hardening. Through the same "attractive graces" that produced her self-consuming conceptions—Death and his pack of "yelling Monsters" (II, 762–66, 795)—Sin thus reflects the deadly kind of "love" her father and son have for her, which is a narcissistic reduction of the divine, life-giving love which all three inversely mirror in each other.

Nevertheless, once he has sufficiently recovered from his initial shock to learn "his lore" (815) from his daughter, Satan gladly "claims" this dreadful duo—for a price. Bartering his recognition of them for their own acceptance of the wages of sin (their further brutalization in exchange for the spurious liberation that any acceptance of their "double" betrayer and begetter must reap), he only further increases their mutual hardening and psychic decay.[58] These effects are already implicit in Satan's answer "smooth":

> Dear Daughter, since thou claim'st me for thy Sire,
> And my fair Son here showst me, the dear pledge
> Of dalliance had with thee in Heav'n, and joys
> Then sweet, now sad to mention, through dire change
> Befall'n us unforeseen, unthought of, know
> I come no enemie, but to set free
> From out this dark and dismal house of pain,
> Both him and thee, and all the heav'nly Host
> . . . .
> And bring ye to the place where Thou and Death
> Shall dwell at ease, . . .
> . . . there ye shall be fed and fill'd
> Immeasurably, all things shall be your prey.
>   (II, 817–24, 840–41, 843–44)

Trusting in these false promises to free them from a perpetual state of famine that can be filled neither in hell nor on earth, Sin and Death thus await a new world of light and bliss even as their father effectively consigns them to forces far beneath those of "original darkness" (984). Yet if for all three the prospect of an ascent to light is clearly a hallucinatory reversal of their entropic decline, the material effects of this delusion are not in themselves unreal.

In another sense, however, their "ascent" is far less real than the mixture of "pregnant causes" forever "imbroiled" by Chaos and Night. Unlike the elements contained in a realm bordered by light (1035–39), satanic darkness contains a positive form of negation whose degrees of fire and ice increase in geometrical proportions inconceivable in a "nethermost Abyss" (956) capable of neither geometry nor proportion. Its real yet also mixed darkness thus presides over a quite different state of entropy, an "Eternal *Anarchie*" where dimension, time, and place are lost, but where its negentropic "confusion stand[s]" (II, 896–97) so as *not* to fall. In this sense Sin and Night represent the consorts of two utterly different kings. While the darkness of Sin constructs a progressively deepening abyss where, as her sire later discovers, "in the lowest deep a lower deep / Still threatning . . . opens wide" (IV, 76–77), the darkness of Night is visited by ceaselessly alternating forces, "Light-arm'd or heavy, sharp, smooth, swift or slow" (II, 902)—alternations again not unlike the "grateful vicissitude" (VI, 8) of heaven itself. Here, however, the rapid reversions of matter are more violent, alternately sinking Satan into their depths, then blasting him back "as many miles aloft" (938). Nevertheless, since none of Night's "four Champions" ever achieves "Maistrie" (898–907), momentary combinations of "Fire and Nitre" can by "ill chance" (935–37) advance Satan's progress, but can permanently sustain it no more than they can sediment into his fire and ice.

In fact, from a scientific viewpoint, the very presence of fire and nitre in Chaos associates it with the natural, nondestructive, and random entropy of primal matter, and not with the negations of hell. Because of the privilege that contemporary science granted to analogy, "'exhalations'" common to "the evaporation of water and other materials" were thought to govern both "the report of the explosion of gunpowder and the peal of thunder," leading to the conclusion that thunder and lightning were similarly produced by "particles of sulphur and niter in the air."[59] The universal distribution of these chemical reactions then allows their random "reports" to be contrasted with their purely inimical uses, perverse distillations of unformed substance such as those Satan and his demons use to convert heavenly rays to cannon fire. In contrast with Moloch's hellish oath that God shall yet "hear / Infernal Thunder, and for Lightning see / Black fire and horror shot with equal rage" (II, 65–67), Chaos and Night's state of "ruinous" noise (921) merely *resembles* a war they can never wage. Threatening no throne but their own, without external interference theirs are empty "horrors" incapable of lasting creation *or* destruction—all sound and no fury, much thunder and no lightning.

Only with richly appropriate irony, then, does Chaos sympathize with Satan, confusing his own *un*arrayed confusion with the determined disarray of the forces he sees falling "With ruin upon ruin, rout on rout, / Confusion worse confounded" (995–96). Whatever his "natural" sympathies with this melee, no concerted effort on his part can actually affiliate him with Satan, since his entropic drives are limited by the very "illimitability" (892) of the contrary material energies (both positive and negative) that define his state.

Consequently, he can neither accurately recognize *nor* aid a fiend whose banishment from light consists in the pseudoliberation that is limitation itself: fire, ice, and destructive entropy. Rather than real assistance, his pathetic offer of "all I can . . . [to] serve, / That little which is left so to defend" (999–1000) merely marks Chaos's inevitable confusion in the face of a ruin whose direction and "speed" (1008) are far better organized than he can possibly imagine. His utter ineffectuality in the face of evil (or good) is further underscored by the earlier allegory of the faithful angel Uriel, the angel of the sun/Son who, because hypocrisy is an "invisible" evil, unwittingly renders far more aid and comfort to the enemy than Chaos can provide his mistaken "friends" (III, 682–84, 722–35).

Thus, if like Satan he thinks himself "impaird" (V, 665) by the recent encroachments on his realm, *un*like him Chaos actually opposes more, not less, order. While Satan champions the static "Orders and Degrees" (V, 792) that the new heavenly order has leveled, Chaos prefers the "hubbub wild" (II, 951) of the endless dissonance which he correctly associates with demonic ruin, but which he incorrectly assumes is identical to his own. Again, his very "illimitability" makes it impossible for him to conceptualize the process whereby satanic misrecognition inevitably decays into psychic dissonance, a regular and predictable process, the metaphysical consequences of which are intimately and nonrandomly bound to their physical causes. This difference is further compounded by the fact that these discordant effects are the dialectical by-products of a form of decay inherently alien to Chaos: a degeneration wherein the extremes of objectification and projection—diseases of too much consonance—precipitate their own inversion—diseases of too much dissonance.[60] As a result, Chaos is ultimately as inept as he is confused: a true "anarch" and no monarch, he completely miscalculates the fact that the Infernal Triad will encroach upon his territory far more than the heavenly forces now at rest. As parts of a mimetically extended personification allegory, the contrasting "dissonances" of Chaos and Satan, his guest, have of course been signaled by their initial appearances—the Anarch's "faultring speech and visage incompos'd" (989) sharply distinguished from the tyrant's darkly "obscur'd" but still fiery brightness and glory (I, 591–94).

Finally, then, although Chaos's erratic entropy does and must contrast with heavenly irregularity (V, 622–24) and its counterpart, an earthly fertility "wild above Rule or Art" (V, 297), its differences from the hyperorganized depredations of satanic fire and ice go far deeper. As appropriate to an unformed, neutral state of matter, some residual parallels with negative entropy remain in Chaos's "dreadful halls of gloomy night" (*Theogony*, 744)— for even if the noisy combustions of Chaos are less pernicious than those of hell, neither can induce the peaceful generation that results from an *ordered* alternation of dark with light. Yet despite its lack of the benign dichotomies and potential syntheses that organize heaven and earth, Chaos's greater distance from hell is imaged in the stark contrast between its comical vehemence and hell's harshly repetitive reverberations. When Sin gives birth to her "inbred enemie" (II, 785), her outcry "Death" echoes throughout her dungeon's caves, finally rebounding upon herself (787–89) with deadly effect. First taking the hollow no-shape of a form possessed only of a "lust and rage" (791) to repeat himself—and consequently his father—by raping his mother, Death's repetition of Sin punishes her repetition of Satan's image through the "ceaseless cry" (795) of their devouring sons, the hounds of hell. This dissonance, one that at once reflects and repeats their "hollow" affections, contrasts with Chaos's "hollow dark assaults [upon the] . . . ear" (953) in its complete lack of any potential for the *kindly* rupture (VII, 419) inherent in its "pregnant causes." The cruel ruptures of a Sin-ful body can give birth only to sterile Death, the scourge but not the source of cosmic life which Chaos so eminently provides (VII, 90–93, 220–21).

While these ruptures increasingly alienate their victims from light, chaotic entropy remains fertilely receptive to reorganization in the presence of *either* light or darkness, as it does when the Son's golden compasses prepare the way for earth's dark warmth (VII, 225–36), and later when Death's "Mace petrific, cold and dry" (X, 294) paves a passageway to hell. Yet, unlike the rival who comes to pacify but not to tame the "Deep" (VII, 216) but like his own son, Satan perverts chaotic fluidity by colonizing the winds of fire and nitre that had once played havoc with him, in turn only intensifying the destructive fire and ice of the internal hell they inhabit regardless of where they crawl, creep, or fly (IV, 75). By placing the nutritive properties of hot, cold, moist, and dry in the crucible of his lust and rage, Satan can create no indeterminate or mutable domain, but only the truly hostile chaos of the northerly comet that presides over pestilence and war. Extracted from but essentially unlike the merely uncreative entropy of Chaos and Night, his anticreative entropy can produce *only* icy thunders and burning wastes, not the generative storms whose lightning brings the rain.[61]

Thus if satanic entropy or downward flux has a temporal materiality as real as that of Chaos and, like it, operates through attractions of like kind, "Faction," or "Clann" (II, 901), it also differs in that its attractions are regularly and irreversibly degenerative. Lacking the benign capacity of the chaotic matter that responds to the Son's voice as he comes to create the earth (VII, 221), this negative form of entropy thrives only upon those elements "purg'd" from it: "the black tartareous cold infernal dregs / Adverse to life" (VII, 238–39). If originally part of nature's balance, these dregs are further congealed and "reduced" by their satanic "reducers," while its true begetters (like the Son) merely return them to Chaos, the state prior to the "fluid Mass" (237) of the womblike earth, its own prematerial womb and chemical source.[62] Ancient but not subject to old age, chaotic entropy declines from its benignly random condition and becomes destructive only in the presence of evil. No more intrinsically inimical to God than the heavenly subsoil diverted into satanic implements of war, Chaos's entropic state is then fully consistent with the *Christian Doctrine*'s position that "original matter was not an evil thing, nor . . . worthless: it was good, and it contained the seeds of all subsequent good[:] . . . a confused and disordered state at first . . . [that] afterwards God made . . . ordered and beautiful" (YP VI, p. 308). More than that, it is also logically opposed to the "hot" of Sin and the "cold" of Death, that is, the negation of random entropy inherent in satanic fire and ice.

Hence the relevance of Frost's "Fire and Ice" as an alternate thermodynamic version of the same recreation myth to which Milton's Chaos adds both scientific substance and prophetic reaffirmation. Yet unlike Frost's, Milton's evolving universe accords even negative entropy a positive potential in maintaining the wisest of Providence's provisions: the primeval *im*balance of uncreated matter, the reactive check on the balances of the rest of God's creation. Because even the most "eccentric" of angelic dances (V, 623) cannot in themselves nullify the overorganization of satanic energies, only through Chaos's ability to further decompose and "digest" the self-consuming fires of these "Hell-hounds" (X, 616, 636) can primal entropy be restored. In this most voluntaristic of all theodicies, higher spiritual agencies cannot destroy lower and more degenerate ones, but the latter's "heavier" and "colder" energies must be allowed to succumb to the "grave" inherent in the downward drift of their own momentum. Then, freed at last from Satan's "Universe of death . . . / Where all life dies, death lives, and nature breeds / Perverse" (II, 622, 624–25), the fundamental alterability of primal entropy provides the cosmic agency whereby "Heav'n and Earth renewd shall be made pure" (X, 638) from its source—in Chaos's womb.

In current physics we are told that within the attenuations of difference Chaos expands into the vast samenesses of interstellar and even interior spaces. Ultimately, then, Chaos is like hell, an everywhere. However, unlike hell, *in potentia* its universal physical properties remain essentially on the side of the life rather than the death principle, as Adam and Eve later discover. By affiliating its vacuities with those of divine freedom, Milton makes his reformed Chaos far more positive than negative, a medium of ambivalence and negation, but also of creative regeneration, in that very equivocation becoming productive. These and related equivocities indicate that while spatial directions like "up" and "down" preserve some of their old allegorical force, his poem's multiple ontological schemes mandate that both space and time now

have merely local and relative meanings: Satan falls by "rising" to the challenge of conquering earth by invading Chaos, the Son rises by "falling" to
serve a sinful race *after* he has descended into its deep, while Raphael both
falls and rises in the process of faithfully informing mankind of the chaos of
physical and moral "space" evolving out of and into "one first matter." Even as
in myth this movement remains ethical, though here the normative processes
of myth have been reversed: moral meaning is not projected onto the symbolic
screen of the physical universe, but the laws of natural action and reaction
have become the paradigm for the "physics" of moral law. For matter now
presupposes two contrary but not antithetical vectors: its originally "steady-
state" in the subatomic forces of chaos (or dark matter) has the potential either
to explode in the superatomic evolution of the galaxies (or of angels), or to
implode under the downward gravitational pull of entropy (or of demons). Yet
since in principle matter is always conserved, it is also subject to reconfigura-
tion after the death of stars like Lucifer/Satan. But like this very name the
negentropic principle only equivocally presupposes a closed system—by no
means a stable "being" much less a stable model of the universe. From this
final perspective, then, Milton's poetic version of protochaos theory suggests
that the canonical is always in some sense contemporary. The ordered integration of the angels' celebratory dance with the irregular/regular dancing stars
of the heavens, open-ended as it may be in its freedom and irregularity, also
elliptically reconciles the poem's oppositions and antitheses—but only in the
decentered "loopiness" of perpetually evolving "vagancies" outside of which
Milton's androgynous angels can scarcely be imagined at all.

The University of Memphis

NOTES

1. All quotations from *Paradise Lost* are from *The Complete Poetry of John Milton*, ed.
John T. Shawcross (New York, 1971) and will be cited in the text by book and line number, or
page number where applicable.

2. Almost certainly Frost's poem reflects the speculative turn to physical cosmology inspired
by that heightened awareness of an ultimate entropic doom, a turn found, for example, in works
ranging from the concluding sections of Nietzsche's *Will to Power*, the final chapters of *The
Education of Henry Adams*, to T. S. Eliot's "Rhapsody on a Windy Night," and, to take an
example of an even more pessimistic twist, the entropic overdeterminations of Thomas Pyn-
chon's novels.

3. The word *negentropy* was suggested by Léon Brillouin to avoid some of the confusion
caused by the apparently equivocal implication of an entropic process that may simultaneously
be destructive and constructive. See his discussions in "Information and Entropy," *Journal of
Applied Physics* 22, no. 3 (1951): 334, 338, followed by "Life, Thermodynamics and Cybernet-

ics," *American Scientist* 37 (1949): 554, and "Thermodynamics and Information Theory," *American Scientist* 38 (1950): 549. But Claude Shannon, *Mathematical Theory of Communication* (Urbana, 1959), defines anything that interferes with univocal meaning as entropic "noise," preferring to avoid using two words for the one force, since what breaks things down also builds them up within the selfsame. Both aspects of entropy are currently registered in cultural and literary studies, though most often with an emphasis not on the positive aspects of negentropy but rather its deconstructive potential, as, for instance, in N. Katherine Hayles, *Chaos Bound: Orderly Disorder in Contemporary Literature and Science* (Ithaca, N.Y., 1990).

4. For a useful statement of the same point in metaphysical terms (that this quasi-"alchemical" process is "not mere metaphor"), see D. Bentley Hart, "Matter, Monism, and Narrative: An Essay on the Metaphysics of *Paradise Lost*," *MQ* 30 (1996): 16–27 (quote p. 22).

5. The details of this "chaotic" self-construction are recorded in Milton's sonnets (particularly *How Soon Hath Time* and *When I Consider*) as well as in prose "digressions" in such works as *The Reason of Church-Government.* Alternatively, Mindele Treip, *Allegorical Poetics and the Epic: The Renaissance Tradition to "Paradise Lost"* (Lexington, 1994), has outlined the complex coordinates of what reception aesthetics would call his "horizon of response." For a theoretical formulation of reception aesthetics, see, for instance, Hans Robert Jauss, "Literary History as a Challenge to Literary Theory," in *The Critical Tradition: Classical Texts and Contemporary Trends,* ed. David H. Richter (New York, 1989).

6. The intellectual background of this theology is discussed in far more detail in my " 'Boundless the Deep': Milton, Pascal, and the Theology of Relative Space," *ELH* 63 (1996): 45–78.

7. Ilya Prigogine and Isabelle Stengers, *Order Out of Chaos: Man's New Dialogue with Nature* (Toronto, 1984). On the commonplace awareness that one should supplement Genesis with Lucretius in reading Milton's cosmogony, see Stephen Fallon, *Milton Among the Philosophers: Poetry and Materialism in Seventeenth-Century England* (Ithaca, N.Y., 1991), p. 247.

8. Most historians of science now find seventeenth-century *and* modern science demonstrating the discontinuous progress originally posited by Thomas Kuhn, *The Structure of Scientific Revolutions* (Chicago, 1962). For Milton's place in this ambiguous progress and the unreliability of older, more linear models of scientific evolution, see Harinder Singh Marjara, *Contemplation of Created Things: Science in "Paradise Lost"* (Toronto, 1992), esp. pp. 7–8, 14. According to Jacob Bronowski, both scientific and literary discoveries—which as most contemporary historians of science now agree include rediscoveries—obey essentially the same principles: in either case, "the mind decides to enrich the system as it stands by an addition which is made by an unmechanical act of free choice." See *The Identity of Man* (New York, 1971), p. 136, which, in proposing the way that great science and literary minds work, was itself far ahead of the positivist models of scientific progress dominant when Bronowski wrote. For a book-length study of Milton's monistic "free-will" defense, see Dennis Danielson, *Milton's Good God: A Study in Literary Theodicy* (Cambridge, 1982).

9. These self-referential consequences here properly belong both to the future work of the author and to a projected collaboration. An extended correspondence with Michael Fixler on an earlier draft of this essay regarding lacunae in its "chaos theory" turned out to be so dense with convergent possibilities that in time it became clear that neither of us could retreat into any kind of exclusivity or conventional proprietary rights regarding our pooled insights and arguments. This article then is in some sense the first installment of a more official collaboration on a larger and more theoretical project. Consequently, in some passages there can be no excessive differentiation of what is properly mine or Fixler's, although anyone who wishes may compare my earlier work, " 'Pregnant Causes Mixt': The Wages of Sin and the Laws of Entropy in Milton's Chaos," in *Arenas of Conflict: Milton and the Unfettered Mind,* ed. Kristin McColgan and Charles Durham (London, 1995), parts of which are reprinted in the present essay by permis-

sion of Susquehanna University Press. On autopoesis, see Humberto Maturana and Francisco Varela, *Autopoesis and Cognition* (Dordrecht, 1980).

10. The theoretical project mentioned in the note above examines how the metaphors of interpretive reading themselves use the bipolar play of entropy and negentropy in self-organizing order out of incoherence. We are part of the canonical process into which the chaotic literary process and all its artifacts "naturally" fall as aspects of larger self-organizing cultural systems. This paradigm is based upon the so-called Gödelian problematic, the best nonspecialist account of which is in Douglas Hofstadter, *Gödel, Escher, Bach, the Eternal Golden Braid* (New York, 1976). More specifically, however, it draws upon Wittgenstein's reduction of the complexity of the Gödelian matter into the incommensurable modes of saying and showing. See the texts cited in "Wittgenstein's Remarks on the Significance of Gödel's Theorem," in *Gödel's Theorem in Focus*, ed. S. G. Shanker (London, 1988), p. 181. That we have hardly yet begun to assess the profound implications for literary theory and all literary interpretation of this development is ably suggested in a preliminary way by David Wayne Thomas, "Gödel's Theorem and Postmodern Theory," *PMLA* 110 (1995): 248–61. For a historical perspective upon the revolution in the philosophy of language, see also Robert Markley, "Representing Order: Natural Philosophy, Mathematics, and Theology in the Newtonian Revolution," in *Chaos and Order: Complex Dynamics in Literature and Science*, ed. N. Katherine Hayles (Chicago, 1991), pp. 125–48, esp. pp. 134–37.

11. As shall appear below, I do not mean to dispute that Milton's universe is monistic, merely that it retains far more equivocity than would appear from unproblematically positive recuperations of Chaos. On Milton's Chaos as "more real than Sin," though not evil, see Fallon, *Milton Among the Philosophers*, pp. 190–91. Other "material" defenses of Chaos include Michael Lieb, *The Dialectics of Creation: Patterns of Birth and Regeneration in "Paradise Lost"* (Amherst, 1970), and John Peter Rumrich, *Matter of Glory: A New Preface to "Paradise Lost"* (Pittsburgh, 1987), pp. 14–25, who generally defends Milton's matter as an aspect of divine glory, or *kabod*. More problematic is Rumrich's "Milton's God and the Matter of Chaos," *PMLA* 110 (1995): 1035–46, which is at once exemplary and potentially misleading. Certainly, as Rumrich suggests, "For Milton nothing can exist without indeterminacy" (1044); but for Milton not all indeterminacies are equal. Chaos's passive and randomly mutable entropy is thus fundamentally distinct from the hermaphroditic deity which Rumrich regards as "espousing" it; for *even more* than his "one first matter" (itself more formally stable than Chaos), God remains *potentially* active even in his absence or "retirement" from putting forth his goodness. While God proclaims that "Necessitie and Chance / Approach not mee, and what I will is Fate" (VII, 172–73), Chaos is distinguished by its *conjunction* of necessity and chance, so that what it "wills" is *not* fate. These remarks are extended in my response to his essay in the Forum, *PMLA* 111 (1996): 468–69, to which, in the same issue, Rumrich responds.

His attempt, however, is admirable in that views of Chaos as "hostile" predominate in a critical tradition that unself-reflexively associates disorder with evil; A. B. Chambers, "Chaos in *Paradise Lost*," *JHI* 24 (1963): 82, assumes that Chaos is therefore sinfully "at war . . . with heaven and with the world," and A. S. P. Woodhouse, "Notes on Milton's Views on the Creation: The Initial Phase," *PQ* 28 (1949): 229n30, suggests that it at least has "some affinity with, evil." Similar theses are presented by Walter Clyde Curry, *Milton's Ontology, Cosmogony, and Physics* (Lexington, Ky., 1957); and Regina Schwartz, *Remembering and Repeating: Biblical Creation in "Paradise Lost"* (Cambridge, 1988), pp. 8–24.

12. *The Reason of Church-Government*, in *Complete Prose Works of John Milton*, 8 vols., ed. Don M. Wolfe et al. (New Haven, 1953–82), vol. I, pp. 751–52; hereafter cited in the text as YP followed by volume and page numbers.

13. In general, as allegorical "capital *C*" personas, Chaos and Night will be referred to as "he" or "she," but as principles as lowercase "its." Although there has been less speculation about

Night than Chaos, it seems fairly safe to assume that she is allied with the Anarch as an even darker and more vacuous phase of prematter, the first stage of an *ex deo* process whereby the Almighty (like Plato's demiurge) fills Night with matter *in potentia*, as Chambers, "Chaos in *Paradise Lost*," pp. 55–84, believes. Afterwards, as Fallon, *Milton Among the Philosophers*, p. 191, explains, creation proper occurs when "God adds to prime matter forms, 'which . . . are themselves material' (*CP*:308)."

14. For Torquato Tasso, see *Discorsi del poema eroico*, Book II, p. 78; here translated and quoted from Treip, *Allegorical Poetics and the Epic*, p. 147, where she persuasively argues for Tasso's influence upon the implicit theory of Milton's subsequent epic.

15. As Keith F. W. Stavely, "Satan and Arminianism in *Paradise Lost*," in *Milton Studies* XXV, ed. James D. Simmonds (Pittsburgh, 1989), notes, Satan's ability to continue to desire evil over good, to choose "freely what it now so justly rues" (IV, 72) even after escaping hell-bent to subdue earth is also one of the most remarkably Arminian and antideterministic aspects of the poem (pp. 125–39).

16. In this, Milton's divergence from Spenser, who in the *Mutabilitie Cantos* condemns flux as nature's bane, is most pronounced, as it may be from Shakespeare as well—if we are to believe William Carroll, *The Metamorphoses of Shakespearean Comedy* (Princeton, 1985), that the latter suspected although did not outright condemn metamorphosis and especially chaos.

17. For a contemporary appropriation of a Lucretian Venus/Mars diad, see Michel Serres, "Lucretius: Science and Religion," in *Hermes: Literature, Science, Philosophy*, ed. and trans. Josué Harrari and David F. Bell (Baltimore, 1982), pp. 98–124.

18. In my forthcoming book, *The Ruins of Allegory* (Durham, N.C., 1998), I discuss the extent to which the kind of reading Samuel Johnson imposed upon the allegory of Milton's poem had the effect of muting the specifically equivocal resonances in the role of such figures as Chaos and Night, Sin and Death, as agents of choice in the cosmogonic process. Yet Milton's "scientific" reading program in *Of Education* would have suggested to his students, allegorical forces like Empedocles' Love and Strife not only precede but in many ways transcend Aristotelian ortho-doxy by providing more flexible conceptions of natural process and flux, all of which stem ultimately from Hesiod's loose but suggestive association of Eros with Hades. In fact, Hesiod, according to Charles Osgood in *The Classical Mythology of Milton's English Poems* (New York, 1900), furnished Milton with more material than any other classical author, and (as I argue below) supplied some central elements of Milton's Chaos. On this point, see Mark D. Northrup, "Milton's Hesiodic Cosmology," *CL* 33 (1981): 305–20, though like so many commentators he oversimplifies both Hesiod and Milton's poem by straightforwardly identifying Chaos with evil. *The Presocratic Philosophers: A Critical History with a Selection of Texts*, ed. G. S. Kirk, J. E. Raven, and M. Schofield (Cambridge, 1983), pp. 17–20, cites not only a late addition to Hesiod (*Theogony* 734–819) in which Night seems to be prior to Chaos, but also some related Orphic and other early speculations in a similar vein.

19. Thus while ardent neoclassicists like Maureen Quilligan, *The Language of Allegory: Defining the Genre* (Ithaca, 1979), insist these figures have no real existence or agency, this is clearly not the case. Not only does Milton's "nethermost Abyss" (II, 956) ponder its alternating allegiance to God and Satan, but Satan's own progeny do the same. Sin "convinces" Death not to attack his father, and Satan "persuades" her to hand over her "fatal Key" to hell (II, 725).

20. From this perspective, the Son's punitive expulsion of the demons from heaven can also be regarded as a naturalistic reaction, a natural "revulsion" of creative energies from their anticreative counterparts comparable to what happens when creation repels the "black tar-tareous cold infernal dregs / Adverse to life" (VII, 238–39). A strikingly similar process occurs when Adam's banishment is explained as the "ejection" of his corrupt elements by "those pure immortal Elements that know / No gross" in Eden (XI, 50–51).

21. Thomas McAlindon, *Shakespeare's Tragic Cosmos* (Cambridge, 1991), pp. 16, 23, 263.

22. On its "transcendent" qualities, see Angus Fletcher, *The Transcendental Masque: An Essay on Milton's "Comus"* (Ithaca, 1971).

23. For similar readings of this simile and its surrounding passages, see John Carey and Alastair Fowler, *The Poems of John Milton* (London, 1968) p. 940, X, 289–93, X, 293–96.

24. The speciousness of this liberation becomes especially apparent later, when Sin looks forward eagerly to the "Monarchie" in which she shall "divide / Of all things" (X, 379–80) with Death and Satan, when in fact their bridge (or *pontifex*) to earth will allow them to "share" their new world only in the most negative sense of division: segregating, despoiling, exploiting, and reducing the richness of its potential. Compare also the Shawcross edition, which comments that Sin has here "fallaciously contrasted" (or reduced) concepts of "squareness and circularity . . . male, female; imperfect, perfect; justice, mercy" (p. 460n38).

25. See Anna K. Nardo, *Milton's Sonnets and the Ideal Community* (Lincoln, 1979), pp. 4–26 (quote p. 13), whose convenient summary of the Weber-Tawney-Hill account of this paradigm shift is generally accurate. For a critique of this paradigm's political tenets, see Sharon Achinstein, *Milton and the Revolutionary Reader* (Princeton, 1994).

26. A similar process seems to take place when Satan diverts heaven's "spiritous and fierie spume" (VI.479) into the cannon fire that "releases" the reciprocal reaction of the divine thunderbolt, which poetically "creates" the hell fires that await him.

27. Here I would agree with Fallon, *Milton Among the Philosophers*, pp. 12–13 (as I have in the companion essay to this article; see note 5 above), that the disparagement of Milton's natural philosophy by Arthur O. Lovejoy, *The Great Chain of Being: The Study in the History of an Idea* (Cambridge, Mass., 1936), p. 164, can be traced directly to the latter's antipathy "to the principle of plenitude [and] to that of sufficient reason, the two principles anchoring the great chain" of the mainline Christian Greek tradition—but by no means the exclusive one, as Lovejoy assumes.

28. A primary example is Regina Schwartz's misconception in *Remembering and Repeating*, pp. 24–26 which, while acknowledging the importance of entropy, argues that the atomist legacy in which it originates is necessarily infernal because it "substitutes chance for providence" while "sacred history speaks, not of entropy, but of disobedience; not of the random collision of particles, but of redemption" (p. 26). Yet since there *is* in fact no uniform voice of sacred history, there can hardly be any "inevitable" association of atomism or entropy with evil. As Rumrich, "Milton's God and the Matter of Chaos," similarly observes, critics steeped in this legacy too often "unjustifiably assume Milton's endorsement of traditional Western and philosophical attitudes toward matter" and "alterity" (p. 1036).

29. For a further exploration of these points, see Debora Shuger, *Habits of Thought in the English Renaissance* (Berkeley, 1990).

30. See Amy Mandelker, "Semiotizing the Sphere: Organicist Theory in Lotman, Bakhtin, and Vernadsky," *PMLA* 109 (1994): 385. Mandelker here notes Lotman's apparently inadvertent echo of *Areopagitica*, when he argues that "noise both within and outside the text can lead to the emergence of new levels of meaning neither predictable from linguistic and genre conventions nor subject to authorial mastery." Like Milton, he too ascribes a "sacral-sexual character" to semiosis, as a passionate rather than objective form of "intercourse . . . required for something new and meaningful to be created" (p. 391).

31. As Richard Jones demonstrates in *Ancients and Moderns: A Study of the Rise of the Scientific Movement in Seventeenth Century England* (Berkeley, 1965), though the Reformers generally supported an empiricist agenda, their thought remained very deeply informed by various strands of theology and/or mysticism. In *Contemplation of Created Things*, Marjara takes the argument still further, showing the impossibility of utterly distinguishing Aristotelians and "Scholastics" from anti-Aristotelians and empiricists, as Jones tended to do.

32. On the revolutionary novelty of the idea of emergent revelation, and by implication, of the idea of an emergently free creativity in events and in nature, see Michael Fixler's discussion of the position of the Dissenting Brethren (with whom Milton was aligned) in the Westminster Assembly in *Milton and the Kingdoms of God* (London, 1964), pp. 119–21.

33. Quilligan, *The Language of Allegory*, p. 179. For a similar if less extreme position, see Fallon, *Milton Among the Philosophers*, pp. 182–84, and Gordon Teskey, "From Allegory to Dialectic: Imagining Error in Spenser and Milton," *PMLA* 101 (1986): 9–23. For Milton's confrontation with Hobbes through Samson's "chaotic" inspiration, see my forthcoming essay, "The Phoenix and the Crocodile: The Dialectic of Miltonic Covenant and Hobbesian Social Contract in *Samson Agonistes*," in *The Literature of the English Civil Wars*, ed. Claude Summers and Ted-Larry Pebworth (Columbus, Mo., 1998).

34. Here Milton's vision reprises the formulation that occurred to him when he first proposed writing a poem "doctrinal to a nation" in *The Reason of Church-Government*, wherein he imagines that the glorified saints should not be "confin'd and cloy'd with repetition of that which is prescrib'd, but that our happiness may orbe it selfe into a thousand vagancies of glory and delight, and with a kinde of eccentricall equation be as it were an invariable Planet of joy and felicity" (YP I, p. 752). Here Milton describes an eternity which as in the paradises of his poem cannot be imagined without the "grateful vicissitude" of diurnal and emotional ("yet sinless") alteration, which *only* to the satanic mind appears as the "hateful siege / Of contraries" (IX, 121–22).

35. For a complementary consideration of the poem's temporal dimension, see Hart, "Matter, Monism, and Narrative," pp. 24–25.

36. See John Rogers, "Milton and the Mysterious Terms of History," *ELH* 57 (1990): 281–305.

37. See John Ray, *Three Physico-Theological Discourses* (London, 1693), p. 6; quoted also in Markley, "Representing Order," p. 130.

38. In every case, divine creativity has both masculine and feminine aspects, the male godhead "engendering" female powers that in turn produce masculine ones with which they conjunctly rule, just as Night rules with Chaos. Although making *use* of traditional sexual symbolism, these male and female powers seem to be conceived as at once mutual and sovereign, or, as R. A. Shoaf, *Milton, Poet of Duality* (New Haven, 1985), might put it, as dual but not dualistic. The masculine force of the "Eternal Coeternal beam" (III, 2) generates the cloudy tabernacle addressed as "shee," but "eldest" female Night's seems to have given birth to Chaos's kingdom (II, 894). Similarly, while Milton's masculinist "God is light" (III, 3), an inseminating force, the Son's energies have feminine implications, since they alone "ineffably" receive the full light of God (VI, 719–22). Ultimately, however, divine light retains some of its old privilege over even a fecund darkness, thereby reasserting some of its old hegemony. For an examination of the textual evidence behind this thesis, see my "Demystifying Disguises: Adam, Eve, and the Subject of Desire," in *Renaissance Discourses of Desire*, ed. Claude Summers and Ted-Larry Pebworth (Columbia, Mo., 1993), pp. 237–58. For the contrary argument highlighting its feminine hegemony, see Rumrich, "Milton's God and the Matter of Chaos," see pp. 1043–45, esp. note 14.

39. Taking a few liberties with Milton's word order, my use of this quotation reflects Adam's own perplexity in the matter. As his question to Raphael suggests, clearly he, too, has difficulty imagining

what cause
Mov'd the Creator in his holy Rest
Through all Eternitie so late to build
In *Chaos*, and the work begun, how soon
Absolv'd, if unforbid thou maist unfould.   (VII, 90–94)

In this way both Chaos and God are recognized as part of a holy but not wholly inexplicable mystery, one that inevitably links the "boundless deep" of God (VII, 168) to the "vast immeasurable Abyss / Outrageous as a Sea" (VII, 211–12), the chaotic "Deep" (VII, 216) extracted from his own nature.

40. For Shoaf, see note 38 above. For a brief history of this complex paradigm, see Brian Rotman, *Signifying Nothing: The Semiotics of Zero* (New York, 1987). As he points out, even Socrates' declaration that " 'all that I know is merely that I know nothing' was ironically allowing 'nothing' to puncture a certain ideal of self-knowledge in which one knows 'all.' " As a result, "it creates . . . a fissure, a hole in the full indivisible knowing 'I' at precisely the point where such an 'I' has to cognise 'nothing' in relation to itself" (pp. 61–66). Milton's place in this tradition is indubitable; in his second prolusion he refers to Pythagoras as "a very god among philosophers," and in his third prolusion he attacks scholastic (that is, Aristotelian) philosophy. See YP I, pp. 234–48; and, of course, *Il Penseroso*.

41. On "nothing," Rotman, *Signifying Nothing*, pp. 70–73, 77–78, also cites the alternate and much older example of the *Zohar*, which Denis Saurat, *Milton, Man and Thinker* (New York, 1970), has claimed as an influence upon Milton. Although the *form* of this "influence" has been largely disproved, Rotman's quotation from exegetical commentaries on the nature of God according to Kabbalah has a decidedly Miltonic ring. For a useful summary of the conflicting traditions about the void in the Greek/Christian and later Jewish tradition, see Rotman, *Signifying Nothing*, pp. 60–78.

42. See Kirk et al., *The Presocratic Philosophers*, p. 20. Here Milton's pre-Newtonian assumptions are also strongly evident: rather than spatializing time in the mode of this mechanics, he atomistically *and* relativistically temporalizes space. For a discussion of Newtonian spatialization, see Prigogine and Stengers, *Order Out of Chaos*, pp. 17–18.

43. This and all subsequent Greek translations are taken from Kirk et al., *The Presocratic Philosophers;* for their comparable conclusions on the location of Chaos, see p. 41.

44. See Rotman, *Signifying Nothing*, pp. 61–63. Within the pre-Socratic tradition there is already a conflict between those of the Eliatic school (primarily Parmenides and Zeno) who emphasize the fundamental unity of being so as to make motion itself a paradox, and others like Heraclitus and Empedocles who make flux, strife, or some combination of love and strife the foundation of cosmic existence *and* freedom. See again Kirk et al., *The Presocratic Philosophers*, p. 194.

45. Hence, as Rotman *Signifying Nothing*, points out, Augustine reasons that God has no part of the void *or* of the lack that must have existed before Creation, since "in creating the world God also created time itself, so God, being outside of time, could never have lacked what he always had" (p. 64).

46. Lucretius, *The Nature of the Universe*, trans. Ronald E. Lathan (Harmondsworth, U.K., 1951), p. 33; on the elenchus, see Kirk et al., *The Presocratic Philosophers*, p. 433.

47. Lucretius, *The Nature of the Universe*, pp. 35–36, 40.

48. A similar if not specifically Heraclitan function of holy fire (*not* to be confused with Satan's icy fire) is suggested by Michael Fixler, "Milton's Passionate Epic," in *Milton Studies* I, ed. James D. Simmonds (Pittsburgh, 1969), pp. 167–92. As Fixler notes of a supporting text in Milton's second Ad Leonoram poem,

In the elemental system of universal correspondences . . . fire is the purest and highest element in the harmonic tetrachord of the basic elements, corresponding to the music of the spheres, which tonally is the fourth or top note in the tetrachord of universal musical essences . . . By the same token fire corresponds with the fourth and highest of the poetic raptures, the love of God, so that the fiery spirit of prayer circling the heavens like a

Neoplatonic daemon of celestial influence is one and the same with the inspiration of visionary poetry. (P. 181)

As Fixler suggests, this is a Neoplatonism fused with Puritanism (p. 191n21), which, as I argue above, itself presupposes a fusion of contemporary with ancient scientific atomism (the latter, of course, having its own set of mystical associations and beliefs in which Milton had an early and obvious interest).

49. For the importance and novelty of this conception of God, see Stephen Fallon, " 'To Act or Not': Milton's Conception of Divine Freedom," *JHI* 49 (1988): 425–49, and also my " 'Boundless the Deep,' " 45–78.

50. On Heraclitus, see Kirk et al., *The Presocratic Philosophers,* pp. 191–93 (quote). For Prigogine and Stengers's position, see *Order Out of Chaos,* p. 14.

51. On reintegrative flux in modern theory, see Prigogine and Stengers, *Order Out of Chaos,* pp. 131–76.

52. Although Shawcross numbers this *Sonnet XI,* I here defer to the more common numbering.

53. See Marjara, *Contemplation of Created Things,* pp. 96–100 (quote p. 97). While seeming to endorse something like this position, Marjara remains vague and inexplicit about the "(absence of) nature of the most vague ontological entity in *Paradise Lost* " (p. 96). Ironically, the same resistance to vacua and adherence to Aristotelian orthodoxy—particularly the idea that "Nature abhors a vacuum" underlies Lovejoy's exasperation with Milton; see *The Great Chain of Being,* note 27 above.

54. For Chaos as a "place" paralleling the deity's, see Shawcross, *The Complete Poetry of John Milton,* p. 392n21. Milton's rejection of the idea of God as *actus purus* is well known; see the *Christian Doctrine,* YP VI, p. 145. For a similar argument on these theological points, see Rumrich, "Milton's God and the Matter of Chaos," p. 1043.

55. Marjara, *Contemplation of Created Things,* p. 234.

56. John Carey and Alastair Fowler, *The Poems of Milton,* p. 552, II, 943–47 (quote), take these hybrid symbols from an allegory of Raban Maur's (Migne cxi, 342), but also note that the "legend of the 'gold-guarding griffins' in Scythia, from whom the one-eyed Arimaspi steal, was often retold out of Herodotus (iii 116) and Pliny (*Nat. hist* vii 10)." In contrast, heaven's golden floor is usually understood as representing the free righteousness of the Son, the "ground" of his being literally "misconceived" and misappropriated by demons like Mammon and Satan.

57. See Shawcross, *The Complete Poetry of John Milton,* p. 289n36.

58. For this aspect of Satan, see John T. Shawcross, "The Mosaic Voice in *Paradise Lost,*" in *Milton Studies* IV, ed. James D. Simmonds (Pittsburgh, 1970), pp. 25–26, and Samuel S. Stollman, "Satan, Sin, and Death: A Mosaic Trio in *Paradise Lost,*" in *Milton Studies* XXII, ed. James D. Simmonds (Pittsburgh, 1986), pp. 101–20. According to Stollman, "Sin and Death and their encounters with Satan act out one of Milton's major doctrines, namely, his . . . antinomian view of the Mosaic Law and of the Law's impediment of the attainment of Christian liberty" (p. 101).

59. See Harinder Singh Marjara, "Analogy in the Scientific Imagery of *Paradise Lost,*" in *Milton Studies* XXVI, ed. James D. Simmonds (Pittsburgh, 1990), p. 86.

60. For a suggestive consideration of how satanic or sinful narcissism causes *copia* to degenerate into a "mere copy," see Shoaf, *Milton, Poet of Duality,* pp. 27–29.

61. Since, as Marjara, "Analogy in the Scientific Imagery of *Paradise Lost,*" notes, "the images of feeding interrelate the earth with the heavens" (p. 89), one might also suppose that hell alternately "cannibalizes" both Chaos and earth.

62. Both the physical composition and the metaphysical valence of these "tartareous" dregs remain much in question. As Shawcross, *The Poems of John Milton,* p. 394n25, points out, the

reference suggests both something hellish or from Tartarus, or something sedimentary, like the residue of wine making. Yet even these allusions seem less unequivocally evil than has often been assumed, as both the grape and also the Titans who inhabit Tartarus may also be taken as protean life symbols, forces that are ambiguously "adverse to life" (239) in its most orderly forms, yet also subterraneanly connected with the more violent energies of destruction and rebirth associated with Satan, Sin, and Death. Such mercurial residues also figure in the alchemical "projection" of the philosopher's stone, as detailed in my forthcoming book, *The Ruins of Allegory.*

THE LADY IN THE GARDEN:
ON THE LITERARY GENETICS
OF MILTON'S EVE

Donald M. Friedman

A S W E H A V E B E C O M E , in recent years, increasingly conscious of the contingency of our methods of interpretation, it has also become increasingly clear that the history of literary genres is paralleled by the history of our understanding and description of literary genres. Almost forty years ago, G. R. Hibbard gave a name to a kind of poem that Renaissance writers knew very well, but had neglected to name while they worked at reviving and revising some of its classical models. He announced the existence of "The Country-House Poem of the Seventeenth Century," and thereby added a dimension both to the critical scope of a genealogical literary category, "The Sons of Ben," and to the explanatory resources of historical and cultural studies.[1] Indeed, Hibbard gave patriarchal pride of place to "To Penshurst," a position Jonson would have claimed in any case, and traced the family line through Carew and Herrick, among others.[2]

Although "Upon Appleton House" is usually also included as a scion, the nature of Marvell's family resemblance appeared, then as now, characteristically puzzling and slightly suspect—a putative parliamentarian cadet branch of a primarily royalist stock. More recently, Alastair Fowler, as part of a larger enterprise of bringing the outlines of the georgic mode out of the shadow of Renaissance pastoral, like some restorer of paintings darkly varnished by time, has instructed us to seek precision by speaking of "estate poems." He reminds us that Carew's "To Saxham," Herrick's panegyric to Pemberton, and "To Penshurst" itself, address themselves to much more than particular country houses—although both the words "house" and "estate" sound, for the period, similar overtones of broad political, social, and spiritual status. Moreover, Fowler has supplied an extended taxonomy of the genre in his anthology, differentiating its various themes, forms, and identifying parts.[3] He argues that during the major period of its efflorescence, which extends from the emergence of Stuart neoclassicism to the rather different Augustanism of the early Hanoverian era, the poem in praise of the architecture of house and landscape engages profound considerations of issues at the center of the century's currents of change, revolution, and restoration. It addresses such issues as the grounds of authority legal, collective, and personal; the definition of the rights of property; the ratios of power and desire between the sexes; and, held over, so to speak, from the debates of Elizabethan pastoral genres, the double-helixlike productive interdependence of whatever was defined as the natural and the artificial, or cultivated, deliberate, and conscious.

Even a cursory reading of Jonson, Carew, Herrick, Marvell, or indeed Mildmay Fane and others who contributed to the georgic/pastoral mode will easily sustain Fowler's contentions. I want, rather, to focus attention on a small episode or epicyle in the history of the genre, one that occurs during a comparatively odd episode itself in British history—the Interregnum. The period seems to have produced several evanescent literary types, almost as if writers were conscious at some level of the precarious, time-shifting quality of the times they were living in.[4] In particular, some poems written in the early and middle 1650s, although they may not constitute a group, let alone a subgenre, may nevertheless have played a part in shaping Milton's portrait of Eve in *Paradise Lost,* a part, to be sure, that sounds a fairly faint note in the grand orchestration of classical, biblical, and literary models he called upon in his epic.

For while Milton reminds us (by filling our minds with remembered images and echoing symbols) of the multifarious imaginings of Paradise that have fed the Western imagination since before literary art, he also invites us to see and respond to his Eden not only as God's "pleasant garden" (IV, 215) but also as "A happy rural seat of various view" (IV, 247).[5] The absence of a personal possessive pronoun is, I think, pointed and deliberate. While it is God's garden, it is also designed to serve as the "place" (IV, 246) of man's government, the location and source of his delegated power to rule over the creatures of this lesser creation. In this sense Eden, though it of necessity lacks the house that conventionally stands for the quality of the family that inhabits it and expresses its relation to inherent authority in its chosen architectural style—Eden is meant to be the site of Adam and Eve's capital (compare *PL* XI, 342–43); it is both the locus and the sign of their regnal authority. It might be more accurate to say that their "country house," their "rural seat," is figured in the nuptial bower that is the scene of their private lives;[6] its architect is, of course, nature under the guiding hand of God. Milton need not be troubled by the negative imperatives that drive Jonson's opening lines in "To Penshurst," where "not" and "nor" exorcise the work of the "foreign architect" whom Marvell will later turn away from the "sober frame" of Nunappleton. The description of Pandemonium in Book II does all that needs to be done to distinguish between infernal building style and the "architecture of paradise."[7]

Barbara Lewalski includes the country house poem in the extensive catalog of generic forms she discovers in *Paradise Lost* on the grounds that we are conducted through the purlieus of Eden much as Jonson and Marvell lead us through the several parts of the estates of Penshurst and Nunappleton.[8] But her major point of comparison, understandably, is that between Milton's Paradise and the pastoral idyll, the *locus amoenus* in its many transformations. My present argument accepts and assumes the multiple lines of descent from classical pastoral and early Renaissance European versions of the imagining of *otium* and innocence. I am concerned, rather, with a relatively minor variation on those major themes, one that has to do at the same time with the figure of the female in the garden and with the place of that garden in the representation of the estate as a seat of power and influence with respect to its surrounding social reality—that which lies without its walls.

For it seems that the peculiarities of "Upon Appleton House" for example, are not to be explained comprehensively by concentrating solely on Marvell's peculiar poetic sensibility, the temper of mind that generated what Rosalie Colie called his "poetry of criticism," nor by focusing on the apparent vagaries of his political allegiances, nor even by thinking closely about the impress of Lord Fairfax's career and immediate presence on the poet's revisionist inclinations in matters of literary genres.[9] We should, I think, also consider the life history of the genre Jonson recreated so vigorously with his paean to the Sidney household. What did it mean for this kind of poem, for instance, that Carew adopted it as a way of meditating on the significance of the withering of Charles's halcyon days under the "night, and cold abroad" during the years of private rule, and the "raging storms . . . and fierce tempests"[10] of the ill-fated Bishops' Wars? What happened to the genre, that is, as and after the social and ecclesiastical structures which had upheld the meaning of the country house had been recast and largely dismantled?

Barbara Lewalski has also written on the country-house poem per se, but with a view to illustrating the place of the central female figure in the genre's depiction of social reality.[11] She notes, for example, that Penshurst's Lady Sidney is praised for her fertile role in preserving the family standards in "the mysteries of manners, arms and arts,"[12] but while Carew was an intimate of the Crofts family, Sir John's wife is in no way distinguished in the general praise of Saxham, nor does Lady Kent appear at Wrest, despite her high place at the Jacobean court and her patronage of poets during Charles's reign. In examples by Aemilia Lanyer, Lovelace, and finally Marvell, Lewalski demonstrates the tight connection between the representation of woman and the specifics of her position and power in the family represented by the estate at the center of the poem's conception. All of them participate to some extent in the habit of pastoral that associates the female figure with generation (as an avatar of Venus Genetrix) and with the imposition of order on nature's wild or untamed fertility. Somewhat paradoxically, while the Jonsonian country-house poem, like the Spenserian gardens that lie not invisibly beneath it, makes much of an inherent tension between conscious art and unthinking creativity, it also tends toward an unemphasized reconciliation in the figure of the woman in the garden, who stands simultaneously for the intrinsic force of the natural and for the civilizing power that uniquely gives that force human shape, direction, and purpose. At the same time, none of the female figures, however prominent or faded into the social background, can escape symbolic resonance with the Virgin or Eve, or with their inescapable, and inescapably ambivalent, connotations of innocence (and the loss of it). A similar ambivalence exists within the conventions of presenting women as wielders of power to members of a social stratum in which that power was traditionally occulted. The ambivalence was also legal and public, in that the economic rights of women remained severely limited during the period while their domestic responsibilities, in both great houses and yeomen's homes, grew along with the recognition of marriage by individual choice rather than dynastic imperative. In short, the aura of interpretation that surrounded both symbolic and real women in the middle of the seventeenth century in England was rich in possibility and difficult to resolve with clarity. Some of the traces of that blurred, aureate discourse can be found, as well as in the weightier poems we have been considering, in a few fugitive lyrics by a few distinctly minor poets, lyrics published not many years before, we think, Milton resumed his interrupted task of composing the epic that he hoped "aftertimes" would not willingly let die.[13]

To begin with a poem that acts as a point of transmission of the Jonsonian pastoral epideictic, and in its manner promises the style and viewpoint of the Augustan continuation in "Cooper's Hill" and Pope's "Windsor Forest," Waller published "At Penshurst (I)" in 1645, contemporaneously with Milton's initial volume.[14] It was addressed to "Dorothea," the object of his fruitless courtship some years earlier—Dorothy Sidney, daughter of the lord of Penshurst to whom Jonson had written his poem; he later changed the name to "Sacharissa," as he also changed "her" power to an unspecified one that he held responsible for the "peace and glory" of the gardens of Penshurst Place. Indeed, her power is such "That it became a garden of a wood," the transformative agency that can, Waller asserts, "civilize the rudest place." Such is her presence, he goes on, that it "beauty too, and order, can impart, / Where nature ne'er intended it, nor art" (9–10). Trees bow and crowd around in recognition of her magnetism; like Amphion she makes "fair figures from a confused heap" (18). Waller has gone beyond Jonson's compliment to Barbara Gamage Sidney's "huswifery," seen as a precious adjunct to her husband's management of his estate,[15] by attributing to the lady in the garden (a garden she is credited with having created) a capacity that can be defined only by negation—it exceeds the traditional terms of comparison, outstripping both nature *and* art. He also introduces mythological notes appropriate to the classical goddesses, notes that will be struck more commonly as the socio-political significance of the aristocratic country seat becomes more problematic as the Stuart period goes on.

Robert Heath went up to Cambridge in 1634, two years after Milton had become an M.A. and retired to study at Horton; Heath's *Clarastella* was published in 1650, along with his *Elegies, Epigrams,* and *Satyres,* all from the shop of Humphrey Moseley. We know precious little about Heath, and nothing at all about his Clarastella. But when she is "walking in her Garden,"[16] we are told, Flora smiles and Ceres yields to "The greater goddess of the two." Clarastella, in what was swiftly to become a convention, inspires the flowers to define themselves by their behavior; that is, the lily grows pale at the whiteness reflected from the lady's candid visage, the rose blushes red with modesty, and the pansy hangs its head out of shyness. The poem ascends to its height of hyperbole as Clarastella assumes the "life-inspiring breath" of the "warm sun," redeems the flowers from death, and "bids them live" so that they may proclaim to the world the source of their "sweets." The lady herself is never described; her beauty is sublimated into a conceit of seemingly divine power, the power not to impose order on the wanton or unruly but to vivify the essences of flowers. Although Flora and Ceres people the poem, the mythic Persephone hovers not far from its enamelled surface. "On Clarastella Walking in Her Garden" distills and typifies a major trope of the hybridization of the estate poem and the Edenic pastoral; the relation of female creatrix and emblematic flora grows toward the center of the evolving genre.

Nicholas Hookes's *Amanda* appeared in 1653; but as his heroine walks in the garden, her effects on cultivated nature are reminiscent of the blazons and pastoral compliments of earlier, untroubled times.[17] Lilies stand on tiptoe to see her, and the tulip that for Marvell was an instance of contemporary man's luxurious appetite for novelty, for Hookes was merely a "short dwarf flower" that "did enlarge its stalk" and "shoot an inch to see Amanda walk." The furthest reach of analogy is to "some royal amorous queen" riding in state to Parliament; and as if in hectic embarrassment, fig trees put on modest aprons, and bees mistake her lips for their honeyed hive. But Hookes reads these signs not as testimony of Amanda's command over the natural scene, but as a libertine invitation and incitement by the flora and fauna for him to "give [his] dear a new green-flowered gown."[18]

The *Poems* of William Hammond, friend of Thomas Stanley, appeared in 1655; and in "The Walk" Hammond reversed Hookes's trope by urging the denizens of the garden traversed by his mistress to instruct her in the meaning of her powers by reflecting the qualities she had bestowed upon them.[19] The point is that from the sound of whispering, kissing boughs, and the sight of the embraces of "twining woodbines" she is to learn the nature of the "sweet joys" she energizes in her creatures. This vicarious courtship is based firmly in an erotic creation myth, so that the "beauteous stains / Nature adorns the Spring with, are but all / Faint copies of this fair Original" (6–8), and the proper hierarchic relation is defined: "She is a moving Paradise, doth view / Your greens, not to refresh herself, but you" (9–10). The flaw in the analogy is revealed in terms that look forward to Pope's Belinda: "She is, alas! too like the Sun, who grants / That warmth to all, which in himself he wants" (13–14).

Even in so minor an example, it is worth noting that the familiar pastoral blazon, the icon of Flora "Peering in April's front," has been touched by the conceptualization of what James Turner calls the "locodescriptive poem of the postwar years."[20] The divine mistress now moves through a scene whose beauties are images of her ontogenic essence. To the role of goddess of fertility has been added the responsibilities of a female demiurge; and as we will see, the traditional iconic connection between femaleness and burgeoning nature is expanded to encompass the need to control, shape, and order the created. To what extent these poems about or addressed to women seen moving through a natural realm peculiarly theirs have to do with the interregnum history of a nation becoming accustomed to a monarchless state is a question worth considering, as is, perhaps, their relationship to the varied periodic revivals and revisions of memories of the reign of Elizabeth throughout the early Stuart era.

Thomas Stanley, whose tutor was Lord Fairfax's scholarly uncle William, is perhaps best known for his history of philosophy and for his abilities as a polyglot translator. His place here is earned by his version of a large part of Theophile de Viau's *La Maison de Sylvie,* Englished as "Sylvia's Park"[21] in 1651. To what by now is a set of conventions of praise for a female figure of authority placed in the shaped natural setting of a park—a fusion of artifice and enclosed wildness—Stanley adds a fevered meditation on his own role as poet and praiser. For instance, the conceit of frozen waters as mirrors, often cited as one possible stimulus for Marvell's images of the reflecting river at Nunappleton, the "jellying" of the halcyon's azure shadow, and even Mary Fairfax's vitrifying power over nature, if examined closely, can be seen to work out an identification between the poet's writing and the preservation of Sylvia's essence:

These floating Mirrours, on whose Brow
    Their various figures gently glide,
For love of her shall gently grow,
    In faithful Icy fetters ty'd.
This cheerful Brooks unwrinkled face,
Shall smile within its Christal case,
    To see itself made permanent,
And from Times rage secur'd, the deep
Impression of my Cyphers keep,
    And my fair Princess form present.   (71–80)

At the last, however, Stanley surrenders to the more familiar compliment of attributing to Sylvia the excellence the park contains:

Each drop that from these Fountains flows,
Each Flower that in these Gardens grows,
    The fruit on every Tree or Wall,
Are the just subject of all praise:
What then must be the glorious raies,
    Of *Sylvias* Eyes, that guild them all.   (225–30)

Somewhere between the blazon of seduction and the ceremonious worship of the female as nature goddess lies John Cleveland's "Upon Phillis walking in the morning before Sun-rising,"[22] which went through nine issues during its first year of publication and through more than a dozen editions between 1651 and 1658. Whether Marvell consciously "Clevelandized" or not, he could hardly have been unaware of the trees which stood "like yeomen of her guard," and, in striking self-reflexiveness, "wooden carkases were grown / To be but coffins of their owne" (11–12). Cleveland's exaggeration trope makes of Phillis a competitor with Venus to outrun the sun, and in bringing such beams of light to nature that it responds as if to the now-deposed ruler, who has been "cramp't" by her miracles. So "the winged Choristers began / To chirp their Matins" and "The wakened earth in Odours rise / To be her morning Sacrifice" (15–16, 19–20). But this Phillis is unwilling to upset the order of things, and "With-drew her beames" lest her presence "Should wed October unto May; / And as her beauty caus'd a Spring, / Devotion might an Autumne bring" (50–53). Like Marvell, Cleveland makes us conscious of the potential for disruption that lies within the power to give order to the natural, the kind of power that the Mower discovers in Juliana, who "displaced" his mind, or the power which, in a different context, strikes Satan "stupidly good" as he gazes at Eve (*PL* IX, 265).[23]

Of all the ladies who were observed walking in their gardens during the years between the execution of Charles I and the death of Cromwell, none is more likely to have been known to Milton than Mary Fairfax, daughter and sole heir of Thomas Lord Fairfax, in her character of demiurge of the estate of Nunappleton, the poem "Upon Appleton House," and the poet's meditation on the past and future of her house and of the garden of the world.[24]

Milton, as is well known, wrote in his capacity as Secretary for Foreign Tongues on behalf of Marvell the job seeker, after he left Fairfax's employ as Mary's tutor. It wasn't until 1657 that Marvell actually got the job; but it seems only reasonable to suppose that Milton was able to acquaint himself with the younger poet's work, even if the Nunappleton poems had been written primarily to show to Fairfax. At the very least, the author of the sonnet to "Cromwell, our chief of men" a year earlier (and of another in praise of the Lord General only four years before that) must have been interested in Marvell's impressions of the retirement of Cromwell's military predecessor, and of his daughter, the tutor's charge. Whether he would have appreciated fully the younger poet's *genera mixta* of epideixis, pastoral, estate poem, epic structure, pastiche, satire, comedy, and self-reflexive meditation is more difficult to decide.[25] What he would have found, in any case, is a poem that promises to show how the family's history illuminates and prophesies its future, but that meanders (and calls attention to its meanderings) through many scenes and places before recalling itself to its ultimate task, which it performs by interrupting itself to introduce "The young Maria" in line 651 of a poem of 776 lines.

The interruption is both literal and ironically comic; the poet, "Abandoning my lazy side" (643), is stretched out by the river's side, contemplating that "crystal mirror" (636) of the river, in whose surface "all things" "doubt / If they be in it or without," (637–38) and the fishes are twanging at his "Lines." But "away" go his hooks, his "quills, / And angles—idle utensils" (649–50), as he realizes that his pupil is abroad. Unlike Stanley and Theophile his original, or the others we have encountered whose poems intervene between their subject and *her* subjects, Marvell identifies himself implicitly with the subjected state. His behavior is like the world he has inhabited so comfortably, an "easie philosopher," until now: "See how loose Nature, in respect / To her, it self doth recollect" (657–58). For what Mary Fairfax does, above and beyond the effects of the other ladies who walk in gardens in the 1650s, is to transform nature, to perfect it, to fix it in a state that reveals both its original state and its telos, a state in sharp contrast to the apparent formlessness and disconnection the poem thus far has moved through, and to the unruly shambles it has become, in the retrospective view of the civil wars the poem assumes.

But like Milton, Marvell does not habitually depart abruptly from the literary traditions he examines; and so he approaches the completion of his circle of celebration of the Fairfax family by way of the compliments generic to the garden poem with a lady at its center:

> 'Tis she that to these gardens gave
> That wondrous beauty which they have;
> She straightness on the woods bestows;
> To her the meadow sweetness owes;
> Nothing could make the river be
> So crystal pure but only she;
> She yet more pure, sweet, straight, and fair,
> Than gardens, woods, meads, rivers are. (689–96)

In short, while Mary is conceived as the generator and donor of all intrinsic natural qualities, she outgoes them in their very haecceity, a move that puts in question the "reflection trope" and opens the way toward Milton's conception of Eve as source, archetype, but at the same time unmatchable exemplum of her scions.

But Marvell only gestures toward that degree of hyperbole, because his primary obligation is to fulfill the purpose of the estate or country-house poem, which is not only to honor the house in terms both appropriate and contingently decorous, but to provide auspicious auguries for its future. The particular circumstances of the Fairfax family during the years of Marvell's sojourn at Nunappleton made this a more-than-usually challenging task; Mary was the only child of the marriage, and Lord Fairfax had broken the entail on the estate so that she alone could inherit, an action that elicited disapproval and dire predictions from his father. The question of her marriage, for these reasons, was even more urgent and obscure than it would have been for any prominent estate owner, whose daughters could normally look for a substantial dynastic arrangement. In this case Mary herself occupied the position customarily held by the oldest son and heir apparent; the fortunes of a single young woman would determine the future of the Fairfax family's standing, even though the name would die out in Mary's line.

The consequence for the resident poet-tutor-observer was that the young woman, always in Marvell an object of impossible yearning and shadowed potential, had to be presented as complete in herself, already formed and capable of commanding the "world" that Nunappleton includes and represents. And so, while he meets expectations by having the natural scene respond to Mary as to a benefactor: "Therefore what first she on them spent, / They gratefully again present; / The meadow carpets where to tread; / The garden, flow'rs to Crown her head" (697–700), he also dissociates and, so to speak, desexes her with respect to those expectations. Mary "disdains" to be praised for "lesser" beauties than wisdom, and " 'scaped the safe, but roughest way" from the "Trains" of love; she must await another "Fairfax" as she plays the avatar of Isabella Thwaites—in other words, she must undergo a sacrifice like the "sacred Bud" cut from the *"Fairfacian Oak,"* to preserve her name under the name of another (stanzas 89–93).

The poem thus reaches its conclusion not on a note of prophetic triumph, but by turning from, after acknowledging, the pressures upon Mary Fairfax that render the called-for celebratory terms leaden and unusable. It turns instead to the estate itself, the "woods, streams, gardens, meads" (752) which have been its errant course, because they have been the scene of her education, and ours. They are charged with persevering as the only evidence of what the created universe was meant to be, what it was until we tasted the "luckless apple." It is now "But a rude heap," made of "Gulfs, deserts, precipices, stone" (764); but Marvell's point is that Nunappleton "contains the same, / But in more decent order tame" (765–66), an order we have observed in the pentagonal design of the Fairfax garden, in the humble concinnity of its house and the Lord who inhabits it, and lately in the effect of Mary's appearance on all of nature, including the fishes and her idling tutor. Nunappleton is praised at the end for being "heaven's centre, Nature's lap, / And paradise's only map" (767–68). We are surely meant to notice that while the first phrase links nature to supernature, and the second figures the conscious design of the human mind as a source of natural fertility, the final phrase admits that the "estate" of man can now be no more than a map, a symbolic representation of an actuality forever lost. Paradise can never be regained, but we can study, visit, and perhaps even shape images of it that can sustain its memory.

How much of this was present to Milton as he composed Books IV and V of *Paradise Lost* is of course impossible to say. In Book XII Michael can promise only "A paradise within," albeit "happier far" (XII, 587); and when (and if) Milton responded to Thomas Ellwood's question, "what hast thou to say of *Paradise found?*" he chose as the scene of restoration the desert of the Son's temptation.[26]

But it seems to me that along with the perdurable images of Eve and the Virgin Mary in the garden of Eden and the *hortus conclusus* of Christian tradition it is beyond doubt that Milton held in mind the figures of pastoral deities, courtly ladies of the country-house genre, and perhaps more recent versions of them, the ladies in the garden. His Eve shares certain qualities, purposes, and dilemmas with many of them; but I believe she also shows the impress of some of the same contextual pressures that were the occasion for the appearance of Hookes's Amanda and Heath's Clarastella, as well as Marvell's Maria.

It seems fairly clear that the Jonsonian mode of "To Penshurst" does not persist in a strong form beyond the reign of James; the Caroline versions of the country-house poem exhibit unmistakably an erosion of even the pretense of confidence in the stability of the monarchy. "To Saxham" is a persuasive example of the withdrawal of epideictic energy into a circle of guardedness and isolation from a surrounding chaos of divisiveness and open warfare; its fires glow "Like suns within," beckoning wandering pilgrims out of the bitter night. Wrest is protected by circles formed by the cooperating hands of nature and art; its waters are guided so that "This Island Mansion, which i' th' center plac'd, / Is with a double Crystall heaven embrac'd" (79–80).[27]

To be sure, most of the somewhat ephemeral poems discussed here were written by disappointed sympathizers of the monarchy; their sense of deprivation and of the disintegration of a social and political order that underlay the manners of the Jonsonian estate poem is easily understandable. But we might also observe that many of them (Hookes, Stanley, Hammond, Marvell, Milton, Stanley—and Eldred Revett and Mildmay Fane, among other poets who wrote of the satisfactions of rural retreat) had Cambridge connections and thus shared that community's perturbed record of political and ecclesiastical allegiances during the decades surrounding and including the years of actual armed conflict. In any event, Marvell fits the "royalist" model only awkwardly, and Milton not at all by the time of the composition of *Paradise Lost*.

Although the larger political-economic issues continue to be investigated and interrogated by an active band of historians, it can perhaps be suggested that the disestablishment of the monarchy and the Church of England during the Interregnum was reflected in one of its manifestations by changes in the status of the country seats of the nobility and the gentry, whose hierarchic relations themselves continued to be revised as the economic and political dislocations of the war years made their effects felt more intensely. Earlier, the decline of the Elizabethan strategy of the royal progress had altered the role of the great house in the play between centralized crown rule and the struggles for survival of the tradition of provincial magnates. Under the Stuarts, the era of the "prodigy house" had passed, and with it one of the foundations of Jonson's ethico-political stance in "To Penshurst" toward the expense of artifice; this is one reason why Marvell's Mower sounds so reactionary and ineffectual a note when he inveighs against garden statuary.

James had tried to urge or force his pullulating courtiers to reside in the country, for reasons both economic and political; but during the years of Charles's private rule and the country's descent toward the ultimate disintegration of civil war, the country seat became increasingly isolated from the network of power and social texture—became, as is clear in Carew's poems of the late Caroline years, primarily a refuge from the inchoate winds of doctrine and debate swirling outside the walls. It is more my speculation than a firm contention that the poetry of the figure in the garden that we have been glancing at is a sign of another kind of retreat, comparable to the withdrawal of poets like Vaughan into an imagined place of worship that was to substitute for the actual church whose disestablishment they had witnessed. That is to say, as the house itself—in all of its dynastic and political significances— disappears from the center of the "estate poem," its locus of meaning and metaphoric power is replaced by the garden. The garden is perhaps the single element remaining from the constellation of emblematic subjects that formed the Jonsonian country-house poem that continues to retain the potency of its multifold inherited meanings. It might even be argued that its ability to speak with unparalleled immediacy and rhetorical economy of a lost but remembered perfection was intensified by the events of the civil war, Interregnum, and Restoration. The garden—image and reality—also held a unique power to allude to the perpetually vexed question of the balance of the natural and the designed, and to blend attitudes toward the realms of divine and human responsibility.

To these considerations may be added what we know of the evolution of garden design in this period. Although authorities disagree over details and dates, it's probably fair to say that the formal, symbolic, and even mathematical Elizabethan garden, and to a large extent some of the Italianate styles of the earlier part of the century were being replaced by gardens that were designed to subject an observer to a series of perspective views while moving through walks and avenues that led to "discoveries." These were gardens that were to be experienced rather than interpreted from a stable viewpoint. Or, to put the matter another way, the experience of coming to a fork in a garden path does not require the kind of knowledge and analysis that are called for in translating an Elizabethan garden knot. Rather, it presents the observer with the necessity of choice, calls for an action; and that action, once performed, registers a change, or at least an actual event, in the life of the observer. If the walker in the garden should later come upon a statue of Venus, or of Hercules for that matter, the meaning of that choice is likely to be more precisely realized; but it is not essential to the experience of the action.

These remarks rely primarily on the scholarship of John Dixon Hunt and Roy Strong, of course; the changes they have traced in English garden design and its ideology during the mid-seventeenth century correspond to changes that were taking place simultaneously in the actual and the symbolic status of the country estates in which those gardens were found.[28] The new Italian gardens were shaped landscapes that contained walks, alleys, groves, sudden shifts of perspective and scale, and which above all were meant to be moved through rather than contemplated from a fixed point—in short, the kind of garden Milton describes in Book IV, containing "hill and dale and plain," "open field" and where the "unpierced shade / Embrowned the noontide bowers"—"this place, / A happy rural seat of various view" (IV, 243–47).

In that garden, whose image is consonant with the actualities of his contemporaries' taste in the rhetoric of horticulture, Milton has placed his archetypal female figure, and has made her move through *his* imagined design in a pattern that sketches out a contemporary condition. But he has done more; he has fitted that pattern to the developing moral experience of Eve as she comes to understand, through choice and action, both what she is and what she is meant to be. It is altogether typical of Milton's uncontainable appetite for inclusion and his inherent drive toward self-differentiation from his literary heritage that he should combine in his figuration of Eve not only the generative potentialities of the classical goddesses and the Marian symbolism of the *hortus conclusus,* but that he should also, if my hunch is right, have incorporated the most recent morphoses of those traditions as he encountered them in the ladies in the gardens of poets like Cleveland, Hookes, Heath, and Marvell.

The generic form of this figure draws on a repertory of tropes and ideas: the female is conceived as enjoying an intimate relationship with vegetable nature, which responds to her by fulfilling its own inherent form, and which she commands by bringing order and design to instinctive forces of growth and creativity; she both represents and embodies the sensuous capacities of human experience, and is thus tutelary to artistic expression and creation; her intelligence is therefore directed at an understanding of the natural world; in all respects she is the "fit help" that God declares is the "likeness" of the male Adam's realm of the animate, the conceptual, the supernatural. Eve is the half of human nature that defines its position between the animals and the angels.

Herein lies a partial explanation of Milton's strategy of giving to his Eve the domain of the garden itself as a site of experience and education—and for the finely detailed process of association that involves her with its flowers and plants. Genesis gave him the myth of Adam's naming of the beasts as a sign of sovereignty; Milton gives Eve the authority to name the flowers, as another instance of the way in which "true authority in men" may nevertheless be "not equal" (IV, 295–96), though equivalently sovereign. The identification of Eve with flowers is of course a commonplace, and can be traced from the moment when she "first awaked" "Under a shade of flowers" (IV, 451), to the morning when she wins Adam over to her concern for the sufficiency of their efforts to govern the green-fused power of the garden that is growing "Luxurious by restraint," to Satan's vision of Eve "Veiled in a cloud of fragrance," "stooping to support / Each flower," "Her self, though fairest unsupported flower" (IX, 425–32). But a comparison of his presentation of Eve with her predecessors can suggest how Milton has both exploited the resources of the contemporary garden poem and transmuted them to serve his epic purpose.

As we have noted, the emblematic female figure in the conventional allegorical garden is the focus of two related but not altogether consonant themes; she stands for the natural forces of fertility, and therefore serves as a surrogate creator; but she also represents the containing powers of social order and convention, which in themselves are implicitly understood to be the foundations of the hierarchical culture of which the country-house poem is an emergent expression in the Stuart period. Thus, the climax of Jonson's praise of Penshurst is his definition of Lady Sidney as "noble, fruitful, chaste withal" (90). Marvell, as we observed, has some discomfort in treating this mildly oxymoronic trope—fertile chastity—mainly because he must pay his compliments to a putatively nubile heiress who must function both as a feminine cynosure and as the guarantor of the continuance of the estate's political power. Mary Fairfax's actual circumstances run exactly athwart the legal and domestic realities of the mid-century, and yet Marvell must compose within a tradition that demands clear distinctions between lines of gender and political power.

He solves his problem partially by placing himself, as awkward, embarrassed, and ineffectual tutor to the phenomenal child, as a foil to her thus-enlarged virtues. He also exploits what in other poems of the kind would have been a disadvantage—the presexual blankness of Mary's femaleness—by the neomythology of explaining Mary's shaping power over the natural scene of Nunappleton as a product of her devotion to "higher beauties," those particularly of wisdom and the command of language. She "gives" "straightness" to the woods and "sweetness" to the meadows, but unconsciously, as she "leads her studious hours" among the very "fields, springs, bushes, flowers" (745–46) which she enlivens almost without noticing.

Clarastella and Amanda, by contrast, stroll through their obedient and adulatory gardens relatively untroubled by concerns about inheritance and dislocated gender roles. They are viewed by male lovers and praisers, whose perspective permits and summons the figures that produce the genetrix, that combination of nurture and seduction concentrated in the multiple valences of Venus. In Hammond and Hookes and Heath, garden flora crowd around the perambulating ladies, receiving and reflecting their essences in a process of reciprocity that both confirms the unspoken identity between the female and the natural and at the same time serves as the hyperbolic presentation of the desired beautiful object. Both the centrality of the female figure and the reflexive dialectic of these poems are allowed full play by the absence of the kind of social and even political tensions that can be found in the country-house or estate poem per se. Although—*pace* some deconstructive theory—it is not easy to substantiate claims on the basis of a lack, we might infer that the appearance of this mini-genre during the Interregnum is a sign of withdrawal from the large national implications that poems set in gardens of country estates had under the Stuart monarchs. These ladies parade in splendid isolation from the events occurring about them; the landscapes they inhabit turn inward upon their inhabitants, and the garden itself becomes the totality of the natural world through which we move. Gone are the fields, the farms, the prospects, the legendary trees, officious animals, mowers and reapers—in other words, the world of actions and events which surrounds, if it does not invade, poems like "To Penshurst," "To Saxham," and "Upon Appleton House."

The ways in which the portrait of Eve in *Paradise Lost* seems to draw upon many variations of the themes and conventions we have been exploring should be fairly obvious to readers of the epic, given the unusual, specific, and extensively detailed identification Milton establishes between Eve and the flora of Eden. She is, in any case, the archetypical "lady in the garden"; and it is Milton's typical way to unpack and repack his archetypes, so that we are made aware simultaneously and continually of how much of what we know has been mixed in the compound of his poem and how strikingly it has been transformed into something we have not known until now.

What is different about Milton's Eve in the garden of Eden is equally striking and revealing, however—Eve is presented to us as a gardener rather than as the source of the essences of the flowers she tends. Nancy Armstrong and Leonard Tennenhouse have pointed out that "the world in which Milton leaves the reader at the end of *Paradise Lost* is a world of work"; but it is equally, and perhaps even more importantly, the case that the world of Adam and Eve before the Fall is a world of work.[29] There is no mistaking the significance of this departure from the dominant pastoral conventions which Milton knew full well and honored in various ways: it is insisted upon repeatedly in conversations between divine and human characters, and it is, of course, the ultimate source of the argument that leads to the separation of the two on the morning of Eve's encounter with Satan. To Adam, as he explains to Eve (IV, 618–32), their "sweet gardening labour" (IV, 328) is that which distinguishes them from other creatures and thus is the outward sign both of inherent human dignity and of the benevolence of "the ways of God to man."

But it is also clear that the particular labor enjoined upon them is also necessary to the preservation of their "estate" in Eden in an immediate, practical way. Their task is not a purely gestural demonstration of hierarchical responsibility, but the imperative to "reform" the nature which surrounds and nourishes them. Characteristically, the verb is charged by both moral and architectural energies; as the walks and alleys of Eden are "overgrown" their growth becomes "wanton," the blossoms and dripping gums which are elsewhere described as "Groves whose rich trees wept odorous gums and balm" (IV, 248) are perceived as "unsightly and unsmooth," asking "riddance, if we mean to tread with ease" (IV, 632).

Adam's unease, and the worry that drives Eve to press the need to make their "pleasant task enjoined" (IX, 207) more efficient, are responses to a view of nature markedly different from the one that prevails in the pastoral versions of Edenic experience that underlie the "garden" poems we have been considering. It is reminiscent of the twisted argument of Comus who, whatever his immediate strategy with the imprisoned Lady, exhibits what seems to be a genuine Miltonic anxiety about a nature which, lacking the control of appetite, will be "strangled with her waste fertility" (728), when buried diamonds would "come at last / To gaze upon the sun with shameless brows" (734–35). This is a nature which, so far from being the benign and bountiful provider limned in Book IV, is a kind of compost heap, eternally generating the forms of life but containing also the potential for monstrous and overwhelming productivity, if not constrained by the work of arts that are the product of consciousness.

The work of Adam and Eve, then, is much more than the symbol of their sovereignty; it is also the strictly necessary exercise of rational government over the created world that nurtures and serves them. It is interesting to note that when, in Book V, Eve offers to prepare a meal for Adam and the affable angel, Raphael, Adam hospitably exhorts her to

> bring forth and pour
> Abundance . . . [for] well we may afford
> Our givers their own gifts, and large bestow
> From large bestowed, where nature multiplies
> Her fertile growth, and by disburdening grows
> More fruitful, which instructs us not to spare. (V, 315–20)

But Eve more observantly replies,

> small store will serve, where store,
> All seasons, ripe for use hangs on the stalk;
> Save what by frugal storing firmness gains
> To nourish, and superfluous moist consumes. (V, 322–25)

In other words, while Adam sees the fruits of their labor as a semiotic system that articulates the complex relations between heaven and earth, Eve has acquired the practical knowledge appropriate to managing the actual affairs of their life in Eden.

By a similar token, when Eve urges their separation in Book IX, she has in mind not only the need to "lop . . . , or prune, or prop, or bind" (IX, 210), but the proper division of labor between her and Adam. He is to take care of the symbolic actions of winding woodbine or directing "the clasping ivy where to climb" (IX, 217), and thus to reenact their marriage and her dependence upon him as the (unmentioned) elm. But she proposes to "find what to redress"[30] in "yonder spring of roses intermixed / With myrtle" (IX, 218–19), where Satan eventually spies her "Veiled in a cloud of fragrance" (IX, 425).[31] There she is observed "upstaying" the variously colored roses which "Hung drooping unsustained" (IX, 430); unlike other ladies who give life and essential qualities to the flora they walk past, Eve is the agent who props them against their intrinsic weaknesses, who enables them to embody beauty and give their fragrance to the airs by sustaining them, as the twining symbols of domestic dependence are sustained by the elm that Adam finds for them.

Perhaps the most concise expression of Eve's particular relation to the flowers that throughout the poem define her sphere of agency and the nature of her mode of understanding occurs in Book VIII. In a frequently noted passage, Eve leaves Adam to converse with Raphael because, Milton tells us, she would rather hear his knowledge from her husband's lips interspersed, as they would be, "with conjugal caresses." But immediately before this, we learn that she goes off, in fact, to inspect "her fruits and flowers, / To visit how they prospered, bud and bloom, / Her nursery" (VIII, 44–46). We have seen how the lilies turn white at the sight of Clarastella's cheek, how Sylvia's eyes "gild" the flora of her garden, how all of Nunappleton "recollects" itself at the approach of Mary Fairfax. When Eve appears, however, "they at her coming sprung / And touched by her fair tendance gladlier grew" (VIII, 46–47). In other words, in response to its nurse the natural world of growing things grows, fulfills its intrinsic nature, becomes more like itself under her tutelage. Milton intensifies the point by his play on "gladlier," in which the attributed delight of the flowers on encountering Eve is registered as more emphatic and healthier growth. The natural response to the hand of Eve is for vegetation to grow better and happier.

The identification with nature which we have seen as a basic trope in earlier poems about ladies in gardens has thus been revised in Milton's version. Flowers do not simply reflect the specific beauties of the female figure, nor do they court her by acknowledging her creative powers. Eve tends a garden that God himself planted "in the east / Of Eden" (IV, 209–10). It is separate from her and lesser; but she is responsible for its proper development, which implies and requires judicious control of its inherent tendency to unlimited growth. She may name the plants, as Adam has the animals; but she neither makes the flowers nor determines their essences. If anything, the reverse is true in the metaphoric thematics of the poem; for nowhere is the nature of Eve's identification with flowers more tellingly placed than at the moment when Adam realizes the import of Eve's "fatal trespass" (IX, 889). A few lines earlier in expectation and "Waiting desirous of her return," he "had wove / Of choicest flowers a garland to adorn / Her tresses" (IX, 839–41).

But as he takes in the significance of Eve's story, her "countenance blithe" and distempered, flushing cheek, "From his slack hand the garland wreathed for Eve / Down dropped, and all the faded roses shed" (IX, 892–93). In Adam's unfallen world, "choicest flowers" are abstract and generic, like his thinking about the relation between duties and desires. But with the realization that everything has changed in the instant of comprehension, those flowers become the rose; that is, their meaning is distilled into the henceforth eternal symbol of transiency and fragile beauty. Eve's sin has, before our eyes, and beyond her hands, created the symbolism of the rose and thus created for all the rest of time a fissure between the human consciousness of its original responsibility for nature's welfare, and uncomprehending nature, which has suffered unwittingly for the failures of its sovereigns.

Milton thus restores to the poem of man's estate, and through his revision of the female figure at the center of the natural scene, the dimension of social and political implication that had distinguished it in its earlier manifestations. That dimension has been enlarged to embrace a world in which the accoutrements of monarchy, including the patriarchal "house," have been diminished, and in which the potency of individual choice has replaced as a major structural member the tacit agreements and definitions of the world of analogy, allegory, and inherited, hierarchical position. While drawing upon the reinterpretation by Interregnum poets for his figuration of Eve as the solitary female figure in the landscape, and while responding to Marvell's idiosyncratic version of the estate poem as historical critique, Milton opens the genre of praise of a "happy rural seat of various view" to the uses and needs of a world of entrepreneurship and forms of labor that dominate the natural. But, as so often in Milton, within the revisionary can be discerned the shapes of other models that have been absorbed, rejected, and transformed.

Eve was always meant to be "fairest of her daughters" (IV, 324), but it may be that at the moment of her second creation she was closer to some of them than we have understood, and that, in a recursion altogether typical of Milton, some of her daughters helped to shape her representation in *Paradise Lost*.

University of California, Berkeley

NOTES

1. G. R. Hibbard, *Journal of the Warburg and Courtauld Institutes* 19 (1956): 159–74.

2. The chronological precedence of Jonson's poem has been challenged by the accession to the canon of Aemilia Lanyer's "The Description of Cooke-ham," composed probably circa 1609–10, and published in 1611. See *The Poems of Aemilia Lanyer: Salve Deus Rex Judaeorum*, ed. Susanne Woods (Oxford, 1993), pp. 129–38; the text is also reprinted in Fowler, *The Country House Poem*, for which see note 3 below.

3. Alastair Fowler, *The Country House Poem: A Cabinet of Seventeenth Century Estate Poems and Related Items* (Edinburgh, 1994).

4. Compare, for example, the curious exchange poems between Henry King and a "Mr. Hen. Rainolds" in the voices of a "Blackmoor Maid" and a "fair boy"; John Cleveland has a "Fair Nymph scorning a Black Boy" in a poem published in 1647 and reprinted 1651 and 1653. The subject seems to have fascinated the contrarious Lord Herbert of Cherbury, who wrote several poems on the theme of "black" or "sunburned exotic beauty." King's and Cleveland's poems, as well as William Hammond's, can be found in volume 3 of *The Caroline Poets*, 3 vols., ed. George Saintsbury (Oxford, 1921). Lord Herbert's are included in *The New Oxford Book of Seventeenth Century Verse*, ed. Alastair Fowler (Oxford, 1992). The standard editions of these poets are: Henry King, *Poems*, ed. Margaret Crum (Oxford, 1965); *The Poems of John Cleveland*, ed. Brian Morris and Eleanor Withington (Oxford, 1967); and *The Poems, English and Latin, of Edward, Lord Herbert of Cherbury*, ed. G. C. Moore Smith (Oxford, 1923).

5. Compare D.M. Rosenberg, "Milton's *Paradise Lost* and the Country Estate Poem," *Clio* 18, no. 2 (1989): 123–34, and Hugh Jenkins, "Milton's *Comus* and the Country-House Poem," in *Milton Studies* XXXII, ed. Albert C. Labriola (Pittsburgh, 1995), pp. 169–86, both of whom also consider the place of labor in *Paradise Lost*. Quotations of Milton's poetry are taken from *The Poems of John Milton*, ed. John Carey and Alastair Fowler (London, 1968). Passages from *Paradise Lost* are cited by book and line numbers in the text.

6. Compare Rosenberg, "Milton's *Paradise Lost* and the Country Estate Poem," pp. 130–31.

7. The phrase is William Alexander McClung's, in his *The Architecture of Paradise*. (Berkeley, 1983).

8. Barbara Lewalski, *"Paradise Lost" and the Rhetoric of Literary Forms* (Princeton, 1985), p. 181.

9. Rosalie Colie, *"My Ecchoing Song": Andrew Marvell's Poetry of Criticism* (Princeton, 1970).

10. "To Saxham," line 33; "To my friend G. N. from Wrest," lines 2, 4. All citations to Carew refer to *The Poems of Thomas Carew, with his Masque Coelum Britannicum*, ed. Rhodes Dunlap (Oxford, 1949).

11. Barbara K. Lewalski, "The Lady of the Country-House Poem," in *The Fashioning and Functioning of the British Country House*, ed. Gervase Jackson-Stops et. al. Studies in the History of Art, vol. 25, Center for Advanced Study in the Visual Arts: Symposium Papers, X (Washington, D.C., 1989), pp. 261–73.

12. "To Penshurst," line 98, in *The Complete Poems of Ben Jonson*, rev. ed., ed. George Parfitt (Harmondsworth, 1988). The poem may also be found in Fowler, *The Country House Poem*, pp. 53–62.

13. According to Edward Phillips and John Aubrey, Milton began the composition of *Paradise Lost* about 1658 and completed it in 1665; see Helen Darbishire, ed., *The Early Lives of Milton* (New York, 1932), pp. 13, 72–75. For Gordon Campbell's recent arguments supporting the date 1658, see William Riley Parker, *Milton: A Biographical Commentary*, 2nd ed., ed. Gordon Campbell (Oxford, 1996), p. 1052.

14. Fowler, *The Country House Poem*, pp. 181–83.

15. It was in fact closer to mismanagement. Lady Sidney was so devoted to the maintenance of Penshurst and so capable in its affairs that Robert Sidney's letters are filled with expressions of gratitude, respect, and regret that she chose not to share his frequent stays in London.

16. Fowler, *New Oxford Book of Seventeenth Century Verse*, p. 585.

17. Nicholas Hookes, "To Amanda Walking in the Garden," in Fowler, *New Oxford Book*, pp. 665–66.

18. J. B. Leishman discusses Hookes, and his admiration for Cleveland, in *The Art of Marvell's Poetry* (London, 1966), pp. 241–44; he calls the manner of "Amanda" "pastoral hyperbole" (p. 80).

19. William Hammond in Saintsbury, *The Caroline Poets*, vol. 2, pp. 489–90.

20. James Turner, *The Poetics of Landscape* (Cambridge, Mass., 1979), p. 62.

21. Fowler, *The Country House Poem*, pp. 272–79. The present text is that of *The Poems and Translations of Thomas Stanley*, ed. Galbraith Miller Crump (Oxford, 1962), pp. 156–63.

22. Morris and Withington, *Poems of John Cleveland*, pp. 14–15; also in Saintsbury, *Caroline Poets*, vol. 3, pp. 35–36.

23. "The Mower to the Glowworms," line 15, in *Andrew Marvell: The Complete Poems*, ed. Elizabeth Story Donno (Harmondsworth, 1972), p. 109. All citations to Marvell are taken from this edition.

24. "Upon Appleton House," in Donno, *Andrew Marvell*, pp. 74–99.

25. Marvell criticism is replete with discussions of the genres to which "Upon Appleton House" should be assigned; almost any essay, let alone the many books that address the poem, will suggest more than one.

26. Darbishire, *Early Lives of Milton*, p. lvi.

27. Wrest Park, Bedfordshire, was the seat of the De Greys, Earls of Kent. Carew appears to have retired there after the first Bishops' War; it is from there that he writes to his friend, "G. N." See Dunlap, *The Poems of Thomas Carew*, p. 257. "To my friend G. N. from Wrest," is on pages 86–89.

28. See John Dixon Hunt, *The Figure in the Landscape: Poetry, Painting, and Gardening During the Eighteenth Century* (Baltimore, 1976); *Garden and Grove: The Italian Renaissance Garden and the English Imagination, 1600–1750* (London, 1986); *Garden History: Issues, Approaches, Methods* (Washington, D.C., 1992); Roy Strong, *The Renaissance Garden in England* (London, 1979).

29. Nancy Armstrong and Leonard Tennenhouse, *The Imaginary Puritan: Literature, Intellectual Labor, and the Origins of Personal Life* (Berkeley, 1992), p. 111.

30. Moments before (IX, 205), Eve had spoken of the obligation to "dress" the garden, to "tend" the plants and flowers; it seems that as she speaks she becomes more apprehensive about the uncontrolled burgeoning of her charges, and so the task becomes to "redress" them.

31. Fowler, *The Poems of John Milton*, p. 881n9, explains the association of myrtle with Venus's modesty and the multiple significances of the rose with respect to fleshly beauty and its evanescence.

"WITH OTHER EYES": LEGACY AND INNOVATION IN FOUR ARTISTS' RE-VISIONS OF THE DINNER PARTY IN "PARADISE LOST"

Wendy Furman and Virginia Tufte

No Man has Ever Thought in This, (as in Other Respects) like *Milton*. O that he had Painted! and as he Conceiv'd!

Jonathan Richardson (1734)

And I know that This World Is a World of Imagination & Vision. I see Every thing I paint In This World, but Every body does not see alike. . . . As a man is, So he Sees. As the Eye is formed, such are its Powers.

William Blake (1799)[1]

SINCE ITS FIRST publication in 1667, *Paradise Lost* has challenged the visual imagination; and since 1688—the year of its first illustrated edition—it has been thought of, perhaps beyond any other work of European literature, as an illustrated poem. More than two hundred artists have illustrated Milton's works; about 150 have made at least one design for *Paradise Lost*, a number illustrating all twelve books of the epic.[2] Gustave Doré wins the honors for the largest set of published illustrations for *Paradise Lost*: fifty plates guide our vision through the 1866 edition—fifty powerful images which have been so frequently reprinted and reproduced that, to many of us, Doré's brooding landscapes, his "firm opacous Globe," his agonized, soliloquizing Satan sum up the Milton of our earliest and most vivid acquaintance.

In our own century, by contrast, the largest series of illustrations is the twenty-nine wood engravings made by a little-known English artist named Mary Groom. The engravings were produced for a fine-printed ten-book edition of the epic, published in London by the Golden Cockerel Press "on the Eve of the Coronation of King George the Sixth and Queen Elizabeth of England on the 12th May, 1937."[3] More than a hundred male artists illustrated *Paradise Lost* between 1688 and the Golden Cockerel edition; Mary Groom appears to be the first woman to give visual form to the poem.[4] The edition in which her work appears was a spectacular one: limited to two hundred copies, with numbers 1–4 printed on lamb vellum full-bound in white pigskin, and 5–200 printed on Batchelor paper "hand-made from pure linen rag with an appropriate Tree & Serpent watermark," half-bound in black pigskin. Reviews of the volume were enthusiastic, although most centered on its technical excellence and few undertook a critique of Groom's interpretation of the poem. However, one reviewer, Humbert Wolfe of *The Observer* for August 8, 1937, suggested that an appreciation of her work might require a special degree of sophistication in the viewer: "Did that admirable engraver Miss Groom see Milton plain—or did she perhaps see him coloured? Or, if we criticise, is it because . . . we are too ridden with our own conceptions of Milton to see him with other eyes?"[5]

Other eyes, of course, are exactly what each of Milton's illustrators has in some degree brought to the poem—if only in the already profoundly difficult sense of coming literally to *see* Milton's unseen and largely unseeable cosmos. The challenge, and the opportunity, facing the visual artist is all but overwhelming. First, there is the challenge of Milton's unmatched *sublimity,* which drew so many eighteenth- and early-nineteenth-century artists to his epic: "*Milton's* Pictures," wrote his eighteenth-century artist-biographer Jonathan Richardson, "are more Sublimely Great, Divine and Lovely than *Homer's,* or *Virgil's* or those of Any Other Poet, or of All the Poets, Ancient, or Modern."[6] Milton's sublimity, however, has been achieved at length and in time, in sonorous moving periods; conversely, as Lessing famously if controversially asserted in 1766, "The artist can never seize from ever-changing nature more than a single moment." Whereas the poet can lead the reader "through a whole gallery of pictures, as it were, up to the last one," only that last, and somehow exemplary, moment can be portrayed by the visual artist. Thus, Lessing continues, whereas poetry

depicts a visible and progressive action, the various parts of which happen one after another in point of time, the [visual] artist on the contrary, depicts a visible and stationary action, the various parts of which are developed side by side in point of space. Now, seeing that painting, owing to its signs or means of imitation, which it can combine in space only, is compelled entirely to renounce time, progressive actions, as such, lie without its province, and it must limit itself to simultaneous actions or to more figures, which by their attitudes lead us to infer an action.[7]

Lessing wrote, of course, about the arts of poetry and painting in general. As W. J. T. Mitchell has observed, Lessing's "space" and "time" distinctions should not be "abstracted from one another as independent, antithetical essences" (*Iconology,* p. 103). But Lessing's distinctions are nonetheless useful to point up the task faced by literary illustrators—a task to which Milton's illustrators have addressed themselves in a number of ways, from the literal synoptic narratives of John Baptist Medina in 1688, to the radical mythic "primitivism" of Mary Groom in 1937. Some, like Louis Cheron (1720) and Francis Hayman (1749), have produced conventional, decorative (though highly influential) designs to accompany the text; others, like William Blake (1807, 1808) and Mary Groom, have produced coherent visual *readings* of the epic, forcing us to see it in new and often challenging ways. Most have to some degree attempted to *interpret* the text—have engaged, as Joseph Wittreich has put it, in "a form of nonverbal criticism."[8] That nonverbal criticism, like its verbal counterpart—and indeed like the poem itself—partakes of its time and place; participates, as Milton did, both in a complex legacy and in inspired innovation. The visual poet, like the verbal one, must first respond with sensitivity to the givens of the text—a text which in turn has responded to a legacy of its own: biblical, theological, political, literary, and visual. But the illustration is at best far more than a visual transcription of the already legacy-laden text: it is rather a dialogue, with the artist participating fully and creatively in the discussion. Thus the history of Milton illustration becomes an intertextual/interimaginary meeting: a symposium not unlike that of Adam, Eve, and Raphael in Eden; a heady interanimation (to use Raphael's word) of forces and sources of almost Edenic variety.

Almost any scene in *Paradise Lost* can illustrate the progression of the poem's visual interpretation. (Indeed a history simply of the scenes *chosen* for illustration can illuminate a great deal about each generation's sense of what the poem is "about.") The dinner scene in Books V through VIII of the poem, however—in which God the Father sends "*Raphael,* the sociable Spirit, that deign'd / To travel with *Tobias*" to "Converse with *Adam* . . . as friend with friend"—serves as an especially rich matrix for exploring various facets of the poem and its visual, theological, political legacy: a legacy full of complex implications regarding gender and marriage, divine as well as terrestrial.[9] The scene, as imagined verbally by Milton, is already full of contending impulses—toward conventional patriarchy and gender equality; toward suburban pleasantry and eucharistic mystery—all unified in one vivid image of Adam and Eve's Edenic labor:

> On to thir morning's rural work they haste
> Among sweet dews and flow'rs; where any row
> Of Fruit-trees overwoody reach'd too far
> Thir pamper'd boughs, and needed hands to check
> Fruitless imbraces: or they led the Vine
> To wed her Elm; she spous'd about him twines
> Her marriageable arms, and with her brings
> Her dow'r th' adopted Clusters, to adorn
> His barren leaves.   (V, 211–19)

This image of the vine and the elm, perhaps because of its own long poetic and visual tradition, from the beginning caught the attention of Milton's illustrators; and a number have used it, in varied ways, to interpret the dinner scene. John Baptist Medina, Milton's earliest illustrator, stays close to Milton's surface text, using the image in a simple and fairly literal manner. William Blake, on the other hand, makes of the image a complex system of references, charged with meanings lying deep beneath the surface of the text. Carlotta Petrina, an American artist working at the same time as Mary Groom, plays down the gender implications of the image, while playing up, in a somewhat attenuated way, its theological significance. And Mary Groom suppresses Milton's metaphor, which is not to say she merely leaves it out; rather she *transubstantiates* it into a feminist and mystical model for marriage: human, sacramental, and eschatological. Each artist, whatever his or her milieu and particular theological or political concern, seems to respond imaginatively to the dictum of the poet Paul Valéry that "we must will . . . in order to see."[10] Each artist positions himself or herself before the poem as "other" in a different way and to a different degree; each takes responsibility for seeing, and for showing us, the poem "with other eyes."

I

Before looking—literally—at the ways in which Milton's illustrators have visualized his dinner scene, we need to look at the scene itself, and at the legacy behind it. For before artists could respond to Milton's vision, he himself had first both borrowed and reinvented (1) traditional images of Paradise, both biblical and extrabiblical, literal and allegorical; (2) biblical and extrabiblical prototypes for angels (in particular Raphael) and angelic visitation; (3) classical and Judaic typologies connected to the role of Eve, and by extension to the role of woman—with interpretations, in turn, ranging from the Pauline to the parliamentarian; and (4) the conventional imagery—both classical and biblical, marital and eucharistic—of the mutually dependent tree and vine.

Milton's Paradise is a complex synthesis of a number of sources and ideas, ranging from fanciful and luxurious Italian gardens like the Villa d'Este, as he would have seen them on his Italian travels; to the idea of the *hortus conclusus* embodied in the Song of Songs and traditionally allegorized in terms of the Virgin Mary; to Protestant iconography of Eden, set forth in clear visual detail in sixteenth- and seventeenth-century illustrated bibles.[11] Just such a biblical Eden can be seen in an engraved *Terrestrial Paradise*, dated 1629, which served as a title page to John Parkinson's *Paradisi in Sole*.[12] Lacking the aesthetic lushness of an Italian garden, or of Paradise as painted by such artists as Raphael and Brueghel, this illustration nonetheless comes strikingly close iconographically to the "Silvan Scene" Milton describes.

In the very middle of Parkinson's elliptically-shaped design stands "the Tree of Life, / The middle Tree and highest there that grew" (IV, 194–95); and "next to Life," as in Milton's text, "Our Death the Tree of Knowledge [grows] fast by" (220–21). The engraving also pictures a "River large" running "Southward through *Eden*" (223); and here, too, "morning Sun first warmly" smites an "open field" full of huge, sturdy-looking "Flow'rs worthy of Paradise" (244–45, 241). Most importantly for our purposes, Adam and Eve engage in a biblical, but also perfectly Miltonic, version of Edenic labor: Eve "stooping to support / [*a*] Flow'r of slender stalk" (IX, 427–28)—as "by her attitude," in Lessing's words, we can imagine her, over time, propping "each" of them; Adam leading "the Vine / To wed her Elm" (V, 215–16)— as vines, already so wedded, cluster around larger trees to both left and right.[13] Gardens like this one, along with the lusher gardens of Italy and the painters its "lantskip" inspired, gave literal shape to Milton's Eden—and in turn to the latter-day Edens of artists, who needed models of their own as they sought to bring, perhaps more accurately to *return,* his "visible" verbal scene to visual life.

Biblical paradises, moreover, were fraught with allegorical significance, from sources accruing over a millennium and a half: from St. Augustine to seventeenth-century emblem books. The palm tree, for instance—just to the left of the Tree of Life in our prototypical engraving—was simultaneously an image of marital fecundity and itself, in John Prest's words, a "favourite candidate for the tree of life" (*The Garden of Eden,* p. 78). Virtually everything in Paradise, moreover (including, of course, the palm), points typologically to the New Testament—to the "one greater Man / [who will] Restore us, and regain the blissful Seat" (I, 4–5) not yet lost (at least not temporally speaking) in the pictured scene. Augustine, for instance, "referred to Christ as the tree of life, the saints as fruit trees, and the four gospels as the four rivers of Eden" (ibid., p. 21). And each object in Paradise, each animal and plant, can be an emblem of "both good and evil," as Diane Kelsey McColley has demonstrated, forcing the viewer to make "interpretive choices reenacting the primal choices of Adam and Eve" ("Iconography," 115). McColley sums up the emblematic legacy presented in biblical illustrations of Eden:

Seeing nature and human nature as successively innocent, cursed, and blessed again, seventeenth-century literary and visual arts lead us literally and mimetically through these three stages. Their images are complex hieroglyphics of real and daily choices by which we preserve or spoil or renew the world. (Ibid., p. 119)

Such was the legacy inherited by Milton and in turn, both directly and indirectly, by the artists who visualize his Paradise—a Paradise enjoyed, lost, and forever (until the End) in the process of being regained.

The traditions Milton has combined into Raphael's visit are at least as complex as the garden setting within which the visit takes place. First, and most obviously, he has borrowed from the Genesis account of Yahweh's mysterious visit to Abraham, which takes place not in a garden, but on the desert plains of Mam're—as the patriarch, much like Milton's Adam, sits "in the tent door in the heat of the day."[14] As is typical of the earliest Old Testament narratives, the identity of the visiting deity is ambiguous and evocative: "And [Abraham] lift up his eyes and looked, and, lo, three men stood by him: and when he saw *them,* he ran to meet them from the tent door, and bowed himself to the ground" (xviii, 1–2).[15]

Abraham's fallen though faithful response to an angelic guest (*a* guest, though three, as Abraham's greeting, "My Lord," makes clear) contrasts sharply with Adam's more confident prelapsarian approach:

> Meanwhile our Primitive great Sire, to meet
> His god-like Guest, walks forth, without more train
> Accompanied than with his own complete
> Perfections; . . .
> Nearer his presence *Adam* though not aw'd,
> Yet with submiss approach and reverence meek,
> As to a superior Nature, bowing low, . . .   (V, 350–53, 358–60)

The "hospitable intent" of both hosts, however, quickly presents itself—in both cases at least partly in the form of instructions to the wife: to Sarah to "make ready quickly three measures of fine meal . . . and make cakes upon the hearth" (xviii, 6); to Eve to "go with speed, / And what [her] stores contain, bring forth and pour / Abundance, fit to honor and receive / [a] Heav'nly stranger" (V, 313–16). Both narratives, in sum, are at their very root patriarchal, and a somewhat retiring role for Eve is built right into the scene's patriarchal source.

But Milton makes significant alterations as well, showing his attentiveness to more liberating possibilities implicit in the biblical text. First, against the silence of Genesis about Sarah's response, he attributes to Eve both pride and initiative in her skillful preparation of the meal:

> *I* will haste and from each bough and brake,
> Each Plant and juiciest Gourd will pluck such choice
> To entertain *our* Angel guest, as hee
> Beholding shall confess that here on Earth
> God hath dispenst his bounties as in Heav'n.   (V, 326–30; our italics)

Moreover, Milton would have noticed that "Sarah [over]heard [the news that she would conceive] in the tent door, which *was* behind" Yahweh and Abraham (xviii, 10). Thus he revises his source considerably to make Eve legitimate co-auditor (though "retir'd," nonetheless "in *sight*" [VIII, 41]) of all but the "studious" and "abstruse" parts of the angel's discourse. And when she departs—voluntarily, and "not, as not with such discourse / Delighted, or not capable her ear / Of what was high" (VIII, 48–50)—Raphael clearly suggests she has chosen the better part: "solicit[ing] not [her] thoughts with matters hid" (167), and choosing instead to "joy" in the real work of Paradise.[16]

Milton would also have noticed that *neither* Abraham nor his wife eats with the Angel(s): "And he took butter, and milk, and the calf which he had dressed, and set *it* before them; and he stood by them under the tree, and they did eat" (xviii, 8). The Genesis text could suggest to Milton, then, that even Sarah's exclusion from the meal is not so much a matter of gender, as of the changed relations between Yahweh and humankind of both genders after the Fall. Indeed, it is just this loss of fellowship that Milton laments as he turns his "Notes to Tragic" at the beginning of Book IX:

> No more of talk where God or Angel Guest
> With Man, as with his Friend, familiar us'd
> To sit indulgent, and with him partake
> Rural repast, permitting him the while
> Venial discourse unblam'd.   (IX, 1–5)

And finally, Milton would remember that not just Abraham, but Sarah as well, would be included in the New Testament honor roll of Hebrews: "Through faith also Sara herself received strength to conceive seed, and was delivered of a child when she was past age, because she judged him faithful who had promised" (xi, 11). Thus Milton's unfallen Eve "Minister[s] naked" at dinner; and his fallen Eve, like her aged granddaughter in faith, will find consolation—and speak the last human words in the poem—in the knowledge that by her "the Promis'd Seed shall all restore" (XII, 623).

Other sources flow into Milton's dinner scene, along with the already rich and problematic Genesis narrative. John R. Knott Jr. suggests a classical and epic prototype in Aeneas's visit to Evander in the *Aeneid*.[17] And the deutero-canonical Book of Tobit proves to be very important—not just here, as Beverley Sherry and others have noticed[18]—but as a subtext to much of Milton's epic. Tobit is also, significantly, a comedy of marriage—and a comedy of Providence, in which none other than Raphael, "one of the seven angels who stand ever ready to enter the presence of the glory of God" (Tob. xii, 15), is used to show God's grace to the faithful (male and female) and to bring good out of a host of evils. (How poignant it is that one of his greatest deeds is the healing of Tobit's blindness!) Milton explicitly takes issue not only with "the common gloss / Of Theologians" (V, 435–36), but with the book's own theory of angelic nourishment ("You thought you saw me eating," says Raphael, "but it was appearance and no more" [Tob. xii, 19]). And Raphael's explanation of angelic intercession quite clearly matches Milton's image of the intercession of the Son:

> You must know that when you and [the heroine] Sarah were at prayer, it was I who offered your supplications before the glory of the Lord. . . .
>
> I was sent to test your faith, and at the same time God sent me to heal you and your daughter-in-law Sarah. (xii, 12–14)

Several critics have recently begun to recognize more fully Raphael's role as divine healer in Milton's epic—indeed his name means "Yahweh heals"[19]—but none has gotten closer to the crux than Philip Gallagher, who saw Raphael as the harbinger of the Father's special providence and grace:

> The ways of regeneration in *Paradise Lost* are the key to the role of Raphael. In the matter of Adam's regeneration, he is the *angelus ex machina* in a renovative plot requiring three instances of visible divine intervention (the other two being by Messiah [10.47–102] and Michael [11.99–225]). Visiting the unfallen Adam, Raphael *is* "Prevenient Grace descending". . . in anticipation not only of man's repentance . . . *but of his fall as well*. . . . Raphael descends . . . to soften Adam's stony heart before it has hardened, to initiate his postlapsarian regeneration before he lapses.

Thus, Gallagher concludes, Raphael becomes a type of Christ: "his motive has been a true *imitatio Christi:* "immortal love / To mortal men, above which only shone / Filial obedience' (3.267–69)."[20] To some extent each of Milton's illustrators has anticipated Gallagher in attending to this insight— none, we shall see, more fully than Blake and Groom.

With all the nuances present in Milton's variety of sources, what wonder if the meal itself has been read variously by critics, verbal as well as visual, ranging from Thomas Kranidas's reading of the scene as domestic comedy to Mary Groom's portrayal of a eucharistic love feast. Thomas Stroup argued quite early in the discussion that the meal is "hardly a rite"; yet even Stroup hedges his noneucharistic interpretation of the dinner with an emphasis on surrounding acts—Adam and Eve's morning prayer and Raphael's "Hail" to Eve—which seem indeed to have clear ritual significance. Most readers, in spite of their caution in the face of Milton's highly Reformed Protestantism, seem to be forced by Milton's text into at least a quasi-sacramental understanding of the scene, an understanding quite traditional with regard to Milton's Genesis source.[21]

Indeed, Protestantism—though it muted the mystery of the sacrament to the extent that Milton displaces the concept of transubstantiation onto his theory of angelic digestion (V, 433–43)—also worked paradoxically in the opposite direction: if the Reformation on the one hand had secularized the sacred, on the other it had sacralized the quotidian. As Amos Funkenstein has argued,

To various degrees, [Protestantism] encouraged the sacralization of the world, even of "everyday life." Human labor *in hoc seculo* was not perceived anymore as a mere preparation for the future life; it acquired its own religious value in that, if well done, it increases God's honor. So also does the study of this world, by exposing the ingenuity of its creator. . . . The world turned into God's temple, and the layman [sic] into its priests.[22]

For such a vision of the world, of course, Eden would become the perfect laboratory: how better to repair the ruins of our first parents than to return to their unfallen, pretragic understanding of a sacramental meal—a meal which like the poem itself, as Joseph Summers has argued, "must evoke our ordinary responses and then redirect them. . . . It must use our experiences . . . of ritual . . . and recreate them utterly, for the ritual which the poem celebrates must be congruent with freedom."[23] It is precisely this "true filial freedom" (IV, 294) between God and humankind—enjoyed in marital intercourse, whether human or divine; whether in work, in lovemaking, or in sharing a meal—which for Milton comprises the essence of prelapsarian life.

It is perhaps not too surprising, then, that Milton's illustrators have responded so fully to his image of the vine and elm—an image which, because of its own multiplicity of sources, allusively combines the meanings of friendship and marital love, divine and human. To some extent, of course, the image of the vine is archetypal, representing, in the words of Hans-Georg Gadamer, the quality of "being present in sensuous abundance." Thus on ancient Greek and Etruscan pottery, for instance, "there is often," says Stephen Bann, "a precise painterly expression of the exuberance of the vine motif."[24] This pervasive image of abundance has developed in two—and for Milton by no means mutually exclusive—directions.

The first of these directions is the classical one, as developed by the Roman poet Catullus (84?–54? B.C.E.) in his two epithalamia—widely known, translated, and imitated during the Renaissance—"Carmen 61" and "Carmen 62." The vine motif is used mockingly in a verse sung by young men to village maidens who, in a spirit of "reluctant amorous delay," argue for the virgin, as against the married, state: "As a mateless vine grows in vacant field," the young men sing,

> Never lifting itself up, never producing mature grape,
> Its tender body drooping with its own weight,
> Topmost shoot almost touching root,
> No farmers, no oxen tend it.
> When by chance this same vine is joined to husband-elm,
> Many farmers, many oxen tend it.
> So it is with a virgin.

Catullus's other use of the topos, in the formal and stately "Carmen 61," comes far closer to the romanticism of Milton's domestic vision, as the poet calls to the bride:

> Come forth, new bride,
> If it pleases you now,
> And listen to our words.
> See how the torches shake their golden hair.
> Come forth, new bride.
> Your husband does not wish to trifle,
>
> . . . .
>
> Or to lie alone
> Away from your soft breasts.
> But rather, as the pliant vine
> Entwines the trees planted nearby,
> So will he be entwined in your embrace.[25]

According to A. L. Wheeler and Peter Demetz, "this motif literally grows from Italian soil"; for Catullus employs as a metaphor for marriage "a specifically Italian way of training the vine and interprets a viniculture technique as suggestive of human relationships."[26] That vinicultural method was quite literally to *wed* (*maritare*) the vine to a tree—particularly the elm.[27]

In the *Book of the Shepherd* (ca. 140 C.E.), a part of the early Church's scriptures, however, the image of the vine "migrated" from a topos of marriage (a practice far from venerated in the early centuries of the Church's life) to the wider social meaning of *caritas* (charity).[28] Then, in the fourth century, the *Book of the Shepherd* was itself renounced (Demetz, "The Elm and the Vine," pp. 526, 531); and its use of the vine as a largely horizontal image of social charity was replaced in Christian preaching by the far more suggestive Johannine formulation, in which the vine becomes an image of Christ's mystical unity with both the Father and with his disciples:

I am the true vine, and my Father is the husbandman. Every branch in me that beareth not fruit he taketh away: and every *branch* that beareth fruit, he purgeth it, that it may bring forth more fruit. . . . Abide in me, and I in you. As the branch cannot bear fruit of itself, except it abide in the vine; no more can ye, except ye abide in me. I am the vine, ye *are* the branches: He that abideth in me, and I in him, the same bringeth forth much fruit: for without me ye can do nothing. (John xv, 1–5)

The nuances in the Johannine passage spread out in a number of directions. First, the context of the discourse, the Last Supper, places upon it an inescapable eucharistic meaning.[29] (It is, after all, the Johannine Jesus who has said, "I am the living bread which came down from heaven: if any man eat of this bread, he shall live for ever: and the bread which I will give is my flesh. . . . He that eateth my flesh and drinketh my blood, dwelleth in me, and I in him" [vi, 51, 56].) On the other hand, the image serves as well to suggest the deep bond of love and friendship between the disciples and their Lord, and among the disciples themselves: "Henceforth I call you not servants . . . but I have called you friends" (xv, 15); "This is my commandment, That ye love one another, as I have loved you" (12). Also connected to the topos of the vine is the idea of *kenosis*, of sacrifice: "Greater love hath no man than this, that a man lay down his life for his friends" (13). And finally, even the eschatological idea of the Last Judgment is implicit in the image: "If a man abide not in me, he is cast forth as a branch, and is withered; and men gather them, and cast *them* into the fire, and they are burned" (6). But the branches that do bear fruit will be resurrected—to dine in the many mansions of the Father's house (xiv, 2), as Adam and Eve, had they been "found obedient" (*PL* V, 501), would perhaps have done, all their posterity with them, without the tragic detour of fallen history.

To Raphael, at least, that possibility—lost but regained by the loving obedience of the one greater Man in John, chapter xv—is the deepest significance of their shared prelapsarian meal. Angelic and human experience, he suggests, whether of food, of thought, or of love, differ not "but in degree, of kind the same." "Wonder not then," he says,

> what God for you saw good
> I refuse not, but convert, as you,
> To proper substance; time may come when men
> With Angels may participate, and find
> No inconvenient Diet, nor too light Fare:
> And from these corporal nutriments perhaps
> Your bodies may at last turn all to spirit,
> Improv'd by tract of time, and wing'd ascend
> Ethereal, as wee, or may at choice
> Here or in Heav'nly Paradises dwell;
> *If* ye be found obedient, and retain
> Unalterably firm his love entire
> Whose progeny you are.   (V, 491–503; our italics)

If, as the Johannine Jesus says, they abide in the vine. In seeking autonomy—cut off from that vine as from each other—first Eve, then Adam will find only sterility.

Here, then, two images come together: on the one hand as a celebration of relationship, whether marital or mystical; on the other as a warning of the cost of disconnection. Without the elm, the vine is vulnerable; without the vine, the elm is sterile; without the Vine Dresser, and without connection to the true Vine, neither can bear fruit—except the fruit of "Death . . . and all our woe" (I, 3).[30] Artists will respond in a variety of ways to this "visible and progressive" metaphor, as they find it woven throughout Milton's epic—sometimes reading it quite literally; other times reading through and even beyond it, as Milton himself has reread and revisualized his own complex web of sources.

II

Milton's earliest illustrators brought their visual rendering of his poetic narrative very close to the surface of the text. Indeed, their designs often *narrate* the epic: using the late medieval device of presenting "simultaneous actions" and arranging space to indicate temporal progression. Three artists contributed to the first illustrated edition of *Paradise Lost,* printed for Jacob Tonson in 1688: Dr. Henry Aldrich (1674–1710), who probably designed the illustration for Book I and certainly for Books II and XII; Bernard Lens (1659–1725), who designed the illustration for Book IV; and John Baptist Medina (1659–1710), who made the designs for the remaining eight books, including those for Books V–VIII. Medina was born in Brussels of Spanish parents. Having been trained there as a historical painter, he came to England about 1686 and executed the *Paradise Lost* designs shortly after his arrival. In 1688 he settled in Scotland, where he was eventually knighted and became a prominent portrait painter. A number of his portraits can be seen in the Scottish National Portrait Gallery.[31] The somewhat awkwardly engraved illustrations in Tonson's edition rarely do justice to the original designs—which were executed in soft blue, gray, and sepia ink on elegant folio sheets, and which can be viewed today in the print room of the Victoria and Albert Museum. But the printed illustrations nonetheless give us a useful glimpse into the way visual artists working shortly after Milton's death interpreted the poet's vision. Moreover, since they continued to be reprinted for nearly a hundred years, they became the standard for visual interpretation throughout the eighteenth and into the nineteenth century.

Most of Medina's designs present the viewer with more than one scene from the epic, leading one commentator to suggest, in fact, that the artist was

Fig. 1. John Baptist Medina, Synoptic illustration to Book V, engraved by Michael Burghers [or Burgesse]. From John Milton, *Paradise Lost,* 4th ed. (London: Printed for Richard Bentley and Jacob Tonson, 1688). Reproduced with permission from the William Andrews Clark Memorial Library, University of California.

working not from the text itself but from the arguments, or summaries, at the head of each book.[32] A close look at the illustrations, however, reveals his careful attention to the actual poem—often to very specific and visually suggestive lines. In his four illustrations covering Raphael's visit, indeed, Medina manages to underscore for the reader most of the major events, and some of the important themes, in this crucial central portion of Milton's theodicy. In his design for Book V, Medina presents three scenes: Adam and Eve engaged in their morning prayer; Adam's first astonished sighting of Raphael; and Eve preparing dinner at the door of the nuptial bower, as Adam goes forth to meet the angel. In his designs for Books VI–VIII, he goes on to show us "the third sacred Morn" of heavenly battle (VI, 748), when the Son, in the "Chariot of Paternal Deity" (750), drives the rebel angels out of Heaven to the burning lake below; in Book VII, Raphael describing the days of creation (shown in rondels above his narration) to a rapt Adam and astonished Eve; and in Book VIII, Adam in the midst of Paradise, remembering the creation of Eve and discoursing with Raphael about the "Sun" and "fruitful Earth" (91–97)— while Eve, a tiny background figure, goes back to her gardening. In all but the design for Book VI, Medina uses the technique of simultaneous narrative; and the Book V design serves admirably to illustrate his work.

The design (fig. 1) is remarkably unified visually and possessed of a grace reminiscent of Mannerist paintings; yet it is made up of three synoptic vignettes, each depicting an episode in front of the arched doorway to Adam and Eve's bower. In the foreground, Medina shows the pair kneeling in prayer after they have come forth "from under shady arborous roof" (137), and before they begin their day's labors. In the second vignette, slightly back and to the left, Adam stands at the doorway and gazes in wonder at the angel Raphael, descending toward him on a white cloud. In the third vignette, much smaller and further back from the picture plane, Adam, "with submiss approach and reverence meek," greets Raphael, who walks toward the bower—as Eve, already having gathered fruits for the meal, now prepares them for their angelic guest. Medina's Paradise is hilly and lush with Italianate shrubbery, although he has chosen in this design not to portray any animal life. The design seems calculated, rather, to turn our attention to the human significance of the scene, and to the connection between the three "progressive actions" he has chosen to freeze into the simultaneity of space.

An interesting analogue exists to Medina's foreground vignette, that of Adam and Eve at prayer, and casts light on the artist's method of visual interpretation. Indeed, if we compare his design with an engraving of the prelapsarian Adam and Eve by the seventeenth-century Flemish artist Jan Theodore de Bry (after Maerten de Vos, for the Mainz Latin Bible of 1609), we can see at least the *kind* of visual image upon which Medina probably drew as a gloss upon Milton's text.[33] In both engravings, as in the poem,

> Lowly they bow'd adoring, and began
> Thir Orisons, each Morning duly paid
> In various style, for neither various style
> Nor holy rapture wanted they to praise
> Thir Maker.   (V, 144–48)

The composition in the two pieces is similar, but Medina has not simply borrowed from the visual tradition and ignored the verbal text before him: the poses of his Adam and Eve reverse and, more importantly, slightly modify those in the earlier image. In both images, Adam kneels with one knee raised, in Medina's design upon a rock, and clasps his hands before his chest in a conventional gesture of prayer.[34] But in Medina's version his prayerfully bowed head and slightly worried expression depart from de Bry's more cheerful full-faced representation, and place these orisons firmly in the narrative context of the poem. These deft details of "attitude," as Lessing would put it, remind us of the evil dream from which Eve has just awakened—and of the fact that Milton's couple are engaged not only in thanksgiving, but also, perhaps for the very first time, in petition. Indeed, it would seem that we observe the exact moment in which they pray that "if the night / Have gather'd aught of evil," the "Parent of good" will "Disperse it, as now light dispels the dark" (V, 206–207, 153, 208).

Perhaps that is why Eve's posture, too, is slightly altered in Medina's design. In de Bry's engraving, she looks merely open and pious, her hands clasped like Adam's—albeit, Venuslike, over her pudenda. Medina's Eve wears an expression far more ardent, even somewhat beseeching; and her arms cross her breasts in a gesture simultaneously evocative of a penitent Magdalene and a submissive Virgin Annunciate. Neither biblical type, of course, exactly represents her case; for Eve, unlike the Magdalene, is innocent (since "Evil into the mind of God or Man / May come and go, so unapprov'd, and leave / No spot or blame behind" [V, 117–19]); yet unlike the Virgin, she is nonetheless full of "sweet remorse" (134). But like both Marys she is the image of "pious awe, that fear'd to have offended" (135).

This visual allusion to the Virgin Annunciate, moreover, is forced to do double duty in the design. For even with simultaneous narrative, Medina cannot gracefully include every stage of the dinner party. Thus he does not show Eve standing "to entertain her guest from Heav'n . . . On whom the Angel *Hail* / Bestow'd, the holy salutation us'd / Long after to blest *Mary*, second *Eve*" (V, 383–87). Nonetheless, the limits of the medium notwithstanding, one could question whether he has risen to Lessing's challenge: to show us the "last," that is the exemplary, in Milton's "gallery of pictures." For by leaving out that moment, along with the eating of the meal, he both plays down considerably the sacramental meaning of the scene and gives Eve a drastically diminished role.

One could argue quite cogently that Medina intended to do no such thing, for there are elements both here and in his series as a whole that suggest his attentiveness to Eve's importance in the epic. In addition to the typological allusions in her pose, for instance, he also suggests by the composition in this design that the angel's descent occurs as an answer to her prayer, at least as much as to Adam's. For although Raphael descends toward Adam alone in the second vignette, the scale of the angel—exactly matched to the praying couple in the foreground—serves not only to indicate his importance and to unify the composition, but also to tie the three figures together thematically. Indeed, although Raphael comes down from the right, in Medina's drawing as well as in the engraving, he nonetheless echoes the composition of Gabriel's descent in countless Annunciation scenes.[35] Thus the connection between Eve's attitude of prayer and the angel's descent is doubly underscored. In his design for Book VII, moreover, Medina shows Eve actively listening to the angel's account—though Raphael, as in Milton's text, addresses his discourse to Adam. And in Book VIII, the tiny figure of Eve "among her Fruits and Flow'rs" (VIII, 44) suggests that Medina has followed the poet in not taking her self absenting for granted, and in remarking on the grace "that won who saw to wish her stay" (43).

But, for all that, Medina has nonetheless managed to magnify the patriarchal strain in the text—returning it, however inadvertently, to a vision closer to Milton's Genesis source than to the poet's own careful adaptation. In the epic, when the angel arrives at their "Silvan Lodge . . . *Eve* . . . / *Stood* to entertain *her* guest from Heav'n" (V, 377–83; our italics), underscoring the fact that he is her guest as well as Adam's. (Adam, after all, has requested his presence in exactly such terms: "Voutsafe with *us* / Two only, who yet by sovran gift possess / This spacious ground, in yonder shady Bow'r / To rest" [V, 365–68; our italics].) In Medina's visual rendering, however (fig. 2), although Adam and the angel have arrived at the Bower, Eve is pictured, out of phase, at a point earlier in the narrative—exactly the moment, clearly, when "for drink the Grape / She crushes, inoffensive must, and meaths / From many a berry, and from sweet kernels prest / She tempers dulcet creams" (V, 344–47). She seems, indeed, "on hospitable thoughts" so "intent"—so concerned "What choice to choose for delicacy best" (332–33)—that she turns to the shadows of domestic care, away from the light of the approaching angel.

Fig. 2. John Baptist Medina, detail from illustration to Book V. Reproduced with permission from the William Andrews Clark Memorial Library, University of California.

At best she becomes a Martha figure (compare Luke x, 38–42), at worst a household drudge. Thus it is, perhaps, that Charlotte Bronte's *Shirley* bursts out against the poet in an understandable moment of feminist irony:

Milton's Eve! Milton's Eve! . . . Milton tried to see the first woman; but . . . he saw her not. . . . It was his cook that he saw; or it was Mrs Gill, as I have seen her, making custards, in the heat of summer, in the cool dairy, with rose-trees and nasturtiums about the latticed window, preparing a cold collation for the rectors,—preserves and "dulcet creams"—puzzled "what choice to choose for delicacy best; what order so contrived as not to mix tastes, not well-joined, inelegant; but bring taste after taste, upheld with kindliest change."[36]

The charge, fairly leveled at Medina if not at Milton, is not helped by Medina's perfunctory use of the Miltonic vine motif. He picks up the marriage metaphor woven throughout the text, with the woven foliage that frames the bower behind the praying couple; but instead of an elm, he portrays a tree bearing apples, pears, or perhaps quinces. A vine indeed "spous'd about [the tree] twines / Her marriageable arms." But the image here suggests no more than marital fecundity—perhaps even no more than the fact that in seventeenth-century portraits, married couples were typically accompanied by such an emblem. In Medina's illustration, in any case, the emblem is shorn of its complex Miltonic associations: the dignity and importance of prelapsarian labor; the subtle mutual dependence of marriage; the crucial prior dependence of humankind upon their maker; the manifold significance, in short, of the angel's visit in the context both of Catullus's marriage legacy and the legacy of the Johannine Vine.

But Medina, after all, is Milton's first illustrator, undertaking the difficult task of deciding which events in a "visible and progressive action" are to be translated into a "visible and stationary" one. He seems to have been "intent" for the most part, like his Eve in her outdoor kitchen, on that literal and workmanlike problem. In any case he has shown us, often attentively and clearly, three stages in Milton's Edenic dinner party, leaving to other artists the task of discovering in visual terms just what it all might mean.

No one, on the other hand, has accused William Blake (1757–1827) of privileging literal narrative over symbolic meaning. Most would agree with Marcia Pointon's observation that, to an extent not typical of other illustrators of Milton, "Blake incorporated into his designs his own interpretations of the poem," applying an interpretive method consistently more "symbolic" than "representational." Blake was, she concludes, "concerned with the idea rather than the narrative."[37] In contrast to seventeenth-century artists like Medina— or indeed to others of his own century like Burney or Hayman—Blake was, as W. J. T. Mitchell has aptly put it, a visionary rather than a visualizer; a transformer rather than a translator.[38] Such an attitude toward his textual sources accounts for a number of distinctive features in Blake's compositions—features, moreover, with relevance to his (and Milton's) twentieth-century admirer Mary Groom. In traditional simultaneous narrative, Mitchell remarks, the "earliest event in the narrative could be placed in the foreground, and the later events could be placed in increasingly distant perspective planes." What better description, indeed, could be found of Medina's practice? Blake, however, "avoids this kind of illusionism in his designs. . . . As a rule, he concentrates on a few foreground images, often arranged symmetrically, to encourage an instantaneous grasp of the whole design rather than an impression of dramatic sequence."[39]

Behind Blake's different method lies his different theory of time, one which ran counter to the formulation implied in the classical and neoclassical doctrine of *ut pictura poesis*. According to this doctrine, as expressed by

theoreticians like Lessing, the sister arts provided "complementary representations of a dualistic world of space and time"—poetry representing space in
time (and who more sublimely than Milton!); the visual arts, on the contrary,
representing time in space. For Blake, however, says Mitchell, "the dualistic
world of . . . time and space, is an illusion which must not be imitated, but
which must be dispelled by the processes of his art" (Erdman, pp. 60–61).
Thus he seeks to show not sequence, as Medina had attempted to do, but the
whole at a glance, in the perspective of *kairos* as opposed to *chronos* time.
Blake's "mural-like tableaux," as Mitchell puts it,

embody the passage of time not as progression from the near to the distant, . . . but as a
movement from the near to the near. All moments in the sequence are immediate and
"immanent"; just as in the poetry, the prophet-narrator "present, past, & future *sees*"
as an eternal *now*. ("Blake's Composite Art," in Erdman, p. 68)

To portray such a view of time, what better venue than Paradise; what better
event than a meal with a visiting angel; what better symbol than the intrinsically sacramental and eschatological tree and vine?

What Medina has portrayed sequentially in four designs and twelve
vignettes, Blake has undertaken to portray in two versions of one symmetrical
and highly allusive design. Indeed, his design for Book V covers not only the
span of Raphael's visit, Books V through VIII, but also the entire epic—

> Of Man's First Disobedience, and the Fruit
> Of that Forbidden Tree, whose mortal taste
> Brought Death into the World, and all our woe,
> With loss of *Eden*, till one greater Man
> Restore us, and regain the blissful Seat.   (I, 1–5)

To accomplish his end of bringing "present, past, & future" into an "eternal
now," Blake portrayed different moments in the epic, exploring their capacity to represent the whole. Indeed, his two complete sets of *Paradise Lost*
illustrations—one executed in 1807, the other in 1808—often differ in precisely the eternal moment chosen for portrayal.

In his 1807 illustration of Raphael's visit, now in the Huntington Library
(fig. 3), he portrays, as Bette Charlene Werner has suggested, "the moment
when the issue of Adam and Eve's obedience is first raised" (*Blake's Vision*, p.
77). Adam and Eve sit side by side across an ornamental garden table from
their heavenly guest. The table is laden with Eve's "Tribute large" of fruit and
drink; and Raphael has completed his speculative discourse, inspired by the
meal, on the possible transubstantiation of human bodies into spirit (V, 493–
500). From Raphael's pointing gesture—to heaven on the one hand, to the
forbidden tree on the other—it is clear that Blake portrays the exact moment

when he raises the caveat: "*If* ye be found obedient, and retain / Unalterably firm his love entire / Whose progeny you are" (501–03; our italics). The warning arouses in turn a gesture of submission from Eve and one of astonishment from Adam. The Adam in Blake's design, indeed, seems just about to say,

> What meant that caution join'd, *if ye be found*
> *Obedient?* can we want obedience then
> To him, or possibly his love desert
> Who form'd us from the dust, and plac'd us here
> Full to the utmost measure of what bliss
> Human desires can seek or apprehend?   (513–18)

We will soon turn to the complex of eucharistic imagery more explicitly developed in Blake's 1808 version of this scene. But it is hard, in this earlier version, to miss in Adam's gesture a typological foretaste of the words of his twelve chosen progeny—spoken at a postlapsarian Supper instituted, by the one greater Man, to repair the ruins of this one: "Lord, is it I?" (Matt. xxvi, 22). And it is hard not to hear the moving, if ironic, words of Peter: "Though all *men* shall be offended because of thee, *yet* will *I* never be offended" (xxvi, 33).[40] That Supper of the true Vine, in a fusion of *chronos* and *kairos* so congenial to Blake's thought, is still millennia into the future from Adam's perspective; but in terms of Milton's Book III it is already past, in the Son's offer of atonement—and thus it is eternally present in the scene to which Blake calls our attention. Jesus makes one other comment at that Dinner to come—one that sheds light, perhaps, on Blake's 1808 revision of the dinner scene: "Woe to that man by whom the Son of man is betrayed!" (Mark xiv, 21). By whom, Blake seems to ask, does the offense of sin and disobedience come? And in answering that question in his later design, he greatly problematizes the epic's view of gender, as well as of sin and redemption.

Nothing is ever simple in Blake—if for no other reason than that every poetic and visual assertion implies, indeed requires, its "contrary." Thus critics have been half right when they have asserted that in moving Eve to the center of his design for Book V (fig. 4), Blake has underscored her role in the Fall, accentuating, as Werner puts it, "her involvement with Adam's temptation" (*Blake's Vision,* p. 78). But what needs to be taken into account is that as Blake gives central place to Eve's role in the Fall, he also gives central place to her typological role in redemption. In so doing he redefines Paradise; pulls the web of *chronos* and *kairos* even more tightly together; underscores the typological connection not only between Eve and Satan, but also between Eve and the Virgin; and doubles the impact of the vine imagery, newly highlighted throughout the design.

Fig. 3. William Blake, Raphael's Visit to Adam and Eve in Eden (*Paradise Lost*, Book V). 1807 version. Henry E. Huntington Library. Reproduced with permission.

Fig. 4. William Blake, Raphael's Visit to Adam and Eve in Eden (*Paradise Lost*, Book V). 1808 version. Boston Museum of Fine Arts (gift by subscription, 1890). Reproduced with permission.

First, Blake's Paradise, as pictured in both 1807 and 1808, differs radically from Medina's rolling Italianate "lantskip." As Mitchell has noted of Blake's landscapes in general, "Pictorial space does not exist as a uniform, visually perceived container of forms, but rather as a kind of extension of the consciousness of the human figures it contains" (*Blake's Composite Art,* p. 38). In both versions, that human perspective comes from within Adam and Eve's bower—looking out a perfectly clear but Gothically arched window, at the dazzling scene of Eden. Hills and waterfalls in the distance, along with other creatures Adam and Eve have addressed in their morning orison, suggest the richness of the creation:

> Fountains and yee, that warble, as ye flow,
> Melodious murmurs, warbling tune his praise.
> Join voices all ye living Souls; ye Birds,
> That singing up to Heaven Gate ascend,
> Bear on your wings and in your notes his praise;
> Yee that in Waters glide, and yee that walk
> The Earth, and stately tread, or lowly creep;
> Witness if I be silent, Morn or Even,
> To Hill, or Valley, Fountain, or fresh shade
> Made vocal by my Song, and taught his praise.
> Hail universal Lord, be bounteous still
> To give us only good.   (V, 195–206)

Images of goodness abound in both versions of the scene: a flock of sheep, an "unwieldy Elephant"; in 1807, a tiny hart longs for the water stream, while an amusingly repressed-looking lion lies down with the rams. But as in the Paradise of early Protestant bibles, there is also much ambiguous imagery: "aught of evil," as suggested at the end of our parents' prayer, is indeed concealed—in the snake wrapped around the fatal tree, which stands at the very center of both designs.

In the 1808 design Blake has chosen to portray a moment either earlier or later than the moment portrayed in that of 1807. As Werner suggests, Eve may be "preparing to betake herself to her fruits and flowers and to leave discussion, which has grown recondite, to Adam" (*Blake's Vision,* p. 76). In that case, Adam here raises his "studious" and "abstruse" question—one that can hardly have appealed to Blake any more than it does to Milton's Raphael—about the seeming "disproportion" of the noble bodies of heaven officiating light to "this Earth a spot, a grain" (VII, 17). Eve, in response to Adam's analytical impulse, is in that case just about to pre-enact her own tragic act of autonomy, which will lead directly, for Blake inevitably, to the Fall. In short, we are viewing the "two great Sexes [that] animate the world" (VIII, 151)[41]—about to begin the division that, for Blake at least, "brought Death . . . and all our woe." Blake, of course, portrays the Fall itself, the moment the fruit is taken, in his powerful illustration to Book IX—a design iconographically and structurally matched to this one. But he is always most interested in the eternal impulses underlying that symbolic act. And his thinking on the significance of gender to the Fall belongs to an important minority strain in Christian thought—a strain "in which it was maintained," as John Prest puts it, "that the damage was done when woman was taken out of the man and created, and that the division between the sexes was the very first example of scattering and corruption" (*The Garden of Eden,* p. 81).[42] Thus, if the moment portrayed is the moment of Eve's departure, she is indeed, by that very act, already on her way to her tragic encounter with the snake-entwined tree behind her head.

On the other hand, and perhaps more likely, the scene may depict the beginning of the dinner itself—in which "at Table *Eve* / Minister'd naked, and thir flowing cups / With pleasant liquors crown'd" (V, 443–45)—and over which the poet expostulates:

> O innocence
> Deserving Paradise! if ever, then,
> Then had the Sons of God excuse to have been
> Enamour'd at that sight; but in those hearts
> Love unlibidinous reign'd, nor jealousy
> Was understood, the injur'd Lover's Hell. (445–50)

In that case Adam invites Raphael to partake of the feast (V, 397–403); the angel responds with his discourse on spiritual communion; and humankind and angelic are about to share in a foretaste of that eternal banquet. The main text, in other words, points to the eschatological feast: the eternal marriage feast of the Lamb.

But Raphael knows the subtext of this Edenic banquet: the fact that these joyous and innocent notes, before they can return to joy, must turn to tragic. He has come, as Hideyuki Shetaka has noted, to teach Adam and Eve not just what they need to withstand the coming temptation—he knows they will not withstand it—but also what they will need to know to begin the long, hard process of redemption after the Fall.[43] As Gallagher argued, Raphael is the messenger of benign Providence, a type of the Son's *kenosis*—wrapping every image of impending tragedy in the garb of prevenient grace. Gallagher also defined Eve's role as Blake has carefully portrayed it here: the instrument of Adam's fall, perhaps, she is certainly nothing less than "the instrument of [his] regeneration" (*Milton, the Bible, and Misogyny,* p. 129). In the designs of some illustrators, notably Mary Groom, Eve's redemptive work is portrayed as in Milton's epic—through a variety of scenes.[44] In Blake's designs, in keeping with his symbolic rather than narrative approach, her role is portrayed mainly through a network of associations connecting her to the Virgin and to Christ.[45]

The main skein of images will lead us back to Milton's tree and vine. But other motifs also point to the pattern of fall and redemption woven through Blake's design. Palms and lilies frame the bower—calling to mind simultaneously the tree of life, the Son's suffering and triumph, and Gabriel's Annunciation to the Virgin: the *Ave* which will reverse Eve's sin, and which has here been previeniently spoken in Raphael's *Ave* to Eve. As McColley and others have observed, the gourd in Eve's hand has at least three traditional meanings; all are significant in the context of Blake's design. In addition to serving, like Eve herself, as a "vessel pure," it can represent (1) swelling pride and transitory happiness, or (2) a warning (as in Jonah's warning to Ninevah); but it is also (3) "the attribute of pilgrims, . . . including the Archangel Raphael . . . and Christ at Emmaus"—and as such a "prefiguration of regeneration as well as fall" ("Iconography," p. 117). For Blake, clearly, all three meanings apply: in Eve's innocent hand is the approach of impending loss, a warning of that approach, and the prefigured cup of redemption.[46]

With that cup, and with the bunch of grapes in Eve's other hand, we come to the crux of Blake's 1808 conception of the meal, a conception much sharpened and clarified from the 1807 version. Here Blake's garden furniture—a whimsical adaptation of the Chinese Gothic design popular in his time—has become far more explicitly Gothic, resembling the paneling in a church; the table behind Eve has come to resemble an altar.[47] Moreover, the trees overarching the bower are entwined not just with lilies, as in 1807, but with "fruitful vines"; and the backs of the bamboo chairs have been revised to bear stylized grape leaves, tendrils, and even large clusters of grapes. We have seen the topos of the vine as a symbol both of marriage and of Christ's unity with his disciples, ultimately to be expressed in the mystical marriage feast of the Lamb. We have also seen how Milton weaves the two topoi together, as artists using the iconography of Eden had traditionally done.[48] Blake here takes the Miltonic topos to the limits of its potential. Indeed, throughout his *Paradise Lost* illustrations, and in a number of his other works as well, Blake uses the vine as an image of Adam and Eve's Edenic unity.[49] He also, as in his *Pilgrim's Progress* designs, frequently uses the vine with the tree as an image of Christ crucified. To Blake, as Pamela Dunbar has observed, "the gadding vine" is an emblem "of Christ the Saviour" (*William Blake's Illustrations*, p. 69). In fact, as Blake wrote in *A Vision of the Last Judgement*, "All things are comprehended in their Eternal Forms in the divine body of the Saviour, the True Vine of Eternity."[50] In the foreground of

Blake's design, then, the vine represents, as for Milton, the very essence of Eden. If Adam and Eve remain obedient to God and connected to one another, they will be connected to the source of immortal Life—until "time may come when men / With Angels may participate" in the heavenly banquet (V, 493–94). But if, as Raphael knows they will, they separate themselves, they will also be entwined: by the death-dealing snake, parody of the living Vine, coiled about the forbidden tree in the midst of the garden.

Between 1807 and 1808, Blake moved the jarring image of tree and snake further back from the picture plane. But in both designs its centrality is unmistakable: it is the subject finally of Blake's design as of Milton's poem. Yet Blake manages the image in such a way as to make clear it in no way undercuts the image of the vine: as Satan seeks to bring evil out of good, so the Son—also "conceal'd" in the very same image—is already at work to bring "goodness infinite, goodness immense" (XII, 469) out of that impending tragedy. "The vine," says Mitchell, writing of Blake's *Book of Thel*, is "a pictorial and metaphoric relative of both the serpent and the worm, and it participates in the same world of symbolic ambivalence" (*Blake's Composite Art*, p. 105). But in condescending to involve himself in the maze of human error, Christ-the-Vine also returns redemptive ambiguity to the snake: "as Moses lifted up the serpent in the wilderness," says the Johannine Christ, "even so must the Son of man be lifted up: That whosoever believeth in him should not perish, but have eternal life" (John iii, 14–15; reference to Num. xxi, 4–9). Thus the snake coiled around the cross (an image Blake will use two more times in his *Paradise Lost* illustrations: at the Fall and at Adam's prophetic hearing of the Crucifixion) becomes an image of the Savior him-self—indeed of the Savior in the role Raphael has come to portray by his name: "Yahweh heals."[51] And, in a typology almost as old as Christianity, the thorny tree of the knowledge of good and evil becomes the cross of his redeeming death—the crushing of the divine wine that will reengraft all believing branches back onto the life-giving Vine. If death, then, must flow from the elements in Eve's hand, so too will eternal life: by her seed all will be born into the futility of fallen history (Romans viii, 20–23); by her Seed all who seek redemption will find their way back to the marriage feast Raphael has come both to share and to proclaim.

Now we must turn our attention to two artists whose eyes are doubly "other" from the text they sought to interpret: both read Milton in our own century (1935–1937); both, moreover, were women. As women, Carlotta Petrina and Mary Groom perforce read Milton to some extent from the margins of the patriarchal (which is *not* to say misogynic) structure within which the poet, for all his radicalism on religious and domestic issues, un-avoidably worked. Milton himself has been at pains to give Eve a human role and voice—defining marriage in terms of "fellowship" and meet conversa-tion, "rational delight." But he does so in a world, as Suzanne Hull has demonstrated, in which women—on all topics from theology to cooking—take instruction from men; a world in which a standard conduct book for women could be subtitled, "In three several discourses also are three es-peciall vertues, necessary to be incident in every vertuous woman, pithely discussed: namely obedience, chastitie, and *sylence*."[52] Milton then is writing in the context of a deep-seated cultural assumption that "women's discourse," as Herman Rapaport has put it, "is essentially different in kind from man's discourse, that it is at best a counterfeit that must be checked, restricted, and limited."[53] Thus, Margaret Homan's words on woman's condition resonate poignantly with the text of Raphael's visit to Adam and Eve: "There is a specifically gender-based alienation from language," she writes, "that is char-acterized by the special ambiguity of the woman's simultaneous participation in and exclusion from [the male] hegemonic group."[54] If Milton has included Eve in the dinner conversation as full and legitimate auditor—replacing the Genesis tradition in which Sarah merely *overhears* what "Chiefly . . . may concern her Faith to know, / The great deliverance by her Seed to come" (*PL* XII, 599–600); and if he has given Eve a dream to balance Adam's instruction in history by the archangel Michael, we are nonetheless forced to observe that most of Raphael's discourse is directed solely at Adam (as is indicated by the singular *thee* he uses, far more often than the plural *you*, throughout).

Moreover, as we have seen from the example of Medina, the liberating impulses in Milton's text often have been overlooked by the poem's illustra-tors, who have subtly returned our attention to its more traditional surface. Thus Medina, whatever his intention, turns Eve into the Brontes's cook; and Blake, from within his theory of mystical androgyny, suggests—as Milton is at pains to *avoid* suggesting—that apart from Adam she is not sufficient to stand. A number of recent critics have shown that Milton is not the "bogey"-haunted misogynist envisioned by such feminist readers as Sandra Gilbert, Susan Gubar, and Christine Froula;[55] but by the time he is read through the eyes of his male illustrators, he represents for the woman artist a kind of challenge not operative for the men who visualized his text in the first three centuries of the poem's life. Is it true, a woman artist might ask with Julia Kristeva, that Milton's language, indeed language itself, is "a male construct whose operation *depends* on women's silence and absence"?[56] If so, asks Mary Jacobus, "Can women adapt traditionally male-dominated modes of writing to the articulation of female . . . desire?" (qtd. in Heilbrun, p. 42). It may well be significant that the mode of their "writing" is in fact not narrative but visual and symbolic; in any event, Carlotta Petrina's answer to Jacobus's question would seem to be a sad, qualified yes, and Mary Groom's a triumphant one.

Carlotta Petrina (born Charlotte Kennedy in 1901 in Kingston, New York) studied in the late twenties and early thirties in New York City at the Art Students' League and the Cooper Union Art School, and in Paris at the Academie Colorossi and Grande Chaumière. During the late forties and early fifties, she exhibited at the Salon d'Automne in Paris, at the Art Institute of Chicago, and at the Pennsylvania Academy of Fine Arts; in 1952 she had a solo exhibition at La Finestra in Rome. In addition to *Paradise Lost* she has illustrated, among other works, *The Aeneid* and *Henry VI*.[57] Her twelve elegant *Paradise Lost* illustrations, one for each book, suggest two overlapping themes throughout: the immensity and *otherness* of the divine, juxtaposed with the often terrifying smallness of humanity.[58]

In her rendering of the dinner scene in Eden (fig. 5), there is no overt terror. But the relative scale of the three principals—Adam's form exactly echoing Raphael's great arm, Eve the crouch of the angel's great knees—alone suggests that this is no social occasion, where humankind and angel will "converse" as "friend with friend." Rather, Raphael appears to have come, saddened by the futility of his task, for only one purpose: to warn Adam and Eve of their destroyer's presence, and so to fulfill "All Justice" (V, 247). At the moment portrayed, he seems about to begin his "Sad task and hard"; for how, he asks, can he relate

> To human sense th' invisible exploits
> Of warring Spirits; how without remorse
> The ruin of so many glorious once
> And perfet while they stood; how last unfold
> The secrets of another World, perhaps
> Not lawful to reveal?   (V, 564–70)

The tone of Petrina's illustration, unlike Milton's version of Raphael's story, is one of unrelieved sadness. As Lloyd Dickson has observed, in Petrina's dinner scene, the "couple's tender smiles and adoring glances [pictured, though still rather somberly, in her illustration to Book IV] are supplanted by an almost sullen, pensive mien" ("Against the Wiles of the Devil," p. 174).

Indeed the whole scene, the stylized lushness of Eden notwithstanding, has reduced the tensions of Milton's text to a single brooding mood. Paradise, here, is shrunk as by a zoom lens to a decorative pattern of flowers; the typological elm reduced—in keeping with a visual tradition seen in Edward Burney's 1799 designs—to a tree stump, which serves as a table for the

Fig. 5. Carlotta Petrina, Raphael's Visit to Adam and Eve in Eden (Book V).
From John Milton, *Paradise Lost,* illus. Carlotta Petrina (New York: Limited
Editions Club, 1936). Reproduced with permission from the William An-
drews Clark Memorial Library, University of California.

preparation of the meal. Unlike both Medina and Blake, Petrina does not seem to be interested in portraying a particular moment, that "last" picture in Lessing's gallery that is a key to the meaning of the narrative. For although the angel has apparently long since arrived, and is about to embark on the main burden of his discourse, Adam and Eve nonetheless still seem to be engaged in the final preparation of the meal. The feeling of the scene, then, is neither narrative nor quite symbolic: the best term for its images, one appropriate for Groom as well, might be *mythic*.

What, then, is the mythos Petrina has sought to convey? Perhaps we can begin to answer that question by looking at some parts of the Miltonic myth she has chosen *not* to include, even by allusion, in her design. Certainly the sense—so vividly portrayed by biblical illustrators, by Milton and by Blake— that Paradise is the arena of significant action, where we are sufficient to stand, free to fall, and offered a crucial choice, is absent from Petrina's design. Also far from the scene are Adam and Eve's joyous morning prayer; their meaningful labor; their wonder at the sight of the angel's approach; Eve's exuberant "hospitable intent"; their mutual falling to "thir viands . . . with keen dispatch / Of real hunger" (V, 434–37); Raphael's discourse on the "concoctive heat" by which, as he converts human food to angelic nourishment, human beings may one day find the food of Paradise "No inconvenient Diet." Gone, even, for what it is worth, is the one much-cited instance of Miltonic humor: "No fear lest Dinner cool" (396). Adam and Eve, as they present their gifts to the angel, look as somber as—and indeed iconographically similar to—doomed natives of another lost paradise, about to encounter the fair-haired god Cortez and his genocidal throng in a Diego Rivera mural.[59] The comparison is startling; yet in our own decade as we look back on Petrina's time, this bleak representation of the Renaissance seriously contends with that of the vexed, but ultimately positive, representation embodied in Milton's poem. Petrina, like every artist, responds to her own century as much as to the poet's, and the lens she has chosen is a very dark one. It is a lens, in fact, that seems to deny that very choice of vision.

Here we find the irony of Carlotta Petrina. For in some ways she has produced a feminist re-reading of Milton's epic. She has removed from the scene a great deal of its residual sexism—as we have seen it to some extent in the poem, to a greater extent in some of its illustrations. Adam here, in defiance of Milton's text, helps Eve with dinner: *they* have been engaged in the process of bringing "from each bough and brake" the bounties of Eden. Moreover, in the vine, which Eve weaves about the table—and in the grapes Raphael holds, as if to dispense, or at least to ponder them—Petrina makes an allusion to the Eucharist shorn of the classical context that would make Adam an elm and Eve a vine. Here, if anything, they are both, and equally, branches: in Petrina's Edenic church, there seems to be no particular male priestly role. The problem is, where is the Vine to whom they can connect? And, just as importantly, does either of them appear "Sufficient to have stood, though free to fall" (III, 99)? The angel's brooding sorrow seems to suggest absolute resignation before their fate; the pose of their small stiff bodies seems to suggest humility, but also primitive, propitiary dread. It is not that woman is *other* here; that she is on the margin: it is that *humankind,* male and female—*man,* as Petrina herself would say—is diminished, alienated, and marginalized by the terrifying wash of fallen history about to happen, both to Adam and Eve (in Petrina's terrifying Expulsion) and to Europe (in Petrina's terrifying time).

The good news in Petrina's design is that Adam here has no "despotic" power over Eve; the sorrowful news is that no one, not even the enormous but languid angel, seems to have any power to stay the tragedy about to befall them. Only God—the frightening Patriarch Petrina shows in her illustration to the next book: bearing down like a Mussolini, in his Chariot of Paternal Deity—offers the possibility that anyone is in charge.[60] And he is not, like Milton's or Blake's compassionate Word of God, a figure with whom we can identify: neither Adam nor Eve (thank heaven) bears the godlike stamp of his image; rather their bearing suggests a humankind defined primarily as victim—*both* of them silenced, checked, restricted, limited. All these hosts can do is serve an innocent last supper on the threshold of the apocalypse.

Mary Groom (1903–1958) produced her twenty-nine *Paradise Lost* illustrations at about the same time as Petrina executed her set of twelve. But their effect, and the reading of Milton's epic they convey, could not possibly be more different. Groom was born in Essex in 1903, was active as a wood-engraver in the twenties and thirties, and retired from the art form considerably before her death in 1958. She was educated in London—at the Slade School of Art, the Royal College of Art, and at the Brook Green School, under the tutelage of Leon Underwood. A member of a distinguished circle of artists, which included Henry Moore among others, Groom illustrated not only *Paradise Lost* but also *Roses of Sharon,* a selection of Old Testament poems. As the title suggests, one of those poems was the Song of Songs.[61]

That biblical poem became the source of some of Groom's innovations in the tradition we have been following. But the mythic synthesis Groom makes is always her own. Her faithful and witty reading of Milton's Paradise continually shows her deep attentiveness to the text; at the same time, in the poet's own "advent'rous" spirit of revision and innovation, she also delves beneath its patriarchal surface to find its deep structure of feminine consciousness. Her vision, at once humanist and feminist, takes us into what Stevie Davies has called the womb of Milton's cosmos—a cosmos which, in stark contrast to Petrina's, reflects a gentle, kenotic, and androgynous Godhead, and which supports a strong, mutually supportive humanity.[62] At last (because with Milton she must turn her notes to tragic) Groom also expels us onto the subjected plain of fallen history. But first she shows us clearly the role of the feminine in repairing the ruins wrought by a patriarchal satanic consciousness (a kind of consciousness, she suggests, to which we all, men and women, are too easily inclined). And in the end she shows us an Expulsion uniquely attuned to Milton's redemptive and reconciling vision: though driven forward by the "flaming brands" of angelic anger, our first parents walk hand in hand, with a restored harmony born of mutual responsibility and love.

Groom represents Raphael's visit to Eden in two images. In the first, the angel greets our first parents—who in contrast to Milton's text and to Medina's distortion of it—stand side by side before him. Both, Groom visually insists, are "Godlike," of "nobler shape erect and tall"; and in both "thir looks Divine / The image of thir glorious Maker" shines (IV, 288–92). Both, in contrast to Petrina's couple, "in naked Majesty [seem] Lords of all" (290); both greet the angel visitor and both, not just Eve, are hailed in his Annunciationlike gesture as the parents of humankind. Here, as at so many points in her interpretation of the poem, Groom follows Milton *actively:* finding and portraying the liberating implications in his text—as he has found and emphasized them in his own sources, ranging from Genesis to Catullus to Paul. Groom's second illustration of Raphael's visit (fig. 6), that of the dinner party itself, is one of the most delightful and innovative of all her self-consciously "primitive," white-on-black designs. It eloquently demonstrates Catherine Belsey's comment that "if *Paradise Lost* is not a feminist text . . . it can still . . . be read on behalf of feminism."[63] One could also add that if it is not a multicultural text, it can be read, through the eyes of an artist like Mary Groom, on behalf of multiculturalism. A number of sources and many conscious aesthetic decisions have contributed to Groom's re-vision of the scene.

Groom apparently admired Blake as much as she admired Milton.[64] In any case, she has turned, in constructing her own mythic paradise, to the triangular structure of his 1808 design. She also has followed him in interpreting the scene as a eucharist, a love feast—taking the idea even further, or at least in different directions. The table itself at which Adam and Eve sit has evolved from Blake's in two opposite, but complementary, ways. On the one hand, she brings his elaborate and elegant garden furniture back toward Milton's original: "Rais'd of grassy turf / Thir Table was, and mossy seats had round" (V, 391–92). On the other hand—as if unfallen nature herself produced the impulse and the mode, as well as the elements, for sacramental worship—that grassy table here rears itself up in the form of a perfect, albeit reformed, communion table. The table comes complete with a leafy altar-

Oreshades; for these mid-hours, till Eevning rise
I have at will. So to the Silvan Lodge
They came, that like Pomona's Arbour smil'd
With flourets deck't and fragrant smells; but Eve
Undeckt, save with her self more lovely fair
Then Wood-Nymph, or the fairest Goddess feign'd
Of three that in Mount Ida naked strove,
Stood to entertain her guest from Heav'n; no vaile
Shee needed, Vertue-proof, no thought infirme
Alterd her cheek. On whom the Angel Haile
Bestowd, the holy salutation us'd
Long after to blest Marie, second Eve.
HAILE Mother of Mankind, whose fruitful Womb
Shall fill the World more numerous with thy Sons
Then with these various fruits the Trees of God
Have heap'd this Table. Rais'd of grassie terf
Thir Table was, and mossie seats had round,

148

Fig. 6. Mary Elizabeth Groom, "Rais'd of grassie terf / Thir Table was" (illustration to Book V). From John Milton, *Paradise Lost,* illus. Mary Groom (London: Golden Cockerel Press, 1937). Reproduced here with permission from the William Andrews Clark Memorial Library, University of California.

cloth, and behind it Raphael, not Eve, ministers—functioning like a reformed Anglican priest.[65]

One way of looking at Renaissance iconography, upon which both Blake and Groom have clearly drawn for their dinner parties, is of course to ask who is at the apex of the triangle, and why. On the one hand, Blake's centralized design (1808)—with Eve at the apex, between Adam and the angel guest—gives Eve tremendous dramatic power. But as we have seen, innocent though Eve is in this scene, her position is at least partly, and potentially, a "bad eminence" (compare Milton's remark on the enthroned Satan, II, 6).[66] And her central position, though it exalts her—puts her, like the Virgin she prefigures, on a pedestal—in so doing it also isolates her, makes her "the other," while Adam and Raphael are compositionally turned into fellows, if not exactly equals. For Groom, as for Petrina, the angel, not Eve, is the other—although for Groom he is far closer to, and thus more capable of intercourse with, the human creatures he has come to bless: different, as Milton's Raphael has put it, "in degree, of kind the same." Adam and Eve are also, in another sense, both one with, and separate from, each other—in a mutual otherness that does not, as it does for Blake, threaten disaster. (It is no doubt significant that in twenty-nine designs, Groom did not produce one showing the Book IX separation scene.) Indeed, as Groom shows repeatedly elsewhere, it is Adam and Eve's individual strength that paradoxically makes relation, I and Thou, a possibility; for, as Adam recalls telling the Father, "Among unequals what society / Can sort, what harmony or true delight?" (VIII, 383–84). Groom's composition, moreover, harks back beyond Blake, to other models that shed interesting light on her design—specifically two common religious images: typified by Rembrandt's *The Supper at Emmaus* and Raphael's *The Marriage of the Virgin*.

The story of the Emmaus supper is told in the Gospel of Luke (xxiv, 13–32). The risen Lord, on the road to Emmaus, is constrained by two travelers who do not recognize him to stay with them for supper. As they sit at table, however, they suddenly grasp his identity at the very moment he breaks the bread. As in Milton's dinner scene, food has become the vehicle to a whole new level of spiritual understanding. In Rembrandt's very typical rendering of the narrative (1648; now in the Louvre), the three figures make a triangular composition, as in Groom's design. The risen Christ, with light rising from his head in rays not unlike the stars over the head of Groom's Raphael, is about to break the bread that will suddenly reveal his identity to the disciples seated to either side of him—one slightly higher, one slightly lower, as in her composition. There the resemblance between the two works ends, and there may well be an *Emmaus* closer to Groom's dinner scene. But the resemblances are striking enough to suggest that the iconography of Emmaus, with its connota-

tions of eucharistic mystery, was at least in the back of her mind, as it probably was in Milton's. Some of the fruit on Groom's table also underscores
the eucharistic theme. Of the cherries, for instance—one of which Raphael
plucks from a bunch and holds out toward Eve—Mirella D'Ancona writes,
"On account of its red color and juice, the cherry suggested the blood of the
Redeemer. Therefore this fruit was often depicted with a eucharistic con-
notation, especially in the scenes of the Last Supper, and The Supper at
Emmaus."[67] Thus, by a complex iconographic allusion, Groom makes Raphael a type of Christ—his divine condescension to be the guest of two
prelapsarian mortals foreshadowing the *kenosis* of the "Heav'nly stranger"
who will give himself as the host.

Along with eucharistic symbolism, Groom has also used iconographic
allusion to underscore the design's other great theme: that of prelapsarian
marriage. Here the visual analogue, in this case quite possibly the source, is
Raphael's *Marriage of the Virgin* (1504; now in the Brera Gallery, Milan).
And here again, we find a triangular composition—in this case with the center
position occupied by the officiating priest, standing between Mary and Joseph. In spite of the conscious "primitivism" of Groom's style, the composi-
tional similarities are striking: the curve of the Virgin's clothed shoulders
matches the curve of Eve's nude ones; Raphael wears a surplice like that of
the priest, only made of stars; Adam's hair and gesture very closely match
those of St. Joseph. On one level such borrowing is a fine example of Groom's
sometimes almost waggish wit; but the quotation also makes an important
typological point: not only does Eve prefigure the Virgin; Adam likewise prefigures Christ—as their marriage prefigures that second heaven-instigated
marriage to come. For Groom the Fall does not inevitably come by Eve, as
Blake suggests it does. Woman, in Groom's representation of Milton's epic,
bears no particular burden or particular blessing by virtue of being woman,
but is rather simply one of two kinds of equally strong and responsible human
beings. Each of us, like each of our first parents, is responsible for his/her
own choice—a point Groom underscores by being one of the few Milton
illustrators to portray, as he does, two separate falls. Thus a couple, not just
the Virgin, is necessary to symbolize their coming redemption, as Raphael
has hailed a couple in Groom's previous illustration.

In keeping with Groom's emphasis, both feminist and humanist, on
Adam and Eve's equality and individual sufficiency to stand, it is perhaps not
too surprising that she does not use the image of the vine in her design.
Rather, she finds her own mythic structure, though one perfectly faithful to
Milton, to express the way the marriage topos and that of the eucharist come
together in Paradise. Her Adam and Eve are too strong to be satisfactorily
pictured as either branches or vines. But she is as interested as any illustrator

before her in suggesting Milton's Edenic theme: the loving mutuality of the bond between man and woman, between both and God, and the perfection of that bond to come at the Lamb's marriage. She finds her source not in Catullus's epithalamia (although she illustrated classical narratives and probably knew them), but in the great biblical epithalamion: The Song of Songs. A pastoral love song taking place in a lily-strewn *hortus conclusus*, its typological connections to prelapsarian Eden are irresistible. The bride is awakened under an apple tree, where her mother—in Adam and Eve's case the earth herself—has brought her forth (viii, 5). Her passionately sensuous, mutual love with her groom, moreover, not only renovates the tree but explicitly reverses the curse laid on Eve at the Fall: "Thy desire shall be to thy husband, and he shall rule over thee" (Gen. iii, 16) gives way to the lines of the Song: "I am my beloved's, and *his* desire is toward *me*" (vii, 10; our italics). In the Song, in short, a symmetrical reciprocity—in which two equal partners are ravished by their desire for one another—replaces the somewhat lopsided reciprocity in which the bride is called to cling like a vine to her elm.

In Christian typology, of course, the restoration of that perfect reciprocity in love—the recovery, in short, of innocence—is to be brought about by another Bride, prefigured by the bride in the Song. Typologically, she images both the Virgin and Christ's bride the Church; for both, in loving reciprocity with the passionate *kenotic* Godhead, give birth to the Seed who reverses the curse set into motion by the Fall. Thus, for instance, in Fra Angelico's *Cortona Annunciation,* the archangel Gabriel gives his "Haile" (as in the text under Groom's illustration) to the Virgin in the foreground—while in the background, behind the Virgin's little fenced *hortus conclusus*, the archangel Michael drives the grieving Adam and Eve from Paradise. Pre-Fall and post-Fall, the garden is the psychological locus of God's most intimate connection to humankind, begetting and conceiving new life in joyous mutual love. Thus the Song fully embodies—in the love longing and lovemaking of the bride and groom, both literal and figurative—the idea of both Catullus's vine and the Johannine vine, shorn completely of their hierarchical implications. As Francis Landy has pointed out, "the germinal paradox of the Song is the union of two people through love." In the garden of their connectedness, the fluid play of extravagant metaphor "permits the interchange of identity" between two equal lovers; "authoritative patriarchal society" is replaced, in fact *reversed,* by one in which through love "all the fragments of the world cohere, and are granted significance, in a single vision."[68] The Song is, finally, the bible's own great gloss on the idea of Paradise.

Groom has attended in her design not only to this overarching pattern and meaning of the Song, but to a number of its visually suggestive images as well—using them, as is continually her wont, to both humorous and joyously serious effect. First, she has refigured Eden itself as a *hortus conclusus,* bringing the viewer right up into an almost womblike space. (This effect is much heightened in her illustration of Book IV, where Adam and Eve enjoy "thir Supper Fruits" on "the downy Bank" of the "brimming stream . . . damaskt with flow'rs" [IV, 331, 334].) And having done so, she here brings us to the banquet scene of the Song, appropriately a marriage feast: "He brought me to the banqueting house, and his banner over me *was* love. . . . I sat down under his shadow with great delight, and his fruit *was* sweet to my taste" (ii, 3–4). On at least two levels here, Groom's Adam and Eve "taste" love. Their own love, their constant banquet, is "better than wine"; and they gaze at one another with glances that say, "Thou hast ravished my heart, my sister, *my* spouse"; "Thou *art* all fair, my love; there is no spot in thee" (iv, 9, 7); "Behold, thou *art* fair; thou hast dove's eyes"; "Behold thou *art* fair, my beloved, yea pleasant; also our bed *is* green" (i, 15–16). At the same time, they share with the angel in a love that suggests the interanimation of the Trinity. The angel, like Adam, gazes lovingly at Eve—but Milton has re-marked on the wonder that "in those hearts / Love *unlibidinous* reign'd" (V, 449; our italics). Rather, the human and angelic trinity feasts on the love that "by tract of time" will have the power to lead them directly to the banquet of heaven—"*if* [they] be found obedient." Yet it is significant that for Groom here, the point is not the warning, but the loveliness of what was, and of what is to be again. Of all Milton's illustrators, she has been most attentive not just to the tensions, but to the innocent joys of his paradise.

In that spirit of innocent, sensuous joy, Groom also has some visual fun with her text—sexy visual fun at that, as if, with Milton, she were challenging us to imagine love as a "Perpetual Fountain of Domestic sweets" (IV, 760; compare Song iv, 15), completely free of our fallen associations. In that spirit, she puns on Adam and Eve's appearance in terms of the lovers' extravagant imagery in the Song. "This thy stature is like to a palm tree," the groom says to the bride (vii, 7); Eve sits before a palm tree (symbol of both fecundity and eternal life)—as if serving as muse for Adam's inspired simile. "Thy breasts," his thought goes on, are "like two young roes that are twins, which feed among the lilies" (iv, 5). And Eve's breasts *are:* the tilt of the head of the fawn in front of her, is exactly the tilt of her sensuously-pictured right breast. (The strawberry, by the way, which she offers, whether to Adam or Raphael, is a classical symbol both of perfect innocence and of Paradise itself [D'Ancona, *The Garden of the Renaissance,* p. 365]).

Groom uses the iconography of the Song in one more very important, very attentive way. If the Song, as Landy has suggested, is about the overcom-ing of otherness—whether the otherness of gender or the otherness between humankind and the Godhead—it can also be used to expand the meanings of Milton's poem by inviting more readers to the feast. As Petrina has used the image of people of color to suggest the victimization of all human beings by history, Groom uses the description of the bride and groom in the Song to suggest the possibility of mutuality—between strong and empowered people of all races: "I *am* black, but comely, O ye daughters of Jerusalem" (i, 5), says the bride, who also says of her groom, "My beloved *is* white and ruddy" (v, 10). White on black engraving, of course, makes all Groom's figures literally black by definition. However, in most of her illustrations, Eve does not look ethnically "other": here she does, while Adam does not. This Eve calls up images, indeed, of goddess figures such as the Black Madonna. Hundreds of such images are to be found throughout Western Europe, which by their very existence call into question the hegemony of monolithic patriarchal Christianity. They combine all the redemptive associations of the Virgin Mary with more deeply rooted matriarchal values, connected with the earth and with female generativity.[69] Groom and her associates were also much interested in the study of "primitive" masks and figures, including those from the South Seas. Here Raphael indeed looks like a gentle Polynesian deity, Raphael-the-healer (healer, ultimately, of all our human divisions) as medicine man. Groom's use of such figures works very much in tandem with her view of the Godhead elsewhere in the poem: the redemptive Christian myth, she suggests, need not be the exclusive preserve of men, of Europeans, or even of orthodox patriarchal theology, expressed in androcentric language. There is in the Song, in Pentecost, in the mystical experience of love, a *glossolalia* (not unrelated to the word *gloss*, as to a text) by which each of us can hear (or at least *see*) the Word of God in our "own language" (Acts ii, 6).

This unity in diversity—in which the other is not silenced, checked, restricted, or limited—is for Groom what Milton's dinner scene in Eden is all about. She suggests that we need not choose between our gender or ethnicity and our humanity; between language and desire; between our dependence on a higher power and our autonomy and responsibility; between Toni Morrison, perhaps, and John Milton.[70] Milton's gift of Paradise is not a static gift. It partakes of its time, both borrowing from and correcting complex traditions from the past—pointing the way to "true filial freedom" and unity, while never freeing itself completely from its temporal biases. Each generation of Milton illustrators has done the same, by its own best lights: sometimes setting the poem back through overliteral interpretation, more often simply by not being attentive enough; sometimes immeasurably advancing our understanding of the poem's manifold implications. Our century has its biases too; more dangerously it has been distinctly short of vision—especially visions of Paradise. And without such vision, the prophet says, the people perish. If the lamp of the body is the eye (Matt. vi, 22), we could do worse as Miltonists than to attend to his Paradise as mediated by three centuries of visual artists.

Whittier College
University of Southern California

NOTES

Photographs of the Medina, Petrina, and Groom designs were made by the William Andrews Clark Memorial Library, University of California.

1. Jonathan Richardson, from *Explanatory Notes and Remarks on Milton's Paradise Lost by J. Richardson, Father and Son, With the LIFE of the AUTHOR, and a Discourse on the POEM by J.R. Sen.* (London, 1734), p. 40. William Blake in a letter to the Reverend Dr. Trusler, August 23, 1799, in David V. Erdman, ed., *The Complete Poetry and Prose of William Blake*, rev. ed. (Garden City, N.J., 1982), p. 702.

2. See Joseph Wittreich's indispensable overview of Milton illustration in *A Milton Encyclopedia*, ed. William B. Hunter Jr. et al. (Lewisburg, Pa., 1978), vol. 4, pp. 55–78.

3. End note to the Golden Cockerel edition of *Paradise Lost* (London, 1937).

4. John Henry Nash's edition of *Paradise Lost* was published for the Limited Editions Club of San Francisco, with plates by Carlotta Petrina, in 1936. However, Groom had already shown five of her illustrations at an exhibition of the English Wood Engraving Society in 1935. Thus, though Milton's first (and two important) women illustrators are virtually contemporaneous, Groom seems to have been the first to be seen by the public—albeit, to this day, a small one.

5. From the files of press cuttings about the Golden Cockerel Press—owned, and graciously shared, by Roderick Cave of the Victoria University of Wellington, New Zealand. The questions raised by Humbert Wolfe in the thirties seem almost to anticipate the diversity of criticism in the nineties. As a recent critic observes, "theoretical horizons shaped, for example, by class, ethnicity, nationality, sexual orientation, and gender" have made it possible "to look at canonical works with different eyes." See *Visual Culture: Images and Interpretations,* ed. Norman Bryson, Michael Anne Holly, and Keith Moxey (Hanover, N.H., 1994), pp. xv–xvi. For a useful overview of "otherness" as theoretical construct, see Mark C. Taylor, *Altarity* (Chicago, 1987). "Although it recurs throughout the century," Taylor notes, "concern with differentness and otherness is a distinguishing trait of thinkers who can be described as 'postmodern' " (pp. xxi–xxii).

6. *Explanatory Notes . . . ,* in *The Early Lives of Milton,* ed. Helen Darbishire (London, 1932), p. 328. See also Leslie E. Moore, *Beautiful Sublime: The Making of Paradise Lost, 1701–1734* (Stanford, 1990), p. 103.

7. W. B. Ronnfeldt, ed. *The Laocoön, and Other Prose Writings of Lessing* (London, 1895), pp. 20, 83, 89. For an analysis of Lessing's historic "space"-"time" distinction in the arts, and comments by later critics, see W. J. T. Mitchell, *Iconology: Image, Text, Ideology* (Chicago, 1986), pp. 95–115.

8. Wittreich, *Milton Encyclopedia*, p. 56.

9. *Paradise Lost* V, 221–22, 230, 29. This citation and all references to Milton's poetry are from *John Milton: Complete Poems and Major Prose,* ed. Merritt Y. Hughes (Indianapolis, 1957).

10. John Gere, preface to an exhibition of a book dedicated by Henry Moore to W. H. Auden, published for the trustees of the British Museum (London, 1974), n.p.

11. See John Dixon Hunt, "Milton and the Making of the English Landscape Garden," in *Milton Studies* XV, ed. James D. Simmonds (Pittsburgh, 1981), pp. 81–105; Charlotte F. Otten, "'My Native Element,': Milton's Paradise and English Gardens," in *Milton Studies* V, ed. James D. Simmonds (Pittsburgh, 1973), pp. 249–67; and John Prest, *The Garden of Eden: The Botanic Garden and the Re-Creation of Paradise* (New Haven, 1981). Also very helpful on Edenic iconography are Roland Mushat Frye, *Milton's Imagery and the Visual Arts: Iconographic Tradition in the Epic Poems* (Princeton, 1978), pp. 218–55; Diane K. McColley, "The Iconography of Eden," in *Milton Studies* XXIV, ed. James D. Simmonds (1988), pp. 107–21; and *A Gust for Paradise: Milton's Eden and the Visual Arts* (Urbana, 1993), esp. chaps. 2 and 3.

12. Reproduced in Frye, *Milton's Imagery*, illus. 168.

13. We differ with Frye (ibid.), who suggests that Adam is picking fruit in the scene while Eve is picking a flower (p. 240), and with Diane Kelsey McColley, *Milton's Eve* (Urbana, 1983), who proposes that Eve is picking a strawberry, in an act simultaneously symbolic of innocence and lust (p. 5).

14. Gen. xviii, 1 (KJV). The contrast between Adam's bower and Abraham's tent, however, already reveals the difference between a prelapsarian and postlapsarian encounter with the divine. For "dwelling in tents" indicates, throughout the bible, the wilderness journey that is human history after the Fall. The tension of tent dwelling is summed up poignantly by the writer of Hebrews: "For here we have no continuing city, but we seek one to come" (xiii, 14). See Jason P. Rosenblatt's comparison of Raphael's visit and the visit of the angels to Abraham at Mam're in "Celestial Entertainment in Eden: Book V of *Paradise Lost*," *Harvard Theological Review* 62 (1969): 411–27.

15. The italics are found in the original text, as they are throughout unless otherwise noted.

16. Clearly Eve's excuse for leaving the discussion—that "such pleasure [of hearing 'studious thoughts abstruse'] she reserv'd, / *Adam* relating, she sole Auditress; / Her Husband the Relater she preferr'd"—echoes uncomfortably one of St. Paul's most retrograde commands, one he often implicitly disavows elsewhere: "Let your women keep silence in the churches. . . . And if they will learn any thing, let them ask their husbands at home" (1 Cor. xiv, 34–35). But Milton, whatever our difficulty with the image of Eve receiving kisses along with her instruction (VIII, 55–57), has at least tried to allay with tenderness and with Eve's volition the harshness of the apostle's word for postlapsarian women: that it is "a shame for them to speak" publicly and that "*they are commanded* to be under obedience" (xiv, 35, 34). Eve, in contrast, may be quiet but is clearly free to speak; is obedient, but under no one's command.

17. John R. Knott Jr., "The Visit of Raphael: *Paradise Lost*, Book V," *PQ* 47 (Jan. 1968): 36–42. This suggestion has considerable appeal, at least as a secondary strain, since even though this epic meal excludes women altogether, the visit reaffirms the crucial role of Aeneas's fated marriage to Lavinia—and of the "seed" of that marriage, which will be nothing less than the whole of Roman history.

18. Beverley Sherry, "'Not by Bread Alone': The Communication of Adam and Raphael," *MQ* 13, no. 3 (Oct. 1979): 111–14. One could argue indeed—and Mary Groom seems to suggest allusively in her illustrations—that Tobit, of all biblical books, most perfectly underlies and parallels Milton's divinely comic view of Providence throughout the epic. Wendy Furman has argued this point in part in two essays: "'With Dreadful Faces Throng'd and fiery Arms': Apocalyptic '*Synchronisme*' in Three Illustrations of *Paradise Lost*," *Coranto* 25 (1990): 29–31; and "'Consider first, that Great / Or Bright infers not Excellence': Mapping the Feminine in Mary Groom's Miltonic Cosmos," in *Milton Studies* XXVIII, *Riven Unities: Authority and Experience, Self and Other in Milton's Poetry*, Wendy Furman, Christopher Grose, and William Shullenberger, guest editors (Pittsburgh, 1992), pp. 121–62.

19. See Thomas A. Copeland, "Raphael, the Angelic Virtue," *MQ* 24 (Dec. 1990): 117–28,

and Hideyuki Shitaka, "'Them thus employed Beheld / With pity heav'n's high king': God's Dispatch of Raphael in *Paradise Lost*, Book 5.219–47," in the same issue, 128–36.

20. Philip Gallagher, *Milton, the Bible, and Misogyny*, ed. Eugene Cunnar and Gail L. Mortimer (Columbia, Mo., 1990), pp. 148, 150.

21. See Thomas B. Stroup, *Religious Rite and Ceremony in Milton's Poetry* (Lexington, 1968), pp. 30–34. Anthony Low, "Angels and Food in *Paradise Lost*," *MQ* 3 (1969): 135, equivocates a bit more, calling the meal a "solemnity," though not a "sacrament." More recently, Marshall Grossman, *"Authors to Themselves": Milton and the Revelation of History* (Cambridge, 1987), pp. 102–11, has made a very useful analysis of Milton's theology of transubstantiation, arguing that the Protestant poet's view of the mystery is essentially the reverse of Roman Catholic theology on the subject. For Milton, Grossman argues, "Raphael's doctrine of transubstantiation through refinement contrasts with [the] negative transubstantiation that sacrifices spiritual truth to a trivial, material sign"; rather, the "transformation of experience into love and love into faith is . . . the true miracle of transubstantiation" (pp. 110–11). Frye, *Milton's Imagery*, illus. 116, demonstrates the traditional eucharistic interpretation of the Genesis, chapter xviii, scene with a sixth-century mosaic in San Vitale, Ravenna. As Sarah watches from the door of her tabernacle-tent, Abraham offers a pascal lamb to the three haloed guests, each of whom has already been presented with a eucharistic loaf from Sarah's hearth. The reference is made explicit by the juxtaposed typological scene to the right: Abraham about to slay Isaac.

22. Amos Funkenstein, *Theology and the Scientific Imagination from the Middle Ages to the Seventeenth Century* (Princeton, 1986), pp. 5–6.

23. Joseph Summers, *The Muse's Method: An Introduction to "Paradise Lost"* (Cambridge, Mass., 1962; rpt. Binghamton, N.Y., 1981), p. 23.

24. The words of both Gadamer and Bann are quoted from Stephen Bann, *The True Vine: On Visual Representation and the Western Tradition* (Cambridge, 1989), p. 7.

25. Text of the poems from *High Wedlock Then Be Honoured: Wedding Poems from Nineteen Countries and Twenty-Five Centuries*, ed. Virginia Tufte (New York, 1970), pp. 30, 22.

26. Wheeler cited by Peter Demetz, "The Elm and the Vine: Notes Toward the History of a Marriage Topos," *PMLA* 73 (1958): 521–32.

27. Many examples of the topos appear in marriage portraits of the seventeenth century—for example, in a painting by Franz Hals of Isaac Massa and Beatrix van der Laen, ca. 1616, now in the Rijksmuseum, Amsterdam. It is reproduced by David Smith in his *Masks of Wedlock: Seventeenth-Century Dutch Marriage Portraiture* (Ann Arbor, 1982), plate 64. Commenting on the portrait, Smith makes a point of some relevance to Milton: "In mingling marital with romantic love, Rubens and Hals created a theme that was well suited to the middle-class, family-centered culture of the seventeenth-century Netherlands" (p. 154).

28. Peter Brown explores early Christian attitudes toward sex and marriage in *The Body and Society: Men, Women, and Sexual Renunciation in Early Christianity* (New York, 1988), making connections throughout between the renunciation of marriage and the radical redistribution of wealth.

29. The connection between John, chapter xv, and the sacrament was often made explicit in Italian art of the Renaissance. Two excellent examples are Masaccio's *Madonna and Child* and Botticelli's *Chigi Madonna* (both in the Uffizi Gallery, Florence)—in which the child either blesses (Botticelli) or munches on (Masaccio) a bunch of grapes.

30. Use of the vine-elm trope by Ovid (43 B.C.E.–18 C.E.) to suggest a "reciprocal" relationship is the focus of Mandy Green's balanced discussion of Eve in "'The Vine and Her Elm': Milton's Eve and the Transformation of an Ovidian Motif," *MLR* 1, no. 2 (Apr. 1996): 301–16. Green reflects, as we do, that Milton's use of the figure in *Paradise Lost* "seems to anticipate not only the fall but also the movement toward regeneration" (p. 316). For a trenchant analysis of the

shift with the Fall in *Paradise Lost* "from floral to fruitful, from paradise without to paradise within, from innocence to experience, from praise to prayer, from discursive to intuitive apprehension," see Kathleen M. Swaim, "Flower, Fruit, and Seed: A Reading of *Paradise Lost*," in *Milton Studies* V, ed. James D. Simmonds (Pittsburgh, 1973), pp. 155–76.

31. On the 1688 *Paradise Lost* illustrations, see Helen Gardner, "Milton's First Illustrator," in *A Reading of Paradise Lost* (Oxford, 1965), appendix B, pp. 121–31; Suzanne Boorsch, "The 1688 *Paradise Lost* and Dr. Aldrich," *The Metropolitan Museum Journal* 6 (1972): 133–50; and John T. Shawcross, "The First Illustrations for *Paradise Lost*," *MQ* 9 (May 1975): 43–46.

32. Edward Hodnett, *Francis Barlow: First Master of English Book Illustration* (Berkeley, 1978), p. 51.

33. The de Bry engraving is discussed and reproduced in McColley, "Iconography," pp. 113–14. She also uses the engraving as the frontispiece to *A Gust for Paradise* and discusses it in chaps. 2 and 3 (pp. 41, 73–74).

34. After reading an earlier version of this essay, Joseph Wittreich pointed out that Adam appears actually to be in the *process* of kneeling. If so, the same ambiguity about the exact moment depicted appears as well in the de Bry engraving, which may well have served as a prototype for Medina's design: both show Adam with one knee resting rather tentatively upon the ground (whether upon a rock, as in Medina's design, or upon what looks like a raised tuft of shrubbery in the de Bry), while the other hovers slightly in the air. Thus his pose, at the moment depicted, might actually better be described as a "bow" (compare the epic voice's description in V, 144).

35. It is difficult to attribute much importance to reversals of image in engravings, since many artists knew the masters of Renaissance art exclusively or mostly through engraved copies which, by definition, reversed the images. This reversal, of course, could be compensated by reversing the original design (a technique the engravers of 1688 apparently followed, since for the most part their printed illustrations do not reverse Medina's drawings), but often such compensation did not take place. Hence, it could be misleading to make too much of an Adam and Eve praying to the right or left of the garden, or of a Gabriel coming down from the right or left side of the sky.

36. Charlotte Bronte, *Shirley* (1840; rpt. New York, 1982), pp. 314–15.

37. Marcia Pointon, *Milton and English Art* (Toronto, 1970), pp. 137–38.

38. W. J. T. Mitchell, *Blake's Composite Art: A Study of the Illuminated Poetry* (Princeton, 1978), p. 19. Other important studies of Blake as an illustrator of Milton include Martin Butlin, *William Blake* (London, 1978); Pamela Dunbar, *William Blake's Illustrations to the Poetry of John Milton* (Oxford, 1980); Stephen C. Behrendt, *The Moment of Explosion: Blake and the Illustrations of Milton* (Lincoln, Neb., 1983); Bette Charlene Werner, *Blake's Vision of the Poetry of Milton: Illustrations to Six Poems* (Lewisburg, Va., 1986); and Joseph A. Wittreich, *Angel of Apocalypse: Blake's Idea of Milton* (Madison, 1975).

39. W. J. T. Mitchell, "Blake's Composite Art," in *Blake's Visionary Forms Dramatic*, ed. David V. Erdman and John E. Grant (Princeton, 1970), p. 68.

40. The question and declaration appear in all four gospels: See also Mark xiv, 19, and xiv, 29–31; Luke xxii, 23, and xxii, 33–34; John xiii, 21–22, and xiii, 37–38. Thus they seem to be inextricably connected to the Church's memory of the Last Supper. And of course the connection is underscored in the iconography of the meal as represented by Leonardo da Vinci, Castagno, and countless others.

41. An interesting image in light of this reading is the oddly shaped vessel on the table, just behind the gourd Eve holds in her hand. The shape represents a counterbalancing of opposing principles, as illustrated in the Chinese yin-yang symbol—an image, that is, of the duality of the sexes.

42. Blake also suggests this tragic vision of the sexes' division in his scene of the creation of Eve, in which she rises like a sad though lovely emanation from Adam's side. On the other hand, in that design, too, Blake's iconography clearly suggests that in this fall before the Fall, Eve also typologically foreshadows that second Eve whose Seed will restore all that is lost.

43. Shetaka, "Them thus employed," 129–36.

44. In "Consider First," Wendy Furman has discussed at length the ways in which Eve is portrayed as redemptrix in the illustrations of Mary Groom.

45. Indeed, as Dennis Burden, *The Logical Epic: A Study of the Argument of Paradise Lost* (Cambridge, 1967), p. 71, has noted, even apart from Raphael's *Hail*, the very fact of her entertaining an angelic guest puts her in Mary's company.

46. One also cannot overlook the serpentine handle on the gourd, which—as Wittreich pointed out to us in response to an earlier version of this essay—both "replicate[s] the serpent wrapped around the tree in the background" and "force[s] an identification of Eve and the serpent." But like the main serpentine image behind her, it also forces an identification of Eve with Christ. The design is, as Wittreich says, "an extraordinary instance of contraries consolidated within a single image."

47. At the Victoria and Albert Museum, London, several possible prototypes for Blake's garden furniture can be seen—including a bamboo chair once belonging to David Garrick; a Gothic garden chair from Strawberry Hill; and a chair with "roots" extending into the ground. Both Milton and Blake could have known about regal English banqueting houses of the sixteenth and early seventeenth centuries of the kind pictured in *The Gardeners Labyrinth*, 1594, by Dydymus Mountain [Thomas Hill]. The drawing shows benches and table in an arbor, and vines entwined around tree posts that form four arches, with gardeners at work pruning and entwining more vines. The scene is reproduced by Patricia Fumerton in *Cultural Aesthetics: Renaissance Literature and the Practice of Social Ornament* (Chicago, 1991), p. 131. Fumerton's stimulating book does not discuss Milton's Eden, but she makes a point relevant to Adam and Eve in such a setting: these banqueting arbors were "exaggeratedly vulnerable," not protected "within layers of outer rooms . . . [but] detached and exposed" (p. 130).

48. Frye, *Milton's Imagery*, shows a number of images of Eden that include the topos of the vine; perhaps most important for Milton, since he well might have seen them, are the Medici tapestries. See, for instance, illus. 151.

49. See, for example, his 1807 design of Raphael descending; and his 1808 design of Adam and Eve asleep in their bower.

50. Dunbar, *William Blake's Illustrations;* Blake qtd. in ibid., p. 69.

51. Leopold Damrosch Jr., *Symbol and Truth in Blake's Myth* (Princeton, 1980), p. 107, has also discussed this complex of ideas.

52. Robert Greene, 1587. See Hull, *Chaste, Silent, & Obedient: English Books for Women, 1475–1640* (San Marino, 1982), pp. 134, 173; our italics.

53. Herman Rapaport, *Milton and the Postmodern* (Lincoln, 1983), p. 143. His analysis in this section draws heavily on Julia Kristeva's *Des chinoises.*

54. Margaret Homan qtd. by Carolyn G. Heilbrun in *Writing a Woman's Life* (New York, 1988), p. 42.

55. See Gilbert and Gubar, "Milton's Bogey: Patriarchal Poetry and Women Readers," in *The Madwoman in the Attic* (New Haven, 1979), pp. 187–212; and Froula, "Pechter's Specter: Milton's Bogey Writ Small," *Critical Inquiry* 10 (Sept. 1984): 171–78; and Froula, "When Eve Reads Milton," *Critical Inquiry* 11 (Dec. 1985): 328.

56. The formulation is again Homan's—quoted by Heilbrun, *Writing a Woman's Life,* p. 41; the italics are ours. And of course for Kristeva, the question is a statement.

57. Still painting in her nineties, Petrina exhibited her work recently in New York City; in

Saugerties, New York; in Brownsville, Texas (where she now makes her home), and in Mata-
moros, across the border in Mexico. She has also enjoyed critical attention from several Milton
scholars. For a general approach to her work on *Paradise Lost,* see Lloyd F. Dickson, "Against
the Wiles of the Devil: Carlotta Petrina's Christocentric Illustrations of *Paradise Lost,*" in *Milton
Studies* XXV, ed. James D. Simmonds (Pittsburgh, 1990), pp. 161–90. For a detailed consideration of Petrina's Expulsion, see Furman, "'With Dreadful Faces Throng'd,'" pp. 27–29. Also
see Michael Lieb's "'The Chariot of Paternal Deitie': Some Visual Readings," in *Milton's Legacy
in the Arts,* ed. Albert C. Labriola and Edward Sichi Jr. (University Park, Pa., 1988), pp. 50–52.
And, for biographical data as well as insightful comparison, see Bruce Lawson, "Unifying Milton's Epics: Carlotta Petrina's Illustrations for *Paradise Regained,*" in *Milton Studies* XXX, ed.
Albert C. Labriola (Pittsburgh, 1993), pp. 183–218. Virginia Tufte has written and produced,
with cinematographer Mark La Femina, a video biography titled *Reaching for Paradise: The Life
and Art of Carlotta Petrina* (La Femina Films, 1994; 55 minutes), presented on PBS Station
KMBH, Harlingen, Texas, in 1995; on Channel 35, Los Angeles, 1995–1996; at the annual
conference of the National Women's Studies Association at Skidmore College, June 1996, and at
Whittier College, March 1997.

58. See, for instance, her images of the Chariot of Paternal Deity and of the Expulsion, in
Dickson, "Against the Wiles of the Devil," figs. 6 and 12; Lieb, "'The Chariot of Paternal
Deitie,'" pp. 50–52; and Furman, "Dreadful Faces," pp. 27–29. Petrina's own life was engulfed
by tragedy during her work on the *Paradise Lost* designs, when her husband John Petrina was
killed in an automobile accident in August 1935 and she and their ten-year-old son were injured.
Poignantly, her husband remained the model for her Adam (as of the male figures in many of the
later paintings). Just as importantly, she lived on the doorstep of the apocalyptic tragedy of our
century: at close range she witnessed the seeming silence of God—or more terrifying, perhaps,
his complicity—in the conflagration of Europe well underway when her illustrations appeared.

59. As in, for example, Rivera's great cycle of murals on the lost city of Tenochtitlán, in the
government palace of Mexico City.

60. The resemblance of Petrina's deity to Mussolini probably is not coincidental, although it
was subconscious. In May 1992, during three days of interviews at her home in Brownsville,
Texas, the artist told us of seeing and hearing the Italian dictator speak—in the Piazza San Marco,
Venice, where she was living in the early thirties with her Italian-born husband. On the one
hand, particularly in retrospect, she was horrified by Il Duce's policies; but, at the time (and the
designs for *Paradise Lost* were in preparation during that period) she remembers having been
impressed, almost overwhelmed, by his charisma.

61. For a biographical sketch of Groom, see Furman, "Consider First," pp. 123–28. Also
underway in our study of Milton illustrators is a monograph on Mary Groom, based in part on
interviews in England with her brother Thomas Groom; with a number of currently active wood-
engravers, among them Simon Brett and Hilary Paynter; and with Judith Russell—who herself
knew Groom, and who is the daughter of the late Gertrude Hermes and Blair Hughes-Stanton,
artists who were among Groom's closest friends. Collaborating in our work on Milton illustrations is Eunice Howe, Department of Art History, University of Southern California, to whom
we are indebted for advice on many points in the present essay.

62. Stevie Davies, *The Feminine Reclaimed: The Idea of Woman in Spenser, Shakespeare
and Milton* (Lexington, 1986), pp. 175–247. Groom's emphasis on the maternal in *Paradise Lost*
also presages comments by John P. Rumrich, *Milton Unbound: Controversy and Reinterpretation* (Cambridge, 1996), who argues that Milton had "worked out a maternally centered psychology" and that he "elaborates a poetics of generation derived from this focus on the maternal, a
dynamic poetics oriented toward what is not yet known and that assumes toleration—that crucial
Miltonic word—for what cannot be foreseen. It is a poetics of feminine power" (p. 23).

63. Catherine Belsey, *John Milton: Language, Gender, Power* (Oxford, 1988), p. 59.

64. This is one of many helpful biographical insights Wendy Furman gained from an interview with Penelope Hughes-Stanton—daughter of Groom's long-time associate, the late Blair Hughes-Stanton and Anne Ross—in London on August 20, 1990.

65. Chediston Parish Church, where Groom attended regularly, served as warden, and was buried upon her death, has just such a table/altar. Since Vatican II, of course, even priests in the Roman tradition face the congregation as Raphael does in Groom's engraving.

66. Indeed, Groom puts Satan at the apex of her own triangular design in her powerful illustration of Book II: "Satan on a Throne of Royal State."

67. Mirella D'Ancona, *The Garden of the Renaissance: Botanical Symbolism in Italian Painting* (Firenze, 1977), p. 90.

68. Francis Landy, "The Song of Songs," in *The Literary Guide to the Bible,* ed. Robert Alter and Frank Kermode (Cambridge, Mass., 1987), pp. 305, 314–15.

69. See Elinor W. Gadon, *The Once and Future Goddess: A Symbol for our Time* (San Francisco, 1989), pp. 213–18. Gadon notes that in France alone, 302 images of Black Madonnas have been catalogued. We know that Mary Groom often traveled in France, and that throughout her life she was deeply interested in medieval frescoes. Moreover, while Groom was working on the illustrations for *Paradise Lost* in 1935, her mentor and friend Leon Underwood was carving in *lignum vitae* a work titled *African Madonna.* In her feeling for multicultural imagery—and her intuition of it in *Paradise Lost*—Groom, along with Carlotta Petrina, anticipates later Milton critics. See, for example, the observation by J. Martin Evans, *Milton's Imperial Epic* (Ithaca, 1996), that Milton "has invited us to see in Adam and Eve a clear reflection of the first explorers' description of the native Americans" (p. 94).

70. We offer Morrison and Milton as a more or less arbitrary example of the kind of false dichotomy often expressed in debates on canonicity and the curriculum. Yet perhaps it is not so arbitrary after all. Among the writers that Furman regularly teaches, she finds that Milton and Morrison engage her students the most passionately (along with Dante and the Bible). In the two writers, however different, students may well find common experiences: among them (1) a complex and ultimately redemptive exploration of gender, and (2) a grounding in the Bible—especially, perhaps not coincidentally, the Song of Songs.

LINGERING VOICES, TELLING SILENCES: SILENCE AND THE WORD IN *PARADISE REGAINED*

Ken Simpson

DESPITE MILTON'S EMPHASIS on the verbal battle between Christ and Satan in *Paradise Regained*, silence is a recurrent theme in the poem. The poet is "mute" without inspiration; Jesus is led by an inward "motion"; Mary and her son engage in silent meditation; Satan is confounded by the mystery of the Word and the angels praise the Son in songs unheard.[1] Typological associations also draw attention to this thematic undercurrent. On three occasions (*PR* I, 353; II, 16–19, 266–78), Milton associates Jesus with Elijah who, after fasting for forty days, heard God's "small voice of silence" (1 Kings xix, 12), while John Diodati, the Reformed theologian visited by Milton in Geneva in 1639, identifies silence and the Word in his commentary on Elijah's theophany: "the revelation and word of God, were specially joyned to the milde and quiet signe, to signifie unto us, that Gods saving revelation of himself is in the Gospell onely . . . and not in his terrible law."[2] In the *Christian Doctrine*, Milton also refers to Elijah's experience in the wilderness as an example of "divine glory, in so far as mortals can comprehend it," which is consistent with the poet's view that "God is inaudible."[3]

Silence is most eloquent, however, in the pinnacle scene of *Paradise Regained*. Faced with casting himself down and presuming God's protection or attempting to stand and falling to his death, Jesus recites the Word and stands by faith. The simplicity and finality of "he said and stood" (IV, 561) resonate in the silence which ensues, as the poem reaches its climax in the Son's fulfillment of the Father's decree. When Satan falls, silence emerges, between Christ's final words and the silent song of the angels, as the sign of divine presence and the mystery of the Son's nature.[4] Having proven by his perfect obedience and hermeneutic victory that he is both divine and human, embodying both transcendent silence and human words, the Son can begin to redeem mankind and language through his prophetic ministry of preaching the kingdom of heaven. At the same time, Milton shows that Jesus derives all from the Father who "is far beyond man's imagination, let alone his understanding" (*CD*, YP VI, p. 133) and who must be represented by nega-

179

tive attributes like silence, in addition to accommodated expressions like the voice at Jesus' baptism.[5] Thus, the silence on the pinnacle is two-sided: on the one hand, it authorizes and redeems language for the proclamation of the Word by the Word; on the other hand, as a minimal image of the Father's ineffable glory, it is also a reminder that such glory is never fully present in words or the Word. The interplay of silence and speech, especially in the pinnacle scene, represents the difficulty of representing the Incarnation—the irreducible mystery of Jesus' identity.

Critics have emphasized the antithesis rather than the interplay of language and silence in *Paradise Regained*.[6] Steven Goldsmith, objecting to Stanley Fish's claim that in the pinnacle scene "speech finds its apex in silence," suggests that silence is "an emblem of nonexistence."[7] In my view, both Fish and Goldsmith are only partially correct. Fish is right to emphasize the culmination of the temptations in silence, but concludes that language is cancelled in silent "union with God" (Fish, "Inaction and Silence," p. 27). Jesus' silence indicates his unity with the Father's will rather than his essence, and as Protestant traditions of commentary would have suggested to Milton, the temptations prepare Jesus for his preaching ministry, a process through which language is redeemed rather than denied.[8] Goldsmith, on the other hand, rightly stresses this redemption of language for the ministry of the Word in Christ's silencing of Satan in *Paradise Regained,* but neglects other details of the poem, other works by Milton, and Christian traditions of commentary which suggest that silence and the Word are not antithetical. The silencing of Satan and the silence of Jesus on the pinnacle are two completely different events: the first reveals the emptiness of words not linked to the Word; the second reveals the saving power of the Word as well as the inability of words to represent God's presence. By citing Scripture, Jesus demonstrates the renewal of language; by standing, he fulfills God's decree through perfect faith; by standing silently, he discloses the presence of divinity in both his words and deeds. In Christ's silence and speech, Milton invites the reader to contemplate the Incarnation of God in man and the nature of divine representation. Christ is charged to represent the unrepresentable while transcending representation himself since his identity as "God-man" is a mystery of faith.

The problem of representing the Incarnation in *Paradise Regained* has been discussed by James M. Pearce and Ashraf H. A. Rushdy, neither of whom acknowledges Milton's integration of the "meta-argument" of divine representation and the "identity motive" in the pinnacle scene.[9] In fact, the coexistence of silence and the Word in theological traditions and throughout Milton's works generally forms a context in which Jesus' identity as "God-man" and the mystery of that representation are revealed at the same time, creating the formal as well as theological climax of the poem. By representing Jesus from shifting perspectives, Milton emphasizes the mystery of the Incarnation as the union of both divine and human natures, but for Pearce, the two most important passages in which Milton uses this strategy—God's speech in Book I, 130–67, and the angelic hymn in Book IV, 596–635—"form the brackets within which the poem's meta-argument is deployed."[10] Although he does explain that the poem is about representing the Incarnation, Pearce does not clarify how the meta-argument can be used to read the pinnacle scene, or to explain the identity motive, reducing the poem's climactic event to something that occurs between formal brackets. Rushdy, on the other hand, explains the identity motive and maintains the pinnacle scene as a formal climax, but denies that the mystery of the Incarnation is revealed to Satan on the pinnacle. For Rushdy, Jesus "represents something like 'recta ratio' on the pinnacle by virtue of his insistent theocentricity," but the paradox of Jesus' theocentric self-representation is not a fulfilment of his nature— this can only occur in the future when God is fully present and there is no need for mediation. Neither does the pinnacle scene represent the mystery of the Son's identity—this is revealed to Satan in the angelic hymn which follows.[11] The silence on the pinnacle refers to Satan's "amazement," his "absence of reason," while Jesus' standing on the pinnacle is not a miracle revealing his divinity, but a simple, natural act since it is possible, though dangerous, for ordinary human beings to stand there.[12] Rushdy is right to dispel the miracle of Christ's standing, but this is not the only symbol of the mystery of the Incarnation. Nor does Milton's depiction of Jesus as "God-man" reveal the essence of the Incarnation; rather, Milton reinforces the mystery of the Incarnation as the paradoxical coexistence of transcendent silence and human words in Christ. This confounds Satan even though silence and the Word have been associated with Jesus' identity from the opening lines of the poem. It is the mystery of the Son's identity as incarnate Word which "amazes" Satan, an identity clarified through Jesus' refusal to limit his self-representation to satanic or even verbal expression and through Jesus' resolute dependence on both parts of his identity throughout the poem.

The pinnacle scene, then, reveals the incarnate Word as a union of divinity and humanity, of unsayable presence and the words of the Word. Throughout *Paradise Regained*, but particularly in this temptation, Milton balances Christ's renewal of fallen language for his ministry with the silence which is both the origin and purpose of discourse, uniting Jesus' dual nature with his prophetic office of preaching the "Gospel of the kingdome of God" begun immediately following the temptations in the synoptic Gospels.[13] Just as divinity and humanity are joined in the Son, so ineffable presence and human words are joined in his preaching: he has shown, by the end of the poem, that he is worthy of speaking, as well as being, God's Word and can proceed to "Publish his Godlike office now mature" (I, 188).[14] It is no coincidence that the emergence of silence on the pinnacle turns on Jesus' faithful use of Scripture and Satan's attempted appropriation of it, or that Milton chooses Luke's order of temptations but adopts Matthew's "It is written" over Luke's "It is said." "It is written" reinscribes the authority of the Father's silent voice even as Jesus speaks and Milton re-creates that speech. Glossing over the difference between the authoritative, originary text and the speaking subject by having Jesus *say* "it is written," Milton reiterates the difference in essence between the Father and Son while still maintaining the Son's status as God-man. All of these details underline the coexistence of silence and the Word in the Son's nature and prophetic office. Patterns of silence and language in other poems by Milton and in Christian theology also show that the power of the saving Word and the limitations of language are implicit in the evocation of silence on the pinnacle in *Paradise Regained.* Before turning to *Paradise Regained,* then, it is necessary to discuss the theological traditions within which Milton worked since these traditions provide reading strategies which help to explain the mystery of Jesus' identity, a mystery reiterated in the union of divinity and humanity, silence and the Word on the pinnacle.

I

Authors of religious works struggled with the problem of saying the unsayable long before the seventeenth century. Erich Auerbach has commented on the "heavy silence" which characterizes the biblical narrative of Abraham and Isaac.[15] In the Christian tradition, according to Pseudo-Dionysius the Areopagite of the late fifth century, attempts to say the unsayable led to a double tradition of Christian theology in which "what is not said is interwoven with what is said."[16] Dionysius's comment implies an especially incarnational view of textuality. Both transcendent silence and the written, incarnate Word are woven together, are textual. The discourse of positive theology is philosophical and persuasive, clarifying what can be predicated of God in prayer and argument. This kind of "God talk" is possible because God is immanent in the hierarchies of nature and the church, the sacraments, the Incarnation, and the Scriptures.

In a passage foreshadowing Milton's doctrine of accommodation in the *Christian Doctrine* which will be discussed later, Dionysius suggests that as much as can be known about God is revealed in the sacred texts: "generally, then, one must neither dare to say nor conceive anything about the hidden, transcendent essence of divinity except what has been divinely expressed in the sacred sciptures."[17] As the reference to hidden divinity indicates, the tradition of negative theology is mystical and non-verbal since "one must ascribe non-logos to that beyond logos."[18] Even though God is given many names in the Scriptures, the essence of divinity is "not known, not spoken, not named"; in fact, because God transcends speech, it is best to say what God is not, remembering that even this is saying too much:

> God is
> all in all
> nothing in none,
> known to all in reference to all,
> known to no one in reference to nothing.[19]

Whereas positive theology emphasizes volubility since God has been accommodated and dispersed in human speech, negative theology emphasizes silence, since the higher we ascend to God the more our "language becomes restricted" until we are "wholly united to the unspeakable."[20] As antithetical as they seem, both traditions complement each other. According to his own principles, Dionysius never *declares* that positive theology is false. More importantly, the two approaches respond to the paradox of God's immanence and transcendence: dogmatic theology affirms that God speaks in nature, the church and Scripture, while mystical theology denies all affirmations in order to attain silent union with God.[21] To repeat, "what is not said is interwoven with what is said."

In practice, however, Dionysius privileges "what is not said" and, in the process, diminishes the importance of the Incarnation as God's revelation in his Son, the Word made flesh. Other early Christian writers were not as eager to endorse negative theology. Several early fathers of the church, although responding to christological and trinitarian disputes in vastly different contexts, insisted that God's Word was spoken in the Creation and the Incarnation.[22] Ignatius of Antioch, for example, whose works Milton read in Vedelius's 1623 edition, recognized the presence of silence in the Word when he explained that God is revealed in his Son "who is his Word which proceeded from silence."[23] Over two hundred years later, but still before Dionysius, St. Augustine clearly outlined the dialectic between silence and language in *De Doctrina Christiana*:

And a contradiction in terms is created, since if that is ineffable which cannot be spoken, then that is not ineffable which can be called ineffable. This contradiction is to be passed over in silence rather than resolved verbally. For God, although nothing worthy may be spoken of Him, has accepted the tribute of the human voice and wished us to take joy in praising Him with our words.[24]

Three features of Augustine's theology of silence reappear in *Paradise Regained*. First of all, silence represents an epistemological limit and identifies the distance between human understanding and the essence of God. Conversely, silence is the condition of speech and authorizes the use of words in God's service in spite of the limitations of language. Finally, silence is devotional and points to the humility and reverence with which believers should approach their Creator. Questions of influence and source aside, Milton dramatizes this theology of representation in the process of portraying the redemption of language by the Word of God in *Paradise Regained*. The poem itself is evidence of Milton's devotional purpose: Christ's faithful reticence is a model of reverent deference to the Father, in whose service he finds perfect freedom. Moreover, God's ineffability is adumbrated in the decree which is fulfilled in the inaction/action and silence/speech of the pinnacle scene, while Christ's identity as the Word made flesh underwrites the Word which he must proclaim and the words devoted to the Word written by the Christian poet. In each case, Milton demonstrates that silence and the Word are not mutually exclusive, but mutually dependent aspects of representation. Not coincidentally, the seventeenth-century nonconformist community most familiar to Milton when he was writing his epics also emphasized God's silent transcendence of representation.

For many Quakers, silence was the purest form of worship. According to Robert Barclay, "there can be nothing more opposit to the natural will and wisdom of man than this silent waiting upon God."[25] Alexander Parker urges the Friends to "sit down in pure stillness and silence of all flesh" while Isaac Penington the younger, probably known to Milton through Thomas Ellwood while he was at Chalfont St. Giles, asserts that "the ministry of the spirit and life is more close and immediate when without words." Finally, in a passage which could serve as a gloss on the pinnacle scene of *Paradise Regained,* Charles Marshall describes a liturgy of silence: "When a motion is felt, and openings are in the heart, and the power of the Lord is prevailing, then sink down in that in which no vain thought can be hid and stand single and passive . . . and then, in the power which warmeth thy heart, and moveth on thy spirit, enter into thy service."[26] A "motion" of the Holy Spirit led Jesus to the wilderness in the first place, while stillness, silence, and passivity are all associated with him in the pinnacle scene, as Milton explores the poetic and liturgical interplay of silence and the Word within his narrative of identity, Incarnation, and ministry.[27]

It is misleading to emphasize silence too much, however, because as Ignatius's comment makes clear, God has broken silence by speaking the Word at the Incarnation. For Milton and other church reformers of the sixteenth and seventeenth centuries, although not the Quakers, the revelational and incarnational thrust of Christianity was made more explicitly verbal through the identification of the Bible as the Word of God.[28] Like most Protestants, Milton accepts the authority of Scripture as "God's self-revelation" and accommodation to his creatures. In addition, by adopting "Sermo" as a Latin translation of the Greek "Logos" in John i, 1–3 (*CD*, YP VI, pp. 238–39), Milton articulates a threefold rhetorical doctrine of the Word in which the Trinity itself is rhetorical since the Father speaks through the Word with the power and persuasive force of the Holy Spirit (YP VI, pp. 300, 283–84): the Father first expresses himself through the Son, "the word by which God is audible" (YP VI, p. 297); secondly, just as a speaker adapts his speech to an audience, so the Father accommodates his infinite glory by speaking the Word in Creation (YP VI, p. 301); and finally, God accommodates himself to the fallen nature of humanity through the divine "decorum" of the internal and external Word of God (YP VI, pp. 590, 134).[29]

In the *Christian Doctrine*, Milton emphasizes the integrity of God's intentions as they are revealed in the literal images of Scripture, a view that is central to his doctrine of scriptural revelation or accommodation.[30] Because God's essence is beyond human understanding, we should "form an image of God in our minds which corresponds to his representation and description of himself in the sacred writings" (YP VI, p. 133). Even though he acknowledges that the divine nature "transcends everything, including definition" (YP VI, p. 137), Milton also avoids a response of complete mystical silence, since God has revealed as much as he wants believers to know, and rejects allegorical interpretation, since this implies an impious addition to God's revelation. Believers should rest in the words and images of Scripture as they have been revealed, knowing that if they understand and act in accordance with the Word, they will understand and act as God wishes them to—in loving obedience. It is in this sense that the identity of the Son is revealed in *Paradise Regained*. His silence on the pinnacle signals his dependence on the Father for his divinity while his use of Scripture underscores the importance of his human ministry of the Word. The interplay of silence and speech in the pinnacle scene reveals the mystery of Jesus' identity as both God and man but also the extent to which Milton transformed the theological "topos" of divine representation into a powerful poetic symbol.

II

The coexistence of silence and the Word is a persistent theme in Milton's poetry before *Paradise Regained*, surfacing in different ways in *Comus* (540–64), *Upon the Circumcision* (1–5), *Il Penseroso* (55–56), *Lycidas* (176), the Nativity ode (116), and especially *Paradise Lost*. The first four lines of Book

VIII, added by Milton in the 1674 edition of the poem, present a variation on the interplay of silence and speech found in Christian tradition and the early poems. In Book VII, 565–640, Raphael's account of Creation culminates in liturgical sabbath hymns sung by the angels complete with echoes of Psalm xxiv, 9 (VII, 566), Psalm xcii, 5, and Psalm cxlv, 3–4 (VII, 602).[31] Like Dionysius and the Quakers, the angels assert that God is beyond thought and speech; on the other hand, like Augustine they do not rest in "silence holy" but proceed to praise and worship "Jehovah," the "great Creator." At the beginning of Book VIII, Adam stands transfixed as Raphael's voice, and presumably the angelic hymns, linger silently: "The Angel ended, and in Adam's Ear / So Charming left his voice, that he a while / Thought him still speaking, still stood fixed to hear" (VIII, 1–3). This conjunction of silence and voice, where "endings" linger and continue to speak or sing in silence, is even more explicit earlier in *Paradise Lost* when Milton describes the onset of evening in Book IV. Here "Silence accompanied" evening as birds and animals prepared for rest, but silence also accompanied them in a musical sense; it played with and offered accompaniment to the song of the nightingale and "Silence was pleased" (IV, 600, 604). The repetition of the word "still" in these references and elsewhere in Milton's work further emphasizes that the interplay of silence and speech is an intricately developed pattern in Milton's poetry before he uses it as a symbol of the Incarnation and Jesus' identity in *Paradise Regained*.[32]

The extent to which Milton continues to develop patterns of silence and speech in *Paradise Regained* which were present in his earlier works is clear from even a brief consideration of the beginning of the poem. In line 12 he admits that he would be "mute" without the inspiration of the Holy Spirit, the same Spirit who led Jesus into the wilderness, thereby linking his poem with the scriptural and incarnate Word. Just as Jesus will raise Eden in "the waste Wilderness" through his obedience, so too the poet will erect his poetic monument out of silence—his subject has remained "secret," "unrecorded," and "unsung" until now (I, 15–17). The "Hymns" and "Celestial measures" of the angels circling the throne following the Father's decree (I, 168–81) parallel Milton's representation of "sacred Song" in *Paradise Lost* (III, 344–410), while the silence of the angels who "Admiring stood a space" before the song (*PR* I, 169) recalls the silence of the angels before the Son emerges to save mankind (*PL* III, 217–18).[33] The song after the pinnacle scene also alludes to the "marriage supper of the Lamb" (Rev. xix, 9) and the "unexpressive nuptial Song" of *Lycidas* (176), both of which celebrate the kingdom of glory established when Christ will silence Satan with "the terror of his voice" (*PR* IV, 627). Finally, Milton's representation of the Father as a voice at Jesus' Baptism and during his "solemn message" or decree concerning the Son (I,

130–67) illustrates not only the doctrine of accommodation, since "God is inaudible just as he is invisible" (*CD*, YP VI, p. 239), but also the nature of the Son's divinity. Just as a silent idea precedes its vocalization or inscription, so also the Father's silent foreknowledge precedes its revelation in the Word. As a result of Milton's use of the metaphor of speech to describe the Father, Jesus, although divine in his embodiment and enactment of the Word, is temporally and essentially subordinate to the Father's divinity.

Common as it is in Milton's works, however, the representation of Jesus' relationship to the Father as an immediate conversation is more pivotal in *Paradise Regained* than in his other poems because Jesus must demonstrate not only that he is the Son but also that he has acquired "the rudiments / Of his great warfare" (*PR* I, 157–58), or preaching ministry, uniting his nature as the incarnate Word with his office as the preached Word. Much has already been written on Christ's nature in *Paradise Regained*,[34] and it is beyond my purpose either to review or engage it; instead, I will outline three conclusions reached by Milton in the *Christian Doctrine* that influence the interplay of language and silence in the poem: first, that the unity of divinity and humanity in Christ is a genuine mystery (YP VI, p. 420); second, that Christ's divinity is not equal to the Father's (YP VI, p. 215); and third, that both natures are always present (YP VI, p. 228), although the Son's divinity/humanity is not proven until he fulfills God's decree through the exercise of free choice. The identity motive is important, but only to Satan: he knows who the Son is (*PR* I, 356), but he is unable to fathom the unity of divinity and humanity in Christ's nature because it is a mystery of faith. Following Milton's advice to "let mysteries alone and not tamper with them" (*CD*, YP VI, p. 421), Jesus is silent in response to Satan's questions about his nature in the debate leading up to the pinnacle scene (*PR* IV, 500–01, 510–21, 522–30, 538–40), revealing Satan's devotion to "monstrous controversies" and the Son's reverence toward the Father. Satan's real purpose in attempting to learn the Son's identity is much more selfish than his words suggest; he is afraid of the "fatal wound" from the "Seed of Eve" which will drive him from his kingdom (I, 53, 54). To retain his kingdom, Satan attempts to separate words from the Word but is reduced to empty silence, while Jesus demonstrates that he *is* the Word and allows the silence of the Father to speak through him.

Milton likely expected his readers to know that the temptations were meant to prepare Jesus for the proclamation of the kingdom of heaven. John the Baptist's ministry immediately precedes the temptations and Christ's own Sermon on the Mount immediately follows them, at least in the Gospel of Matthew. The temptations are linked to Christ's kingly vocation in the *Christian Doctrine* as well. The temptations and the Crucifixion are two forms of humiliation suffered by Christ to satisfy divine justice and to create his kingdom (YP VI, 438–39), also known as the kingdom of grace and heaven. Although the "reign of grace . . . began with his first advent, when it was proclaimed by John the Baptist," it continues through the spiritual warfare of the church and will lead to the "kingdom of glory" at Christ's Second Coming (YP VI, 624, 436–37). The action of *Paradise Regained*, itself illustrating how the kingdom of Christ is attained by hearing the Father's voice, is framed by the "Kingdom nigh at hand" (I, 20) proclaimed by the Baptist, the kingdom of Christ revealed after the temptations in Jesus' preaching ministry, and still further in the future, the kingdom of glory, which follows the final defeat of Satan foreshadowed in his fall from the pinnacle.

Commentators from a broad range of worshipping traditions were even more specific about the interpretation of the temptations. At his Baptism, Jesus was named by God and anointed by the Spirit "to preach the Gospel to the poore" (Luke iv, 18), while the temptations were a series of verbal and hermeneutic tests to prepare him for this ministry. The Baptism, temptation, and vocation of Christ were seen as a unified sequence of events in the Son's early ministry. For Erasmus, Christ sets an example for God's ministers as he battles Satan through prayer, sobriety of life, and the Holy Scriptures before accepting the sacred task of preaching the Gospel.[35] Lancelot Andrewes argues that Christ began his calling from his Baptism and proved himself "too cunning for him [Satan] in disputing" by showing that "Scriptum est" is the best defense against the distrust, presumption, and idolatry of the devil, the "publisher of infamous reports." William Perkins reminds the clergy that Christ, as the "sole Doctor and Prophet of Gods Church," must be "tempted before he go[es] to preach" just as ministers of the Word must "prepare themselves against Satans temptations."[36]

Milton also emphasizes the exegetical nature of the temptations, especially in the pinnacle scene. Not only is the last temptation the only one in which both characters quote Scripture, but Satan's attempt to have Jesus presume God's protection hides a more insidious sin—the distortion of the text and its meaning. As James H. Sims has clearly shown, Satan abuses Scripture throughout the poem, but his debasement of the text in the pinnacle scene differs from his previous abuses of the bible in two ways: first, it occurs at a climactic moment in the poem and, therefore, is not one misinterpretation among many; secondly, while Satan's other misreadings are for secondary purposes—to gain sympathy for himself or to flatter Jesus, for example—his corruption of the Word on the pinnacle is meant to undermine the silent assent of the Spirit and Word, the source of Jesus' power in all of the previous temptations.[37] Whereas Satan wrests the meaning of the Word to serve his own purpose, Christ shows he *is* the Word by demonstrating that the "Scriptures of God are sufficient in themselves, truly to interpret and expound themselves."[38]

The commentaries of John Calvin and the annotations of scores of other exegetes all mention Satan's "craftie purpose" and Christ's hermeneutic victory on the spire of the temple.[39] The interpretation of the Puritan divines responsible for the widely read *Annotations Upon the Books of the New and Old Testament* is representative:

The devil now seeks to foil Christ with his own weapons, and cites Scripture. . . . There is no charge, or temptation of Satan more pernicious and dangerous, then that which is coloured with misseapplied Scripture, and shew of sanctity. . . . Here appeareth the venom of the old dragon, when he pretendeth the sacred authority of Gods H. word, to lead men to sin, and disobedience to God.[40]

By omitting "all thy wayes" from his reference to Psalm xci, 11, Satan makes the text appear to say that God's people can do anything and expect divine protection. Most commentators, however, argue that the text does not apply to dangers in which people voluntarily throw themselves because "all thy wayes" refers to all the ways of faith set forth by God.[41] Thus, when Jesus cites Deuteronomy vi, 16, he answers Satan's method as well as his intent. He shows that Satan's interpretation must be wrong, otherwise the commandment would be contradicted, and that Satan's intent is to undermine his faith by tempting him to ask God for a sign of his presence. Christ's text refers implicitly to Exodus xvii, 1–7, where the Israelites tempt God by demanding signs of his favor, saying "Is the Lord among us, or not?" In *Paradise Regained*, the question is answered by the voice of silence which emerges after Christ's faithful use of language and Scripture on the pinnacle.

What Jesus must learn throughout *Paradise Regained*, then, is not his own identity or the nature of his kingdom—in his first, silent meditation he reveals the nature of his divine parentage and of his spiritual, eternal kingdom. What he must learn is "How best the mighty work he might begin / Of Savior to mankind, and which way first / Publish his Godlike office now mature" (I, 186–88). Like Milton himself in *Sonnet VII* and *Sonnet XIX*, Jesus must "stand and wait" for the proper time to begin God's work and in this he must be dependent upon his Father's call since his time "is not yet come" (*PR* III, 397). That God's work will begin with Jesus' preaching ministry is underlined throughout *Paradise Regained* by the interplay of language and silence as Jesus uses the word of God to "stand against the wiles of the devill" (Eph. vi, 11).

The centrality of language in the conflict between Christ and Satan is emphasized even before the temptations. Prior to meeting Satan, Jesus learns his identity from Scripture (*PR* I, 259–63), adopts "winning words" for his "duel, not of arms" (I, 222, 174), receives the witness of John the Baptist and the Holy Spirit (I, 25–31), and "audibly" hears his Father's voice pronounce him the "beloved Son" (I, 31–32). Satan interprets the events of Jesus' Baptism in a "carnal" and literal way that reveals his lack of faith and, therefore, his inadequate view of language. He fails to associate God's "Son belov'd" with his "first-begot" (I, 85, 89), stands "Thunderstruck," silenced by the "voice divine" (I, 36, 35), assumes that Christ's kingdom will be political (I, 98–99), and sees the physical dove, "whate'er it meant," but not the Holy Spirit (I, 83). The terms of the conflict are set from the beginning of the poem. By joining his will to his Father's voice, a voice essentially silent but accommodated to human limitations, Jesus correctly interprets the testimony of heaven and gains the "winning words" necessary for his preaching ministry; by denying the authority of the Father's voice, Satan misinterprets God's texts and falls in "shameful silence" (IV, 22), his "train of words" (III, 266) vanishing like "froth or bubbles" (IV, 20).

In the first temptation, Satan tries to separate the Son's office from his nature by asking him to distrust God's providence in the performance of a miracle. Jesus reads the trial typologically, linking his prophetic office with Moses and Elijah and his nature with the manna from heaven given to the Israelites in Exodus xvi, 11–15, but also shows that he fulfills both types since he *is* the "Word / Proceeding from the mouth of God" who has perfect trust in the Father, unlike the Israelites (*PR* I, 349–51). Jesus' refusal to separate his nature and ministry or to use words apart from the Father's plan sets the stage for the struggle between the Word and satanic silence in the following temptations.[42] Not only has the "inward Oracle" silenced the pagan idols, but Christ will reduce Satan to muteness as he withstands the temptation to use his words apart from the spiritual kingdom he has come to proclaim. Having rejected wealth and luxury, Jesus renders Satan speechless: "So spake the Son of God, and Satan stood / A while as mute confounded what to say" (III, 1–2). When he does begin to speak, Satan comes as close as he can to knowing Jesus as the Word, but fails to understand the significance of Christ's kingdom:

> Should Kings and Nations from thy mouth consult,
> Thy Counsel would be as the Oracle
> *Urim* and *Thummim*, those oraculous gems
> On *Aaron's* breast, or tongue of Seers old
> Infallible.   (III, 12–16)

Jesus reduces Satan to murmuring when he denounces glory and later fully reveals the absence of God which is the source of Satan's empty words: "Satan had not to answer, but stood struck / With guilt of his own sin" (III,

146–47). At the beginning of Book IV, Satan is silent once again; he realizes that Jesus will not separate his words from God's Word in order to establish his kingdom prematurely through force. When Jesus rejects the "smooth conceits" of Greece for the eloquence of the Word, his steady progress toward the proclamation of his own kingdom reaches a new level. By insisting upon the connection between eloquence and character and the source of both in God's revelation in his Word and the "Light from above" (IV, 289), Jesus lays down the first principle of language in his spiritual kingdom. Christ's redemption of language, however, reaches its symbolic height in the final temptation.

In this scene, Milton varies the pattern of temptation, Word, and silence in order to emphasize the source of Jesus' authoritative and authentic language in the presence/silence of the Father. Beginning with the Word in an attempt to appropriate the Son's authority, Satan omits phrases and deliberately distorts the text: Psalm xci, 11–15, refers to the angels sustaining the faithful, not catching them if they fall; and he cleverly omits verse 13, which refers to the dragon and adder being trampled under foot, an allusion to Genesis iii, 15, a text Satan has been trying to understand since his opening speech (I, 64–66). When Jesus paraphrases Luke iv, 12, the force of truth linked with the performative Word and his faith that God will reveal his ministry in due time not only confound Satan, but they also open the text to the silence from which the Word has proceeded. Present from the beginning in his decree but speaking only through Jesus' actions, the Father is revealed as the silent source of the inexhaustible, disseminative power of the Word (John xxi, 25).

Whereas Satan's use of language reveals the silent void of faithlessness, the creative presence, which is silent in itself but speaks through the Word, emerges as language is redeemed for the ministry of the Word. Suspended momentarily between heaven and earth, Jesus fulfills the Father's decree and unites his office with the mystery of his nature as the incarnate Word. The song of the angels reinforces the presence of silence as well. The angels celebrate Christ's present victory and look ahead to the apocalypse when Satan's kingdom will be destroyed, but they do so with words only heard by Christ. The song itself, then, represents the apex of Milton's redemption of language since it is only through poetic and fictional re-creation that he can move his fallen readers closer to the "Heavenly Anthems" which otherwise would have been silent.

Our knowledge of Jesus' ministry to preach the kingdom of God as well as of Milton's view of God's silent transcendence both play important roles in a balanced assessment of the pinnacle scene. If we emphasize only the former, we ignore Milton's effort to come to terms with the limitations of language; if we emphasize only the latter, we deny Milton's belief in the saving power of the Word. Milton would have readily agreed with Thomas Wilson's claim that eloquence was "first given by God, after lost by man, and last repaired by God again."[43] In *Paradise Regained*, this redemption of language is demonstrated in Christ's silencing of Satan and, most emphatically, in his faithful waiting as the divine Word upon God's silence in the pinnacle scene. The redemption of language, however, is not an act complete in itself; it is necessary for Jesus' preaching ministry of the kingdom and for the writing of religious poetry. Just as the Son's preaching ministry is sanctioned by God's presence in silence and in the Holy Spirit which initially leads Jesus to the wilderness, so too the poet receives his authority from divine inspiration, the inward Oracle, and the Word of Scripture. By receiving such authority, Milton could write sacred verse in God's silence and in so doing attempt to redeem language from its fallen state. Although we may not be able to hear strains of the divine music in *Paradise Regained*, as perhaps we can in *Paradise Lost*, in the attitude of reverent silence adopted by Jesus before he begins preaching the Word, Milton shows his readers how best to compose themselves to that end.

University College of the Cariboo

NOTES

1. John Milton, *Paradise Regained* I, 12, 290, in *John Milton: Complete Poems and Major Prose,* ed. Merritt Y. Hughes (Indianapolis, 1957). References to Milton's poetry are to this edition and subsequent citations will appear in the text.

2. For this literal translation of "kol demamah dakkah" in 1 Kings xix, 12, see Aharon Wiener, *The Prophet Elijah in the Development of Judaism* (London, 1978), p. 14. For Diodati's view of this passage, see John Diodati, *Pious Annotations of the Holy Bible,* 3rd ed. (London, 1651), 1 Kings xix, 11–12.

3. John Milton, *Christian Doctrine,* trans. John Carey, in *The Complete Prose Works of John Milton,* 8 vols., ed. Donald M. Wolfe et al. (New Haven, 1953–1976), vol. 6, pp. 151–52, 239. All references to the *Christian Doctrine (CD)* are to this edition. Subsequent citations will appear in the text as YP with the volume and page numbers following.

4. Compare Abraham Cowley, "Upon His Majesties Restoration and Return," 137–40, in *The Works of Mr. Abraham Cowley* (London, 1668); and Richard Baxter, *An Apology for the Nonconformist Ministry* (1668), p. 7. For Cowley, the Puritans misread God's providence, finding it in the "fierce thunder" and "violent wind" of the civil war rather than "the still voice of peace" of the Restoration. According to Baxter, the nonconformists have "patiently waited on Gods Providence, in silence as to the pleading of our cause . . . whilest Volume after Volume hath been published against us." Baxter's reading is closest to Milton's since Satan and the established church are more voluble than Jesus and the nonconformists. For Jesus as nonconformist hero,

see Gary D. Hamilton, "*Paradise Regained* and the Private Houses," in *Of Poetry and Politics: New Essays on Milton and His World,* ed. P. G. Stanwood (Binghamton, N.Y., 1994), pp. 239–48.

5. For Milton, many of God's attributes must be stated negatively to "show God is not imperfect as created things are" (*CD,* YP VI, p. 149). He also notes that eternity "is expressed in the Hebrew language by inference rather than by distinct words" (YP VI, p. 144), indicating a possible textual strategy of his own.

6. Two exceptions include Georgia Christopher, "The Secret Agent in *Paradise Regained,*" *MLQ* 41 (June 1980): 137; and Leonard Mustazza, "Language as Weapon in Milton's *Paradise Regained,*" in *Milton Studies* XVIII, ed. James D. Simmonds (Pittsburgh, 1983), p. 214. Silence has fared better in the following studies of other works by Milton: Ronald B. Bond, "God's 'Back Parts': Silence and the Accommodating Word," in *Silence, the Word and the Sacred,* ed. E. D. Blodgett and H. G. Coward (Waterloo, Ont., 1989), pp. 169–87; Gregory F. Goekjian, "Deference and Silence: Milton's Nativity Ode," in *Milton Studies* XXI, ed. James D. Simmonds (Pittsburgh, 1986), pp. 119–35; and Shirley Sharon-Zisser, "Silence and Darkness in *Paradise Lost,*" in *Milton Studies,* XXV, ed. James D. Simmonds (Pittsburgh, 1989), pp. 191–211.

7. Stanley Fish, "Inaction and Silence: The Reader in *Paradise Regained,*" in *Calm of Mind,* ed. J. A. Wittreich Jr. (Cleveland, 1971), p. 42; Steven Goldsmith, "The Muting of Satan: Language and Redemption in *Paradise Regained,*" *SEL* 26 (1986): 125.

8. For the view that Christ's divinity in *Paradise Regained* consists in his unity with the Father's will, see Hugh MacCallum, *Milton and the Sons of God: the Divine Image in Milton's Epic Poetry* (Toronto, 1986), p. 240.

9. James M. Pearce, "The Theology of Representation: the Meta-Argument of *Paradise Regained,*" in *Milton Studies* XXIV, ed. James D. Simmonds (Pittsburgh, 1988), pp. 277–96; Ashraf H. A. Rushdy, "Standing Alone on the Pinnacle: Milton in 1752," in *Milton Studies* XXVI, ed. James D. Simmonds (Pittsburgh, 1990), pp. 193–218; *The Empty Garden: The Subject of Late Milton* (Pittsburgh, 1992). I agree with Rushdy that the mystery of the Incarnation is not revealed by the miracle of Jesus standing on the pinnacle; on the other hand, the "identity test" is central to the action of the poem and leads to a restatement of the mystery of the Son's nature in the coexistence of silence and the Word.

10. Pearce, "Theology of Representation," p. 290.

11. Rushdy, *The Empty Garden,* pp. 317, 316, 270–71.

12. Rushdy, *The Empty Garden,* p. 317; "Milton in 1752," p. 197.

13. Mark i, 14. All scriptural references are to *The Holy Bible* [AV] (London, 1612). Subsequent citations will appear in the text.

14. Douglas Lanier suggests that Jesus' use of silence in *Paradise Regained* reveals Milton's "fear of the independent interpretive afterlife of the written word." Jesus refuses to say what his identity or kingdom are because he knows Satan will misrepresent the radically interior nature of the kingdom and the irreducible mystery of his identity. Jesus' "controlled indeterminacy," in my view, is the silence which reminds the reader of the divine, unrepresentable source of his identity and his ministry of the Word. See Douglas Lanier, " 'Unmarkt, unknown': *Paradise Regained* and the Return of the Expressed," *Criticism* 37 (Spring 1995): 187–212.

15. Erich Auerbach, *Mimesis: The Representation of Reality in Western Literature,* trans. W. R. Trask (Princeton, 1968), p. 11.

16. Pseudo-Dionysius, "Letter Nine," in *Hierarchy and the Definition of Order in the Letters of Pseudo-Dionysius,* trans. R. F. Hathaway (The Hague, 1969), p. 154. Hereafter, I will include references to *Patrologia Graeca,* ed. J.-P. Migne (Paris, 1857), and *Patrologia Latina,* ed. J.-P. Migne (Paris, 1853). I will cite volume and column number as follows: *PG* III, 1105D; *PatL* CXXII, 1113A.

17. Pseudo-Dionysius, *The Divine Names*, in *PG* III, 588C; *PatL* CXXII, 1113A. This is my translation of Erigena's Latin translation in *PatL*.

18. Pseudo-Dionysius, *The Divine Names*, in *The Divine Names and Mystical Theology*, trans. and intro. J. D. Jones (Milwaukee, 1980), p. 177; *PG* III, 869A; *PatL* CXXII, 1154B.

19. Dionysius, *Divine Names*, trans. Jones, p. 179; *PG* III, 871A; *PatL* CXXII, 1155B-C.

20. Dionysius, *Mystical Theology*, trans. Jones, pp. 217, 218; *PG* III, 1033B, C; *PatL* CXXII, 1175B, C.

21. Jones, "Introduction" to *Divine Names*, pp. 22–25.

22. For the complicated development of the Logos in early Christian thought, see H. A. Wolfson, *The Philosophy of the Church Fathers*, 2nd ed. (Cambridge, Mass., 1964), pp. 141–372 passim, and J. N. D. Kelly, *Early Christian Doctrines*, 3d ed. (London, 1965), pp. 83–338 passim. For a lucid treatment of the Word and early Christian mystical theology, see A. Louth, *The Origins of the Christian Mystical Tradition* (Oxford, 1981).

23. Ignatius, "Letter to the Magnesians," in *The Apostolic Fathers: A New Translation and Commentary*, 6 vols., trans. R. M. Grant (Toronto, 1966), vol. 4, p. 63; *PG* V, 669B. As Grant indicates on page 62, most modern translators think that the Latin and Greek texts, which state that the Word does *not* proceed from silence, reflect anti-Gnostic emendation.

24. St. Augustine, *The Christian Doctrine*, trans. D. W. Robertson (New York, 1958), p. 11; *PatL* XXXIV, 21. See also *Corpus Christianorum Series Latina*, ed. J. Martin (Turnhout, Belgium, 1962), vol. 32, pp. 9–10.

25. Robert Barclay, *An Apology for the True Christian Divinity . . . [of the] Quakers* (London, 1678), p. 249.

26. Alexander Parker, *Letters, &c. of Early Friends*, ed. A. R. Barclay (London, 1841); Isaac Penington, *The Works of Isaac Pennington*, 4 vols. (Philadelphia, 1863); Charles Marshall, *An Epistle to Friends Coming Forth in the Beginning of a Testimony* (n.p., 1677). Cited in Richard Bauman, *Let Your Words Be Few: Symbolism of Speaking and Silence Among Seventeenth-Century Quakers* (Cambridge, 1983), pp. 121, 122, 127.

27. For many Quakers, silence was a symbol of crucifixion and mortification as well. William Britten writes of the "pure silencing of the flesh" while Richard Farnsworth praises those who have "crucified the flesh" and are able to "wait upon God in silence from the fleshly birth." See William Britten, *Silent Meeting: A Wonder to the World* (London, 1660), p. 11; and Richard Farnsworth, *The Spirit of God Speaking in the Temple of God* (London, 1663), pp. 4, 11.

28. John Calvin, *The Institutes of the Christian Religion*, 2 vols., ed. J. T. McNeill and trans. F. L. Battles (Philadelphia, 1960), vol. 1, pp. 69–71; Heinrich Heppe, *Reformed Dogmatics*, ed. E. Bizer and trans. G. T. Thomson (London, 1950), pp. 21–30; Martin Luther, *Luther's Works*, 55 vols., ed. and trans. J. Pelikan and H. T. Lehman et al. (Philadelphia, 1958–1986), vol. 36, p. 124; vol. 45, p. 129; vol. 36, p. 34.

29. For Milton's use of "sermo" for the Greek "logos," see *The Works of John Milton*, 20 vols., ed. Frank Allen Patterson et al. (New York, 1931–1940), vol. 14, p. 180.

30. H. R. MacCallum, "Milton and Figurative Interpretation of the Bible," *UTQ* 31 (1962): 400–03.

31. I call these liturgical sabbath hymns (*PL* VII, 565–73, 602–32), not because Milton approved of such forms in his own worship, but because they occur on the seventh day (VII, 592, 634), they offer praise in song to the "great Creator" (VII, 567), and they ritualize a divine event by using liturgical forms such as choral music, incense, scriptural reference, and schemes of repetition (VII, 601, 599, 565, 591–93).

32. A full discussion of the interplay of silence and speech in Milton's poetry before *Paradise Regained* is beyond the scope of this essay, but compare *PL* IV, 598; *PL* VIII, 3; *Comus* 560; *PR* IV, 601 and Jesus' stillness throughout the pinnacle scene. In each case, stillness, silence, and

speech or singing are linked. In *Comus* (548–64), the Attendant Spirit describes how silence overcomes "barbarous dissonance" and then, in turn, is overcome by "a soft and solemn-breathing sound" to the point where "even Silence / Was took ere she was ware, and wished she might / Deny her nature and be never more, / Still to be so displaced" (557–60). Listening in silent entrancement, "amaz'd" (565) like Satan in the pinnacle scene of *Paradise Regained,* he later discovers the origin of the sound—the voice of the Lady.

33. A similar sequence is found in Rev. v, 1–11. No angels volunteer to open the sealed book, the Lamb steps forward, and "the voice of many Angels round about the Throne" is heard in heaven.

34. For a concise overview and analysis of the criticism, see MacCallum, *Sons of God,* pp. 230–38.

35. Erasmus, *The first tome or volume of the paraphrase of Erasmus upon the newe testamente* (London, 1548), sig. Cii.

36. Lancelot Andrewes, *Ninety-Six Sermons,* 5 vols. (Oxford, 1843), vol. 5, pp. 483, 503, 482; William Perkins, *The Works of that Famous and Worthie Minister of Christ,* 3 vols. (London, 1612–1613), vol. 3, pp. 371–72.

37. James H. Sims, "Jesus and Satan as Readers of Scripture in *Paradise Regained,*" in *Milton Studies* XXXII, ed. Albert C. Labriola (Pittsburgh, 1995), pp. 194, 209–11.

38. Perkins, *Works,* p. 394.

39. See the following: *The Bible and the Holy Scriptures Conteyned in the Olde and Newe Testament* [Geneva Bible, 1560], facsimile ed. (Madison, 1969), Matt. iv, 6–7; John Calvin, *Calvin's Commentaries: A Harmony of the Gospels,* 3 vols., trans. A. W. Morrison, ed. D. W. Torrance and T. F. Torrance (Grand Rapids, 1972), vol. 1, p. 140; Diodati, *Pious Annotations,* Luke iv, 10; John Downame et al., *Annotations Upon all the Books of the New and Old Testament,* 2d ed. (London, 1651), Matt. iv, 6; William Fulke, *The Text of the New Testament of Jesus Christ Translated out of the Vulgar Latin by the Papists of the traiterous Seminarie of Rheims. With Arguments of Books, Chapters, and Annotations* (London, 1601); Luke iv, 8; John Lightfoot, *The Works of John Lightfoot,* 2 vols. (London, 1684), vol. 1, p. 498; Matthew Poole, *A Commentary on the Holy Bible,* 3 vols. (London, 1685; rpt. London, 1963), vol. 3, p. 17.

40. Downame et al., *Annotations,* Matt. iv, 6.

41. See the following: Lancelot Andrewes, *Sermons,* p. 522; John Calvin, *Calvin's Commentaries,* ed. and trans. J. Haroutunian and L. B. Smith (London, 1958), p. 166; Downame et al., *Annotations,* Matt. iv, 6–7; Erasmus, *Paraphrase,* sig. Cii^{x}; Geneva Bible, Psalm xci, 11; Martin Luther, *Works,* vol. 1, pp. 107–08; William Perkins, *Works,* p. 393.

42. For the same evidence with a different emphasis, see Goldsmith, "Muting of Satan," pp. 131–36.

43. Thomas Wilson, *The Arte of Rhetorique* [London, 1553], facsimile ed. (Gainesville, Florida, 1962), p. 9.